D. H. Lawrence – see Lawrence's Life, p. xi.

Mara Kalnins is Staff Tutor in Literature, University of Cambridge Board of Continuing Education and Fellow of Corpus Christi College, Cambridge. She has edited *Apocalypse* (1980) and *Aaron's Rod* (1988) for the Cambridge Lawrence edition, *D. H. Lawrence: Centenary Essays* (1986) and is editing *Sea and Sardinia*.

For Tom

D. H. LAWRENCE

Selected Poems

Edited, with an introduction and notes, by
MARA KALNINS
Staff Tutor in Literature,
University of Cambridge Board of Continuing Education
and Fellow of Corpus Christi College

J. M. Dent & Sons Ltd: London
EVERYMAN'S LIBRARY

First published in Everyman's Library 1992

This book is set in Sabon at The Spartan Press Ltd,
Lymington, Hants
Printed in Great Britain by
The Guernsey Press Co. Ltd, Guernsey for
J. M. Dent & Sons Ltd
91 Clapham High Street, London SW4 7TA

British Library Cataloguing in Publication Data is available upon request

ISBN 0 460 87129 3

CONTENTS

LAWRENCE'S LIFE

11 September 1885	Born in Eastwood, Nottinghamshire, son of John Arthur (1846–1924) and Lydia (*née* Beardsall, 1851–1910) Lawrence.
September 1898 – July 1901	Pupil at Nottingham High School.
1902–8	Pupil teacher; student at University College, Nottingham. First publication: 'A Prelude', in the *Nottinghamshire Guardian* for 7 December 1907. Appointed teacher at Davidson Road School, Croydon, in October 1908, where he taught until February 1912.
1909–10	Meets Ford Madox Hueffer in London, September 1909; sequence of five poems 'A Still Afternoon' published in the *English Review* (November). Breaks 'betrothal of six years standing to Jessie Chambers' in November 1910. Engaged to Louie Burrows in December (until February 1912). Death of his mother, Lydia Lawrence, on 9 December 1910.
1911–12	*The White Peacock* published on 19 January 1911. Meets Edward Garnett. Ill with pneumonia in November and resigns his teaching post on 28 February 1912. Meets Frieda Weekley (*née* von Richthofen, 1879–1956) in March and they leave for Germany on 3 May. *The Trespasser* published 23 May 1912. L. and Frieda travel

	to the Tyrol on 5 August and continue to Italy; at Gargnano, Lago di Garda from September 1912 to March 1913.
1913	*Love Poems and Others* (February). April–May in Germany; *Sons and Lovers* (29 May). June–August in England; in July meets Katherine Mansfield, Norman Douglas, Herbert and Cynthia Asquith, W. H. Davies. In August travels to the Continent: Germany, Switzerland and Italy until June 1914.
1914	Marries Frieda Weekley in London on 13 July; they live in London, Buckinghamshire and Sussex. Meets Amy Lowell, Richard Aldington, Hilda Doolittle, S. S. Koteliansky, Lady Ottoline Morrell. *The Prussian Officer* (26 November).
1915	Meets E. M. Forster and Bertrand Russell. *The Rainbow* (30 September) suppressed by court order on 13 November. Meets Aldous Huxley. Moves to Cornwall at the end of the year.
1916	At Higher Tregerthen, Zennor, St Ives, Cornwall. John Middleton Murry and Katherine Mansfield join L. and Frieda in April. *Twilight in Italy* (June); *Amores* (July).
1917	In February refused new passports for America. Visits Nottingham, Derbyshire, London in April. After surveillance, expelled from Cornwall by the military authorities on 15 October; thereafter in London. *Look! We Have Come Through!* (26 November).
1918–19	In London, Berkshire and Derbyshire until November 1919. *New Poems* (October 1918). Very ill with influenza February–March 1919. Writes preface for American edition of *New Poems* (28 August 1919). Leaves England in November for Italy. *Bay* (20 November 1919).

1920	Mostly in Italy until February 1922: Florence, Rome, Capri and Sicily where rents the Fontana Vecchia (March–August). September to the Italian lakes, Florence, Venice and back to the Fontana Vecchia in October; there until April 1921. *Women in Love* and *The Lost Girl* (9 and 25 November, respectively).
1921	Visits Sardinia 5–13 January. *Movements in European History* (February). Visits Germany and Austria (April–August); meets Earl and Achsah Brewster. *Psychoanalysis and the Unconscious* (10 May). At the Fontana Vecchia from September until February 1922. *Sea and Sardinia* (12 December).
1922	Leaves Italy in February for Ceylon and Australia (March–August). *Aaron's Rod* (14 April). August en route to San Francisco; arrives in Taos, New Mexico, in September and remains until March 1923. *Fantasia of the Unconscious* and *England, My England* (23 and 24 October, respectively).
1923	March–November in Mexico (principally Chapala, May–June) and USA (July–October) and Mexico again (October–November). *The Ladybird, The Fox, The Captain's Doll* (11 April); *Studies in Classic American Literature* (27 August); *Kangaroo* (13 September); *Birds, Beasts and Flowers* (9 October). December leaves for England.
1924	In England, France and Germany until departs for New York on 5 March; then to New Mexico at Lobo (later renamed 'Kiowa') ranch, Taos (May–October), and Mexico (mainly Oaxaca, October–March 1925). *The Boy in the Bush* (with Mollie Skinner, 28 August). Death of his father, John Arthur Lawrence, on 10 September.
1925	In February seriously ill with influenza and recurrent malaria. Tuberculosis confirmed.

	Travels back to the ranch in Taos early in April; remains until September. *St Mawr together with The Princess* (14 May). Leaves America in September for England. To Germany and France at the end of October and then to Italy. *Reflections on the Death of a Porcupine* (7 December).
1926–27	Travels in Italy until May when moves into the Villa Mirenda, Scandicci (near Florence) where the Lawrences are based until June 1928. Visits England and Scotland July–September 1926. *The Plumed Serpent* (21 January 1926); *Mornings in Mexico* (June 1927).
1928	In late April/May writes 'Chaos in Poetry' (introduction to *Chariot of the Sun*) and the preface and foreword to the *Collected Poems*. *The Woman Who Rode Away and Other Stories* (24 May). June–March 1930 mainly in France with visits to Switzerland. *Lady Chatterley's Lover* (July); *Collected Poems* (September). Typescript of *Pansies* seized by postal authorities in December.
1929	Writes the introduction to *Pansies* in January and the foreword in April. Exhibition of paintings at the Warren Gallery, London, raided by the police in July. *Pansies* (July; unexpurgated edition August); *The Escaped Cock* (September). Writes most of *Last Poems* in October and *Apocalypse* between October and December (corrected by 9 January 1930).
1930	Dies in Vence, Alpes Maritimes, France on 2 March. [Immediate Posthumous Publications] *Nettles* (13 March); *The Virgin and the Gipsy* (17 May).
1931	*Apocalypse* (3 June).
1932	*Etruscan Places* (September); *The Letters of D. H. Lawrence*, ed. Aldous Huxley (26 September); *Last Poems*, eds

	Richard Aldington and Giuseppe Orioli (1 October).
1933	*The Plays of D. H. Lawrence* (July).
1936	*Phoenix: Posthumous Papers*, ed. Edward D. McDonald (19 October).

CUE-TITLES

The place of publication is London unless otherwise stated.

Burnet	John Burnet, *Early Greek Philosophy*, Edinburgh: Black, 1892; 1908.
COLP	*The Collected Poems of D. H. Lawrence*, 2 vols, Secker, 1928.
COMP	Vivian de Sola Pinto and Warren Roberts (eds), *The Complete Poems of D. H. Lawrence*, 2 vols, Heinemann, 1964.
Letters	James T. Boulton *et al.* (eds), *The Letters of D. H. Lawrence*, 6 vols, Cambridge: Cambridge University Press, 1979–91.
Moore	Harry T. Moore (ed.) *The Collected Letters of D. H. Lawrence*, 2 vols, Heinemann, 1962.
Murray	Gilbert Murray, *Five Stages of Greek Religion*, Oxford: Oxford University Press, 1925.
Nehls	Edward Nehls (ed.), *D. H. Lawrence: A Composite Biography*, 3 vols, Madison: University of Wisconsin Press, 1957–9.
Not I,	Frieda Lawrence, *Not I, But the Wind . . .*, Heinemann, 1935.
Phoenix	Edward D. McDonald (ed.), *Phoenix: The Posthumous Papers of D. H. Lawrence*, Heinemann, 1936.
Phoenix II	Warren Roberts and Harry T. Moore (eds), *Phoenix II: Uncollected, Unpublished and other Prose Works by D. H. Lawrence*, Heinemann, 1968.
Roberts	Warren Roberts, *A Bibliography of D. H. Lawrence*, Rupert Hart-Davis, 1963; rev. edn 1982.

INTRODUCTION

'The clue to all his utterance lies in the sheer appreciation of the instant moment, life surging itself into utterance at its very well-head',[1] wrote Lawrence of the American poet Walt Whitman, and the words are even more true of his own poetic voice. Like Whitman, Lawrence saw the poet as the enemy of convention. For him the task of the poet was both to rid his verse of outworn clichés of form and expression, to become 'spontaneous and flexible as flame,'[2] and to be an uncompromising critic of stereotypes of thought and feeling as well as of outmoded and restrictive social and political forms. This reveals itself in Lawrence's writings in several ways. First, he was fascinated by human psychology, by what he called the '*terra incognita*' of the self, and in his poems as in his fiction he sought to explore the unknown places of the human psyche, to articulate the states through which not only the mind but the body pass, so that they could be understood and become the foundation for renewal in the individual and in human relationships. He saw in the relation between men and women especially '*the* problem of today, the establishment of a new relation, or the re-adjustment of the old one, between men and women',[3] and it was a subject that was to occupy him as a man and an artist throughout his life. Secondly, his art reveals a profound and searching criticism of the political, religious and social structures which have shaped our materialistic and technological age, an age which he saw everywhere increasingly denying the integrity of the individual and impoverishing the quality of human life. And finally he was, as he called himself, a 'passionately religious man',[4] not in the narrow sense of belonging to a particular creed – he rejected the traditional Christianity of his non-Conformist upbringing early on – but in Blake's sense of discovering the infinite in all things. In this sense his later poetry, especially the *Last Poems*, becomes an urgent attempt to give form to visionary experience. Like the fiction and the essays, then, Lawrence's poems span the whole of his life and concerns as an artist, and bear witness to his development into the writer of genius, the prophet and interpreter of our civilisation on which his reputation as one of the most distinctive voices of the century rests.

T. S. Eliot has suggested that 'If you examine the works of any great innovator in chronological order, you may expect to find that the author has been driven on step by step, in his innovations, by an inner necessity, and that the novelty of form has rather been forced upon him by his material than deliberately sought.'[5] Although Lawrence was never merely an impersonal servant of his material he undoubtedly submitted to just such a sense of 'inner necessity'; 'the novels and poems come unwatched out of one's pen' he wrote in his foreword to *Fantasia of the Unconscious*.[6] He was often to refer, at times rather ruefully, to his 'demon', the unknown power of inspiration that drove him and the curious sense he had of the early poems especially, seeming 'to me to come from somewhere, I didn't quite know where, out of a me whom I didn't know and didn't want to know, and to say things I would much rather not have said.'[7] This spontaneity gives Lawrence's art that quality of freshness and directness of expression that many critics have noted. At the same time, however, he was also a stringent self-critic and re-writer. If the vision had not been conveyed fully, if the demon had not had his say, he would revise and recast whole poems, stories, even whole novels, to which the versions of *The Rainbow*, *Women in Love* and the three *Lady Chatterley* novels, for example, attest. It is significant that when he wrote the foreword to his *Collected Poems* of 1928 and acknowledged having extensively revised the early poems for that volume, he should have drawn a distinction between his early verses (written up to 1912) and the later ones, virtually uncorrected, in which he felt he had found his poetic voice in the free verse form which was to be the distinguishing mode of his poetry thereafter. As he said: 'It is not for technique that these poems are altered: it is to say the real say.' In the same foreword he wrote: 'I have tried to establish a chronological order, because many of the poems are so personal that, in their fragmentary fashion, they make up a biography of an emotional and inner life.'[8] It is therefore appropriate to follow Lawrence's development as a poet chronologically through this selection of his poems and to continue the story, 'the biography of an inner and emotional life', with the poems that succeeded the 1928 collection.

Lawrence's early poems, written between 1906 and 1912 and contemporary with *The White Peacock* (1911), *The Trespasser* (1912), *Sons and Lovers* (1913) and the early stories, show the young writer struggling to understand his 'demon' and give it expression. They chronicle his years in Nottingham and London and many of them portray his relationship with his mother ('The Bride', 'The Virgin Mother') and the friends of his youth and early adulthood: Jessie Chambers (the 'Miriam' of *Sons and Lovers*) who first sent his poems to the *English Review* in 1909; Louie Burrows to whom he was engaged for over a year; and Helen Corke from his time as a school teacher in Croydon. In these poems the young Lawrence explores traditional verse forms and experiments with various techniques in his search for a personal style of poetic expression. (His later division in the *Collected Poems* of the poetry into 'Rhyming' and 'Unrhyming' is important, as I will suggest below.) It is true that many of these poems reveal his inability at this stage to use the formal resources of verse, rhyme and metre to express his insights; they rely rather on the sheer intensity of experience, a failure which R. P. Blackmuir criticised in his 'D. H. Lawrence and Expressive Form'.[9] But in others the discipline of experimenting with conventional forms, even when the rhyme and metre are only partially successful, as in 'The Wild Common', can result in a conciseness of expression which anticipates his later craftsmanship in verse. Poems like 'Baby Running Barefoot' and 'Corot' have both an immediacy, an engaging directness of emotional and imaginative response to the world, and a controlled yet unforced construction. They reveal that power 'to transmute the common experience into significance'[10] which Jessie Chambers felt was Lawrence's special gift. Others, such as 'Monologue of a Mother' and the dialect poem 'The Collier's Wife' already show that almost uncanny psychological insight into women which found expression in stories such as 'Odour of Chrysanthemums', in parts of *Sons and Lovers* and later in *The Rainbow*.

Although many of the early poems are derivative and point to his debt to the great nineteenth-century poets, not all of them are merely imitative; like Hardy's poetry, which he admired (though he never shared Hardy's essentially tragic vision of life), the best reveal a distinctively modern sensibility. A poem like 'Dreams Old and Nascent: Nascent', with its echoes of Zola's *Germinal*, already contains themes which were to become increasingly familiar in Lawrence's works: the criticism of crass materialism – the 'ghastly dream of riches' – and the pollution of the earth in the name of economic expediency; the cry for revolution 'not in the name of money or work . . . but of life',[11] as he was later to say, and yet throughout the sense of wonder at the mystery of life which perpetually unfolds itself in pure living creatures. Formally, then, the early poems are uneven and many only make sense in the context of Lawrence's life, but in others the emotion or perception has been recreated into a significance expressed by the poem itself, irrespective of biography.

Many of these early poems, which originally appeared in periodicals, were later collected and published in volume form in *Love Poems and Others* (1913), *Amores* (1916) and *New Poems* (1918) but, like *Sons and Lovers*, they are essentially records of a past and finished life. The importance of the next period, beginning with the devastating impact of his mother's death in December 1910, followed by his own serious illness with pneumonia in the autumn of 1911, and then his meeting and elopement with Frieda Weekley in the spring of 1912, is impossible to exaggerate. It signalled the end of Lawrence's life in the Midlands and the breaking of ties with his family and the relationships of his youth. His decision to become an independent writer living by his pen alone and his commitment to a life with Frieda generated an astonishing creativity and development in his voice as an artist. 1912 marks the division between works which could possibly have been written by other gifted writers, to prose and poetry which we recognise as uniquely Lawrentian. We are henceforth aware, as contemporary readers must have been, of a wholly new voice in English literature.

It is in this next period of experimentation that Lawrence found the free verse form which he thereafter made his own. He was of course widely read in both French and English poetry and was deeply influenced by the poets of the English Romantic movement. But it was above all his reading of Whitman, though he later came to disagree with his doctrine,[12] that helped him to clarify his ideas about the nature of free verse and to achieve that greater technical freedom with which he created his own special form of poetic utterance. In Whitman's poetry Lawrence found what Whitman himself had called 'Nature without check, with original energy',[13] an emphasis on immediate, spontaneous expression which became the cardinal principle of his own writing, poetry that is the 'direct utterance from the instant, whole man'.[14] The letters of 1913 are filled with a sense of excitement and discovery: 'I have always tried to get an emotion out in its own course, without altering it'; and 'it is the hidden *emotional* pattern that makes poetry, not the obvious form,'[15] by which Lawrence did not mean the undisciplined outpouring of states of feeling or intense perceptions but something closer to T. S. Eliot's notion of '*significant* emotion' in poetry – that is 'emotion which has its life in the poem',[16] rather than in the merely specific details of the poet's life. In free verse the poet must bring no received or preconceived elements of rhythm, rhyme, metre or stanza form to his writing: 'I think I read my poetry more by length than by stress . . . I think more of a bird with broad wings, flying and lapsing through the air, than anything, when I think of metre.'[17] The treatment of each poem must develop naturally from the poet's emotional response to his subject matter – 'The law must come new each time from within'[18] – as indeed Coleridge had said: 'it is innate; it shapes, as it develops itself from within, and the fulness of its development is one and the same with the perfection of its outward form . . . for it is even this that constitutes its genius – the power of acting creatively under laws of its own origination.'[19] Here, too, Lawrence's habit of continual, spontaneous revision became a way of embodying that belief in poetic expression and form that itself best realises the fluid and ever-changing emotional pattern. The spontaneous revision is part of a process, but the process is also a procedure with a definitive end, to get 'an emotion out in its own course'. Like the Romantics Lawrence felt that poetry was at once a direct, naïve response to the world of nature and man, and that it was also visionary, a notion akin to Blake's seeing through the eye.[20] The imagination of the poet makes 'a new effort of attention, and "discovers" a new world within the known world';[21] it intuitively shapes and transforms what it has perceived into art.

Looking back in 1928 Lawrence divided the two volumes of the *Collected Poems* into 'Rhyming' and 'Unrhyming'; the former contains the early poems, the latter begins with the poems which tell the early love story with Frieda when they travelled through Bavaria, the Tyrol and Italy in 1912–14. These were later collected in the cycle *Look! We Have Come Through!* (1917). In fact, many of the *Look!* poems are crafted in traditional rather than free verse form and many of them do rhyme, but Lawrence placed them in the 'Unrhyming' section to emphasise the difference between the verse of his youth and that in which he achieved the rhythmical spontaneity of free verse thenceforth characteristic of his poetry, and his sense as an artist that 'to write poetry one has to let oneself fuse in the current.'[22]

So a poem like 'Green', which is rhymed with a regular metre and stanza form, nevertheless reveals Lawrence's aim to convey an instantly felt awareness in a lucid modern idiom. The poem is simplicity itself: the delicate green dawn sky holding sun and moon is contained in the translucent green eyes of the beloved, newly opened and 'like flowers newly seen', where the last phrase contains the heavens, the world of nature and the response of the lover in one clear image. 'Song of a Man Who Has Come Through' significantly combines Lawrence's newly found sense of artistic freedom with the fulfilment as a man that his life with Frieda was bringing him, and also his perception of living in a time of destruction and change for the western world. The opening lines, 'Not I, not I but the wind that blows through me!/A fine wind is blowing the new direction of Time', recall the wind as the Romantic symbol of creativity, life and energy, rather than as the modernist symbol of sterile futility, as in Eliot's *The Waste Land.* Lawrence would have known Coleridge's 'Aeolian Harp' where the image of the wind making music on its strings both expresses the attunement of the poet as a man to nature, and acts as a metaphor for the divinely inspired power of the artist. The timeless biblical and classical references also give the artist's life and message universal relevance. Thus the wind and the chisel signify the yielding of the self, the rock of the ego, to the divine so that one can be reborn and 'come at the wonder' of the Hesperides, the land of the golden apples, which are emblems of eternal youth. The fountain is a symbol for the inexhaustible flow of creativity and of life and perhaps echoes Blake's 'The cistern contains; the fountain overflows.'[23] And the three angels of Genesis (xviii–xx) are emissaries of the divine unknown. In the Old Testament story they appeared before Abraham and Sarah as God was about to destroy the sinful cities of Sodom and

Gomorrah, announcing that the couple would have children in their old age to preserve humanity. So too Lawrence saw his new life with Frieda and his commitment to his art as a hope for a future beyond the present time of imminent war and destruction.

Writing the poems for the *Look!* cycle, his novel 'The Sisters', which was to become *The Rainbow* (1915) and *Women in Love* (1920), and the *Study of Thomas Hardy* (1914), also helped Lawrence to formulate his dialectic vision of things: first, his conception of man as a creature of duality, in perpetual conflict with himself, with the claims of emotion and intuition on the one hand and those of the intellect and reason on the other; and secondly his doctrine of creation through opposition. Both were to inform nearly all his subsequent work. Deeply influenced by his reading of the pre-Socratic philosopher Heraclitus, Lawrence saw conflict, or 'strife' as he called it, as the primary power which creates all things into being, a notion for which Blake's oft-quoted 'Without Contraries is no progression' is an apt epitome.[24] In the novels he expresses this through the quest of the principal characters to create themselves into new being through the continual flux of opposition, to evolve (or destroy) themselves through the deep pressures between and within themselves, and the external pressures of the historical and social conditions of the time. Like Jung, Lawrence saw the human psyche poised between the objective, physical cosmos and the subjective, inner world, with an urgent need to resolve the opposition, to integrate them for the growth and enrichment of the self. In his works he gave this integrating power many names – for example the Crown, the Rainbow, the Holy Ghost – but it was always in essence a creative power.[25] The prose 'Argument' to the *Look!* cycle articulates this sense of transcendence and growth through personal conflict:

> After much struggling and loss in love and in the world of men, the protagonist throws in his lot with a woman who is already married. Together they go into another country, she perforce leaving her children behind. The conflict of love and hate goes on between the man and the woman, and between these two and the world around them, till it reaches some sort of conclusion, they transcend into some condition of blessedness.[26]

At another level it is this clash of opposites which creates art: 'It is most wonderful in poetry, this sense of conflict contained in reconciliation'[27] where 'conflict' not only expresses the tensions in language and in forging the poetic elements which go into the making of a poem, but also suggests that the composition of a poem is a metaphor for life itself, for we are ourselves 'opposites which exist by virtue of our inter-opposition. Remove the opposition and there is collapse.'[28] So in a still wider sense the task of the artist is that of any man and Everyman, to create the self into unique being, to 'create that work of art, the living man, achieve that piece of supreme art, a man's life'.[29]

Thus Lawrence in the first years of his new life with Frieda and at the outbreak of the First World War, a war that for him, as for others of his generation and time, seemed to herald the end of Western civilisation. The letters of the war years are filled with a sense of nightmare and apocalypse:

> So it is the end – our world is gone, and we are like dust in the air . . . Everything has a touch of delirium . . . It is not a question of me, it is the world of men. The world of men is dreaming, it has gone mad in its sleep, and a snake is strangling it but it can't wake up.[30]

Living in poverty in London and then in Cornwall (where he and Frieda were under military surveillance and later expelled) in retreat from a world gone mad, Lawrence rejected humanity for a time and turned to the pristine loveliness of the world of nature, but it is characteristic of him that even the most despairing of his writings during the war should end with the hope of renewal:

> I do really think we shall see this old order collapsing – even in the outer world – smashing right down . . . I want to have some seed of a new spirit really – I know the time is nearly come to sow it. We shall be like Noah, taking all the precious things into the ark, when the flood comes, and disembarking on a new world.[31]

The notion of leaving for 'a new world' is significant, for the cataclysm of the First World War coincided with the shattering of Lawrence's belief in an English reading public who could and would respond to his voice as a writer. Six weeks after its publication by Methuen in September 1915, *The Rainbow*, the novel in which he had articulated his deepest religious belief in marriage as the way to creative fulfilment, was banned for immorality; for the next four years no publisher would touch its sequel *Women in Love*; Chatto and Windus objected to the sexual tone of the *Look!* poems and insisted on deleting two and on the rewriting of others.[32] Henceforth, Lawrence was to write for an international audience, particularly for America, and for posterity: 'a work of art is an act of faith, as Michael Angelo says, and one goes on writing, to the unseen witnesses.'[33] Henceforth, too, he was to feel himself a permanent exile from the land of his birth: 'I am going away from the land and the nation I have belonged to: departing, emigrating, changing the land of my soul as well as of my mere domicile.'[34] In the autumn of 1919 he left England, never to return to live there.

After the nightmare of the war years, the return to his beloved Italy 'was like coming to life again' wrote Frieda.[35] He and Frieda rented the Fontana Vecchia in Taormina, Sicily – 'Lovely, lovely Sicily, the dawn-place, Europe's dawn, with Odysseus pushing his ship out of the shadows into the blue. Whatever had died for me, Sicily had not then died: dawn-lovely Sicily, and the Ionian sea.'[36] It was here that he wrote most of the poems that were later published as *Birds, Beasts and Flowers* (1923). These reveal a dual thematic strand which was to be a feature of the poetry to come: they are at once wonderful evocations of the mysterious 'otherness' of the natural world and its creatures which he saw in Italy and, from the spring of 1922, in his travels to Ceylon, Australia and New Mexico: 'once be disillusioned with the man-made world and you can still see the magic, the beauty, the delicate realness of all other life.'[37] But many of them (for example 'The Evangelistic Beasts') have at their heart a different and serious purpose: to explore the nature of political and religious doctrine and power in human societies and to search for the causes of the *malaise*, as he saw it, of our century.

This quest also informs the novels of the early 1920s – *Aaron's Rod* (1922), *Kangaroo* (1923) and, later, *The Plumed Serpent* (1926) – as well as the non-fiction, such as the textbook he wrote for schools, *Movements in European History* (1921), the psychology essays *Psychoanalysis and the Unconscious* (1921), *Fantasia of the Unconscious* (1922), and his *Studies in Classic American Literature* (1923). Having witnessed the failure of Christianity and democracy in western metropolitan culture, Lawrence addressed himself to the problem of how mankind could create 'a new era of living'.[38] His search was to lead him across the globe to other countries and civilisations and back to old pagan religions and myths as well as to the familiar Christian gospels in the quest for symbols that would refresh the springs of religious and political awareness in modern man. And his fascination with the ancient world and earlier cultures (in particular the Aztec, American Indian and, towards the end of his life, the Etruscan) was not, as has been erroneously suggested, because Lawrence advocated some kind of return to the primitive for us, but because he recognised the unchanging qualities of human nature and the validity of laws which had governed man in the past. These, he argued, must also have value for our century and our civilisation. In his travels he therefore sought to find and to understand the creative and vital forces in nature and human societies which he felt could reshape and regenerate our world.

Something of this quest can be found in the *Birds, Beasts and Flowers* poems and may have influenced their form. As Graham Hough has pointed out, their highly original and idiosyncratic free verse shape has no literary antecedents, though it appears to be related in some way to the prose structure of the imaginative essay, 'in which fragments of external reality – things, people, places – appear, and the effort is to present them with the maximum of objectivity and vividness – yet to offer them as objects of contemplation in themselves, not as elements in a narrative or exercises in self revelation.'[39] Like Lawrence's essays, the central concern of the *Birds, Beasts and Flowers* poems, as Sandra Gilbert has noted, is 'knowledge through meditation: they *essay* to know something, not wholly and extensively, in all its parts and implications, but intuitively, often obliquely, fragmentarily; not through orderly ratiocination, but through emotional perception.'[40] Unlike the essentially expository and tentative style of the essay form, however, these verses achieve an organic wholeness and symbolic unity of expression. Lawrence selects and closely observes aspects of an object in a strenuous attempt to convey its essence, as Cézanne was concerned to render the applyness of an apple.[41] The progress of each poem is then a kind of discovery, often based on a dialogue – the poet with the reader or with himself or the object – in a repetitive, colloquial rhythm which exemplifies the spontaneous poetic process which Lawrence had defined as the nature of free verse in his essay 'Poetry of the Present' (1919) and which also illuminates his prose style.[42] What makes these free verses true poetry however, is that what at first appear to be fragmentary observations are seen by the end of the poem to serve a higher unity, an imaginative and satisfying symbolic wholeness. Then, too, the rhythmic organisation of the lines is not arbitrary, as had been the case with some of the early poems; they are not merely discursive prose broken up into irregular verse form, but can be seen to serve the meaning actively.

The best of the *Birds, Beasts and Flowers* verses – for example the 'Tortoise' poems or a poem like 'Snake', though there are many others – exemplify this poetic method in the highest degree.

He reached down from a fissure in the earth-wall in the gloom
And trailed his yellow-brown slackness soft-bellied down,
    over the edge of the stone trough
And rested his throat upon the stone bottom,
And where the water had dripped from the tap, in a small
    clearness,
He sipped with his straight mouth,
Softly drank through his straight gums, into his slack long
    body,
Silently.

Here the construction of the lines as well as the soft sibilance of the alliteration and the diction ('reached', 'trailed') marvellously imitate the movement of the snake and use the flowing, rhythmic resources of English to the full. The poem begins as a closely observed natural description of the snake and then proceeds to relate the dramatic confrontation between poet and animal. By the end of the poem, however, we are aware of far deeper resonances. The nature of the encounter with the snake, the references to the albatross of Coleridge's mariner and to ancient Mediterranean mythology, combine direct and symbolic presentation; an apparently simple experience comes to stand for a complex imaginative whole, becomes a statement about the 'accursed voices of my human education' and the violated integrity of the non-human world of nature, and offers us an intuitive glimpse of truths which resonate beyond the page of the poem itself.

The years immediately following the *Birds, Beasts and Flowers* poems, published as a volume in 1923, saw very little poetry written, with the exception of the hymns and songs for his Mexican novel *The Plumed Serpent*. It was not until Lawrence had returned to Europe in the autumn of 1925, following his near-fatal illness in Mexico, and settled in the Villa Mirenda outside Florence, that he began writing poetry again. He lived here from 1926 to 1928 and it was here that he also wrote the three *Lady Chatterley* novels. In the autumn of 1927 he was at work revising, and sometimes recasting, the poetry for the *Collected Poems* and in March 1928 he corrected the proofs. It is not surprising that, having reviewed the process of his artistic development for nearly twenty years in the preparation of this collection, Lawrence should now have sought to articulate his ideas about writing a new kind of poetry which became the *Pansies* poems of 1928 and early 1929 and then the 'Last Poems': 'I am doing some little *Pensées* – sort of poems, but really *thoughts* – all in snatches.'[43] In his foreword to *Pansies* he wrote:

> These poems are called *Pansies* because they are rather *Pensées* than anything else. Pascal or La Bruyère wrote their *Pensées* in prose, but it has always seemed to me that a real thought, a single thought, not an argument, can only exist easily in verse, or in some poetic form.[44]

Like Hardy's belief that 'the mission of poetry is to record impressions, not convictions',[45] Lawrence's view of poetry was that it should convey 'a true thought' rather than expound 'a bare idea or a didactic statement'. A 'true thought' records an impression, 'the breath of the moment . . . one eternal moment easily contradicting the next eternal moment'.[46] Thus the foreword goes on to suggest that the subject of a poem should spontaneously determine its form though not in any mechanical sense of formal organisation. Something like this notion of spontaneous expression had been part of Lawrence's doctrine since 1913, as we have seen, but the *Pansies* poems suggest a further development. Lawrence had always seen man as a creature of dual consciousness, with the claims of emotion, instinct and the senses on the one hand, conflicting with those of the intellect and reason on the other. This is revealed in his belief that there are two ways of knowing the universe: 'in terms of apartness, which is mental, rational and scientific, and knowing in terms of togetherness which is religious and poetic',[47] that is, intuitive and emotional. As early as the *Study of Thomas Hardy* and the early versions of *Studies in Classic American Literature* he had wistfully glimpsed the possibility of a 'harmony between the two halves of the psyche. The approach is towards a pure unison between religion and science',[48] between emotion and reason. It was in the last year of his life that Lawrence achieved this integration and understood that both kinds of knowledge are essential parts of the process of human thought and consciousness. Just as he had always seen the body and the soul as conceptually distinct but actually integrated – he called this integrated self in *Fantasia* and elsewhere the 'physical psyche' or the 'biological psyche' – Lawrence came to see the instinctive and intellectual selves as part of the same unity, which he called 'the emotional mind'.[49] The poem 'Thought' shows what Lawrence meant by this integrated consciousness and it is worth quoting in full.

Thought, I love thought.
But not the jiggling and twisting of already existent ideas
I despise that self-important game.
Thought is the welling up of unknown life into consciousness,
Thought is the testing of statements on the touchstone of the
    conscience,
Thought is gazing on to the face of life, and reading what can be
    read,
Thought is pondering over experience, and coming to
    conclusion.
Thought is not a trick, or an exercise, or a set of dodges,
Thought is a man in his wholeness wholly attending.

As David Ellis has shown, one way of considering the *Pansies* poems 'is as a part of a life-long effort to find the literary form which would best allow for precisely this kind of thought. "Pansies" themselves are a consequence of the realisation that it is often the need to organise individual thoughts to an argument which distorts them into a "trick, or an exercise, or a set of dodges".'[50] This awareness shows itself in the fluid and ever-changing voices and forms of the *Pansies* poems, which alter according to the subject, the 'thought'. Poetic values such as these would seem to be far removed from the emphasis on structure and craftsmanship, on techniques such as irony, ambiguity and paradox, seen by Eliot and Empson as the distinctive features of modern poetry. Yet Lawrence is also a particularly modern poet in his range of poetic styles and subjects and in his use of different moods, registers and tones – by turns serious, mocking, reverent, ironic. So the *Pansies* poems are as varied as flowers themselves.

Some reveal that delighted response to the beauty of nature which had been evident from Lawrence's earliest years; others are satiric and epigrammatic; still others are 'real doggerel',[51] as Frieda called them, voicing Lawrence's criticism of contemporary society; or they express a utopian vision, the hope for a future which will foster individual liberty and creativity. Like his last book, *Apocalypse* (1931), many of the *Pansies* poems are vigorously iconoclastic, a radical criticism of the Christian and democratic ideals and the scientific technology that have shaped our civilisation, but they also reveal Lawrence's belief in mankind's power to create 'a new heaven and a new earth' if he can destroy the 'false, inorganic connections, especially those related to money, and re-establish the living organic connections with the cosmos, the sun and earth, with mankind and nation and family.'[52]

Often the poems form clusters and show the working out of a 'true thought' in several forms: for example, the elephant poems, the poems on the making of things, those on revolution and social change, those on old age. The mutations these poems pass through also exemplify what Lawrence called the habit of the emotional mind, its tendency to move naturally in a cyclical process of vision and revision – or as 'thoughts that scurry in different directions yet belong to the same nest'[53] – in the effort to achieve the full expression of an impression. In *Apocalypse* he defined this poetic method more precisely, as one which 'starts with an image, sets the image in motion, allows it to achieve a certain course or circuit of its own, and then takes up another image' and allows 'the mind to move in cycles, or to flit here and there over a cluster of images'.[54] In *Pansies* the result is an almost musical variation in which an image begets another image which in turn suggests a further mood or theme. The thoughts modulate into one another in an associative process which is both natural to the poet and mimetic of the way the consciousness operates.

An offshoot or variety, as it were, of the *Pansies* poems was the series Lawrence called *Nettles* (1930), written in July and August 1929 in response to the all too familiar censorship of his work: 'At present I can do *nothing*: except write a few stinging *Pansies* which this time are *Nettles*. I shall call them nettles'.[55] *Lady Chatterley's Lover* (1928) had been banned, the manuscript of *Pansies* seized by the postal authorities in December of 1928 and Lawrence had had to delete fourteen of the poems for his English publisher Martin Secker. In July 1929 an exhibition of his paintings at the Warren Gallery, London, was raided by the police. The *Nettles* poems are an understandably irritated response to 'all this persecution and insult'[56] and represent a temporary falling-off in quality. As many critics have noted, they are in the nature of angry squibs, attacks on the government, the magistrates and critics and the British public. But the censorship also prompted him to write the important introduction and foreword to *Pansies* where he not only formulated his new poetic method, as we have seen, but also affirmed his belief in the need for people 'to make an *adjustment in consciousness* to the basic physical realities'.[57] Like *Lady Chatterley's Lover*, some of the *Pansies* poems are about the need for a rebirth of physical and sexual consciousness. The 'true thought' comes 'as much from the heart and the genitals as from the head' and 'the fairest thing in nature, a flower, still has its roots in earth'.[58] In a witty, and perhaps unconscious tribute to Lawrence, John Heath-Stubbs has similarly defined poetry in his 'Ars Poetica':

> The intellect shapes, the emotions feed the poem,
> Whose roots are in the senses, whose flower is imagination.[59]

It was in the last months of his life, however, from the summer of 1929 to his death on 2 March 1930 that Lawrence's poetry achieved its fullest and finest flowering. These last months reveal an astonishing outpouring of nearly three hundred poems. They were written in two notebooks which Richard Aldington and Giuseppe Orioli, the editors of the 1932 posthumous collection, divided into MS B and MS A, 'More Pansies' and 'Last Poems', though no such division had Lawrence's authority nor, as several critics have shown, is it borne out by the poems themselves.[60] The critical and scholarly arguments surrounding this question are not the concern of this introduction, but it makes sense, I think, to place all the late verses simply into one category as 'Last Poems'. What does emerge from a reading of these late poems is that they fall into two kinds, though largely irrespective of which notebook they were written in. There are those which are still recognisably 'Pansies', poems derived from experience and psychological insight. These take subjects from the realm of human experience and consciousness which are readily intelligible as part of our ordinary life. But there are others which are imaginative renderings of something which is not derived from specific experience and ordinary understanding. These are the poems on life and death which belong to that rare kind of art which is created by visionary insight.

In his essay 'Psychology and Literature' Jung has usefully defined two kinds of artistic creation, the 'psychological' and the 'visionary'. The former, he argues, deals with all the experiences and emotions, both rational and non-rational, which make up the ordinary life of people, though expressed by the poet with greater clarity and insight than is given to the ordinary person – a notion reminiscent of Coleridge's view of the poet as one who possesses the creative imagination in greater degree.[61] But 'visionary' poets see into that which is beyond the grasp of normal human understanding and their art is different from that of poets who 'never rend the curtain that veils the cosmos . . . never transcend the bounds of the humanly possible . . . But the primordial experiences rend from top to bottom the curtain upon which is painted the picture of an ordered world, and allow a glimpse into the unfathomed abyss of what has not yet become.'[62] It is a view strikingly similar to Lawrence's late essay 'Chaos in Poetry', his review of Harry Crosby's *Chariot of the Sun*.

> The essential quality of poetry is that it makes a new effort of attention, and 'discovers' a new world within the known world. Man, and the animals, and the flowers, all live within a strange and for ever surging chaos . . . But man cannot live in chaos . . . Man fixes some wonderful erection of his own between himself and the wild chaos, and gradually goes bleached and stifled under his parasol. Then comes a poet, enemy of convention, and makes a slit in the umbrella; and lo! the glimpse of chaos is a vision, a window to the sun.[63]

Such a vision, then, reveals something deeper and more primordial, something beyond normal human consciousness yet which cannot be ignored. As Jung goes on to point out, this vision is 'a true symbolic expression . . . of something existent in its own right, but imperfectly known . . . Human passion falls within the sphere of conscious experience, while the subject of the vision lies beyond it. Through our feelings we experience the known, but our intuitions point to things that are unknown and hidden – that by their very nature are secret.'[64] The findings of physics and mathematics since the late seventeenth century have offered humanity an orderly, eminently rational and scientific map of the cosmos, a reassuring picture of a universe which acts by predictable and constant laws, though twentieth century theories on the uncertainty principle of quantum mechanics and recent discoveries on chaos boundary conditions suggest that our comfortable post-Newtonian view of the universe may be a gross oversimplification of reality. At the same time, throughout the history of mankind, the seers, prophets and poets have witnessed to a different world beyond that grasped and understood by the intellect. Our advanced technological age has rejected superstition and metaphysics, has focused on rationally explainable principles of social and political structures and on the way language determines how we see the world. Yet underneath remains a deep fascination with the psyche and the possibility of other modes of being that have haunted mankind since the dawn of consciousness. The visionary poet, like Blake or Lawrence, articulates these intimations through symbol and myth. At one level, of course, the use of symbols is a fundamental process, a way of conveying concepts, of perceiving the world and giving it meaning. But it is also a way of conceptualising that which is beyond the purely material and normally perceived, and it is in this way that symbol functions in many of the 'Last Poems' and gives them form. Poems like 'Shadows', 'Ship of Death', 'Bavarian Gentians', 'Butterfly' and many others imaginatively transcend the ordered, known, visible world; they represent that visionary insight which is humanity's closest approach to what cannot be understood but only obscurely sensed through the physical manifestations of nature and our being. Many of the last poems are visionary in this sense and the repetitive, cyclical style is an attempt to approach an understanding of death and immortality, not through logical statement but through the subtle modulation of associated images and symbols.

Thus a poem like 'Butterfly' eschews formal verse stanza and regular metre and employs an incantatory, repetitive style which perfectly exemplifies that natural, cyclical process which Lawrence defined in 'Poetry of the Present' and *Apocalypse*. The butterfly is clearly a metaphor for the soul; it is also a symbol of resurrection, of transmutation from one state in the physical world (the caterpillar and its chrysalis) into another (the winged creature of the air). The butterfly's movement is from the safe, warm, walled garden with its red geraniums suggesting the life of the body, the world of nature and of human consciousness, to the sea, the unknown, driven by a keen wind 'polished with snow', heralding death and winter. The physical world is evoked with precision – 'We live in the center of a physical poetry'[65] as Wallace Stevens put it – yet it is also used to suggest the numinous. The infinite and eternal are apprehended by associating the very small and ephemeral (the butterfly) with the vast (the sea and air), a daring conjunction reminiscent of Blake:

> To see a World in a Grain of Sand
> And a Heaven in a Wild Flower,
> Hold Infinity in the palm of your hand
> And Eternity in an hour.[66]

The butterfly, the creature of air and emblem of metamorphosis (one is reminded of Ursula and the butterflies in chapter x of *Women in Love*) yet sips the dirt of physical mortality, perhaps an unconscious reference to Whitman: 'I bequeath myself to the dirt to grow from the green I love/If you want me again look for me under your bootsoles'.[67] The present tense of the poem, the incantatory lines, the repeated interrogatives, the butterfly's physical movement imitated by the metrical contrasts of the verse with its complex pattern of rhythmic stresses (for example the irregular speech rhythms suddenly and sharply focused in the anapestic 'till the wínd/slides yŏu shéer/frŏm the arch-crést', contrasted with the unaccented and mimetic 'strange level fluttering') coupled with the symbolic associations of the invisible rainbow and the wind, establish a calm serenity and acceptance of coming dissolution. It is the very reverse of Claudio's fearful 'To be imprisoned in the viewless winds/And blown with restless violence about/The pendant world'.[68] Here surely is a poem in which the apparent simplicity of the unrhymed free verse conceals a highly sophisticated symbolic form and an intricate range of emotional and symbolic resonances which operate in precisely the spontaneous and cyclical way Lawrence had suggested in his essays – resonances which unite the world of physical seeing with that of visionary insight into the unknown and the unknowable.

It is truly poetry, in Lawrence's words, 'at the moment of inception in the soul, before the germ of the known and the unknown have fused to begin a new set of concepts . . . Through it all runs the intrinsic naïveté without which no poetry can exist, not even the most sophisticated. This naïveté is the opening of the soul to the sun of chaos . . . This opening, and this alone, is the essential act of attention, the essential poetic and vital act. In this and this alone, we truly *live.*'[69] So in another and wider sense, the activity of the poet expresses what both the Romantics and Lawrence saw as at once the means and aim of all human existence, the creation and achieving of the self by its own powers. For Coleridge 'the poet brings the whole soul of man into activity'; for Blake 'the Poetic genius is the true Man'; in *Apocalypse* Lawrence expressed the urgent need to awaken and develop the 'poetic intelligence'[70] in every man, by which he meant the cultivation of the imaginative as well as the rational elements: 'Thought is a man in his wholeness, wholly attending.' In their lucidity and accessibility to all readers, these late poems represent the perfect fusion of the poet as craftsman with the poet as visionary and prophet. They achieve what Whitman defined as the greatest art: 'The art of art . . . is simplicity . . . to speak in literature with the perfect rectitude and insouciance of the movements of animals . . is the flawless triumph of art. If you have looked on him who has attained it, you have looked on one of the masters of the artists of all nations and times.'[71]

NOTES

1. 'Poetry of the Present', *Phoenix* 220.
2. Ibid. 221.
3. *Letters* i. 546.
4. *Letters* ii. 165.
5. T. S. Eliot, *After Strange Gods* (1934), p. 24.
6. Foreword to *Fantasia of the Unconscious* (1922).
7. Foreword to *COLP*, *Phoenix* 251.
8. Ibid. 252.
9. R. P. Blackmuir, *Language As Gesture: Essays in Poetry* (1954), pp. 286–300.
10. 'E. T.' [Jessie Chambers], *D. H. Lawrence: A Personal Record* (1935), p. 198.
11. Moore 1110.
12. See *Letters* ii. 129–30; the essays on Whitman in *The Symbolic Meaning*, ed. Armon Arnold (Arundel, 1962), and *Studies in Classic American Literature* (1923) and 'Democracy' in *Phoenix* 699–718.
13. Cited by Robert W. French, 'Whitman and Lawrence', in *D. H. Lawrence and Tradition*, ed. Jeffrey Meyers (1985), p. 105.
14. 'Poetry of the Present', *Phoenix* 220.
15. *Letters* ii. 61; 104.
16. T. S. Eliot, 'Tradition and the Individual Talent', *Selected Essays*, p. 22.
17. *Letters* ii. 102–3.
18. 'Poetry of the Present', *Phoenix* 222.
19. *Lectures on Shakespeare* (1818) in *Coleridge: Selected Poetry and Prose*, ed. K. Raine (1987), p. 239.
20. See Blake's 'Letter to Dr Trusler'.
21. 'Chaos in Poetry', *Phoenix* 255.
22. *Letters* i. 489. Perhaps an echo, too, of Whitman's 'The greatest poet . . . is the free channel of himself', *Leaves of Grass*, ed. Malcolm Cowley (1986), p. 13.
23. 'Proverbs of Hell', *The Marriage of Heaven and Hell*.
24. 'The Argument', *The Marriage of Heaven and Hell*. See also *Letters*

ii. 364: 'I shall write out Herakleitos, on tablets of bronze'.

25. See especially Mark Kinkead-Weekes 'The Marriage of Opposites in *The Rainbow*' in *D. H. Lawrence: Centenary Essays*, ed. Mara Kalnins (1986), pp. 21–40 and his introduction to *The Rainbow* (Cambridge, 1989), pp. xxxiii–xxxvi.
26. *COLP* 6. See also *Letters* ii. 539 (dated 15 February 1916): 'For myself, thank God, I feel myself becoming more and more unified, more and more a oneness. And Frieda and I become more and more truly married – for which I thank heaven. It has been such a fight. But it is coming right.'
27. *Study of Thomas Hardy*, *Phoenix* 478.
28. 'The Crown', *Phoenix II* 368.
29. *Letters* ii. 299.
30. *Letters* ii. 339–40.
31. *Letters* ii. 663.
32. See *Letters* iii. 145–6 and n. 1; 148 and n. 1.
33. *Letters* ii. 602.
34. *Letters* ii. 428.
35. *Not I*, 100.
36. *Phoenix II* 328.
37. *Phoenix* 345. Although this comes from 'Review of *Gifts of Fortune* by H. M. Tomlinson' and dates from November 1926, the quotation accurately expresses L.'s feelings at this time.
38. 'The Spirit of Place', *The Symbolic Meaning*, p. 30.
39. *The Dark Sun* (1956), pp. 205–6.
40. *Acts of Attention* (1972), p. 132.
41. See 'Art and Morality' and 'Introduction to these Paintings', *Phoenix*.
42. See the foreword to *Women in Love* where he writes of the 'continual, slightly modified repetition' and defends it as 'natural to the author: and that every crisis in emotion or passion or understanding comes from this pulsing, frictional to-and-fro, which works up to culmination' *Phoenix II* 276. See also the later preface to '*Cavalleria Rusticana* by Giovanni Verga' where L. speaks of the cyclical movement of thought: 'It is a psychological fact, that when we are thinking emotionally or passionately . . . we do not think rationally: and therefore, and therefore, and therefore. Instead, the mind makes curious swoops and circles. It touches the point of pain or interest, then sweeps away again in a cycle . . . There is a curious spiral rhythm . . . until at last there is the closing-in, and the clutch of a decision or a resolve' *Phoenix* 249–50.
43. Moore 1105.
44. Foreword to *Pansies*, *COMP* 423.
45. F. E. Hardy, *The Life of Thomas Hardy 1840–1928* (1962), p. 377.
46. Foreword to *Pansies*, *COMP* 424.

47. *Phoenix II* 512.
48. *The Symbolic Meaning*, p. 138.
49. *Phoenix II* 237; *Apocalypse and the Writings on Revelation*, ed. Mara Kalnins (Cambridge, 1980), p. 96; 142.
50. David Ellis, 'The Place of "pansies" in Lawrence's poetry' in D. Ellis and H. Mills, *D. H. Lawrence's Non-Fiction* (1988), p. 169.
51. Moore 1106.
52. *Apocalypse*, p. 149.
53. Introduction to *Pansies*, *COMP* 417.
54. *Apocalypse*, pp. 96–7.
55. Moore 1172–3.
56. Ibid. 1173; for the full story of this event see Nehls III 326–95.
57. Ibid. 1111.
58. Introduction to *Pansies*, *COMP* 417.
59. *John Heath-Stubbs: Collected Poems 1943–1987* (Manchester: Carcanet, 1988) p. 377.
60. See Introduction to *Last Poems* by Richard Aldington; David Ellis, *D. H. Lawrence's Non-Fiction*, pp. 158–61; Keith Sagar, *D. H. Lawrence: Life into Art* (1985), pp. 324–54, and *D. H. Lawrence: A Calendar of his Works* (1979).
61. Coleridge, *Biographia Literaria*, ch. XIII–XIV.
62. C. G. Jung, 'Psychology and Literature' in *Modern Man in Search of a Soul*, transl. C. F. Baynes (New York, 1933), p. 157.
63. *Phoenix* 255. Cf. Shelley's 'A Defence of Poetry': 'Poetry . . . strips the veil of familiarity from the world . . . it purges from our inward sight the film of familiarity which obscures from us the wonder of our being . . . It creates anew the universe, after it has been annihilated in our minds by the recurrence of impressions blunted by reiteration.'
64. Jung, op. cit., p. 162.
65. *The Necessary Angel* (New York, 1966), p. 66.
66. 'Auguries of Innocence'.
67. 'Song of Myself', *Leaves of Grass*, ii., 1329–30.
68. *Measure for Measure* III i, 123–5.
69. *Phoenix* 259–61.
70. Coleridge, *Biographia Literaria*, ed. G. Watson (1965), p. 173; Blake, 'All Religions are One'; Letter to Charles Wilson (2 February 1928) cited in *Apocalypse*, p. 19.
71. *Leaves of Grass*, pp. 12–13.

NOTE ON THE TEXTS AND ACKNOWLEDGEMENTS

No wholly authoritative edition of Lawrence's poetry exists, though a definitive one is now in preparation as part of the Cambridge Edition of the Works and Letters. Until then *The Complete Poems of D. H. Lawrence* in two volumes, edited by Vivian de Sola Pinto and Warren Roberts (1964), remains the most complete and accurate to date despite considerable errors of transmission.

The textual history of Lawrence's poems reveals editorial interference and censorship, though happily not to the same extent as that of the novels and essays. Lawrence himself collected, extensively revised and proofread his poetry for the two-volume *Collected Poems* (1928) between November 1927 and March 1928. Volume I, titled 'Rhyming Poems', included *Love Poems* (1913), *Amores* (1916), *New Poems* (1918) and *Bay* (1919); Volume II, titled 'Unrhyming Poems', contained *Look! We Have Come Through!* (1917) and *Birds, Beasts and Flowers* (1923). The extent of Lawrence's revisions and alterations can be seen by consulting Ferrier's *Variorum* and some of the versions in Appendix 3 to *Complete Poems*. For a full publishing history of this, and other volumes of Lawrence's poetry, see Warren Roberts, *A Bibliography of D. H. Lawrence* (1982). Lawrence also prepared his *Pansies* poems for publication but the typescript was seized in December 1928 by the postal authorities on orders from the Home Office, probably as a result of the banning of *Lady Chatterley's Lover*. Although Lawrence revised and retyped the poems, fourteen were omitted from the first edition (July 1929) but restored in a privately printed edition (August 1929). The volume of poems which he next prepared for publication was

Nettles, written as a response to the censorship of *Pansies* and the police seizure of his paintings from the Warren Gallery, London, in July 1929, and published immediately after his death (March 1930). Lawrence's late poems are written in two notebooks in the possession of the Harry Ransom Humanities Research Center, University of Texas at Austin. These formed the basis for the posthumous *Last Poems* (1932), edited by Richard Aldington and Giuseppe Orioli, but that edition is inaccurate, containing both substantive and punctuation errors and in places even omitting whole lines. In his introduction Aldington suggests that Lawrence intended the poems in these notebooks to form two separate collections and he therefore divided them into 'More Pansies' and 'Last Poems'. However, since no authorial evidence for such a division exists the poems in this selection are simply grouped under the heading 'Last Poems'.

The base texts for this selection are the first editions which Lawrence prepared and proofread and which therefore have his authority: *The Collected Poems* (1928), *Pansies* (unexpurgated, 1929), and *Nettles* (1930). The poems in the *Last Poems*, however, have been emended and corrected with reference to the author's two manuscript notebooks. These are the most authoritative texts available until the Cambridge edition of *The Poems of D. H. Lawrence* is completed. The following emendations have been made silently:

(i) clearly accidental spelling or punctuation errors by the typesetter have been corrected;

(ii) accidental omissions, as in final stops and apostrophes in colloquial contractions, have been supplied.

The cardinal principle which must govern any selection is that of doing justice to the author. The poems included in this volume total only a quarter of Lawrence's poetic *oeuvre* and inevitably some have been omitted that have appeared in other selections and anthologies, but the poems chosen do represent the whole chronological range of Lawrence's writing and intend to show the reader something of the diversity and richness of his work. If an emphasis has been placed on the later poems, this expresses the editor's view that these poems may have been undervalued by critics in the past and that they are among the author's finest literary achievements.

Appendix I

Although it is not possible in a necessarily limited selection of Lawrence's poems to include early drafts and different versions, the five versions of 'Ship of Death' and 'Bavarian Gentians', originally published from Lawrence's notebooks as an appendix to the *Last Poems*, are reprinted here to afford the reader an insight into the way his process of vision and revision operated. The base text is that of the *Last Poems* checked against the manuscript notebooks. For other versions and cycles of poems with similar themes which illuminate Lawrence's poetic method, as discussed in the introduction to this volume, the reader is directed to the *Complete Poems* and Ferrier's *Variorum*.

Appendix II

The seven texts printed here represent Lawrence's most important essays on his own poetry. 'Poetry of the Present', written in August 1919 as an introduction to the American edition of *New Poems* (June 1920), first appeared in *Playboy*, numbers 4 and 5 (1919), and was later collected in *Phoenix* (1936) and included in *Complete Poems*. Lawrence's review of Harry Crosby's *Chariot of the Sun* was written on 26 April 1928 with three additional pages added on 29 April and then revised on 1 May. It first appeared as 'Chaos in Poetry' in *Exchanges* (December 1929) and subsequently as the introduction to *Chariot of the Sun* (November 1931) and was again reprinted, with some slight differences, in *Phoenix*. Although technically it is not about Lawrence's own poetry in the sense that the other prefaces, forewords and introductions in this Appendix are, it is included because it is Lawrence's most substantial late essay on poetry and because his ideas here illuminate the distinctive poetic method and style he evolved in his own last poems.

The preface and foreword to the *Collected Poems* were both written in May 1928. The shorter preface was used in the *Collected Poems* and the longer foreword published in *Phoenix*: both are reprinted in the *Complete Poems*. Lawrence wrote an early foreword to *Pansies* in December 1928 in the same notebook as the poems (dated 'Christmas 1928' but this first version only appeared in the *Review of English Studies* for May 1970). A revised, longer version of this piece, printed here, appeared as the introduction to the unexpurgated edition of *Pansies*. In March and April 1929 Lawrence also wrote a shorter foreword which was published with the expurgated edition. Both the introduction and foreword were also reprinted in the *Complete Poems* and *Phoenix*. Finally, in the autumn of 1929 Lawrence wrote a set of prefaces for a new edition of *Birds, Beasts and Flowers* and these are included here for interest. In a rare acknowledgement to Burnet's *Early Greek Philosophy*, which he was re-reading, Lawrence wrote that the prefaces were 'part original and sometimes quotations from the fragments of Xenophanes and Empedokles and others, but I should like it all put in inverted commas, and let them crack their wits (the public) to find out what is ancient quotation and what isn't (It is nearly all of it me)' (letter to Laurence Pollinger, 25 November 1929). The new edition of *Birds, Beasts and Flowers* was published by the Cresset Press (1930) with wood-engravings by Blair Hughes-Stanton. The prefaces here, which also appear in the *Complete Poems*, reproduce that text.

Inevitably, any editor of Lawrence must acknowledge the scholarship of earlier editions and critical studies. Among the former I would like to acknowledge my debt to the editors of the *Complete Poems*, the editors of the Cambridge Edition of the Works and Letters, and Keith Sagar's *D. H. Lawrence: a calendar of his works* (1979). Of the many critical works cited in the bibliography that follows special mention must be made of Sandra Gilbert's *Acts of Attention* (1972), Graham Hough's early study *The Dark Sun* (1956), Keith Sagar's *D. H. Lawrence: Life into Art* (1985), and David Ellis's chapter on Lawrence's poetry in David Ellis and Howard Mills, *D. H. Lawrence's Non-Fiction: Art, Thought and Genre* (1988). I must also thank Laurence Pollinger Ltd and the Estate of Mrs Frieda Lawrence Ravagli as well as the Harry Ransom Humanities Research Center for permission to consult and use the manuscript notebooks of the *Last Poems* for this selection; Cambridge University Press for permission to quote from their edition of Lawrence's letters; and Carcanet for permission to cite the two lines from John Heath-Stubbs's 'Ars Poetica'. My special thanks go to the University of Texas at Austin for a fellowship to enable me to undertake research at the Harry Ransom Humanities Research Center, to George Donaldson for his invaluable criticism and encouragement, to Chris Pollnitz and Lindeth Vasey for helpful advice on editorial matters, and to Gabrielle Firmager for generous help with proofreading.

SELECT BIBLIOGRAPHY

The place of publication is London unless otherwise stated.

WORKS OF D. H. LAWRENCE

(i) MANUSCRIPTS. Two notebooks containing the poems published as *Nettles* (1930) and *Last Poems* (1932) in the Harry Ransom Humanities Research Center, The University of Texas at Austin.

(ii) EDITIONS OF THE POEMS. No definitive edition of the poetry is available until the Cambridge *The Poems of D. H. Lawrence*, eds Carole Ferrier and Chris Pollnitz, is published. Until then the two-volume *The Complete Poems of D. H. Lawrence*, eds Vivian de Sola Pinto and Warren Roberts (Heinemann, 1964) and the first editions are the most authoritative. The first editions are as follows: *Love Poems and Others* (Duckworth; New York: Huebsch, 1913); *Amores* (Duckworth; New York: Huebsch, 1916); *Look! We Have Come Through!* (Chatto and Windus; New York: Huebsch, 1917); *New Poems* (Secker, 1918; New York: Huebsch, 1920); *Bay* (Beaumont, 1919); *Tortoises* (New York: Seltzer, 1921); *Birds, Beasts and Flowers* (Secker; New York: Seltzer, 1923); *The Collected Poems of D. H. Lawrence* (Secker, 1928; New York: Cape and Smith, 1929); *Pansies* (Secker; New York: Knopf, 1929; unexpurgated edition privately printed by Stephensen, 1929); *Nettles* (Faber and Faber, 1930); *Last Poems* (Florence: Orioli, 1932; Secker; New York: Viking, 1933).

(iii) EDITIONS OF THE PROSE WORKS. L.'s complete works are widely available in both hardback and paperback (the latter principally Penguin in the UK and Viking in the USA) but these editions are textually inaccurate, based as they are on the censored and expurgated first editions which all subsequent editions have followed. The authoritative Cambridge Edition of the Works and Letters (general editor J. T. Boulton) is in the process of being published and at the time of going to press has published the following volumes: *Apocalypse and the*

Writings on Revelation, ed. Mara Kalnins (1980); *The Trespasser*, ed. Elizabeth Mansfield (1981); *The Lost Girl*, ed. John Worthen (1981); *St Mawr and Other Stories*, ed. Brian Finney (1983); *The White Peacock*, ed. Andrew Robertson (1983); *The Prussian Officer and Other Stories*, ed. John Worthen (1983); *Mr Noon*, ed. Lindeth Vasey (1984); *Study of Thomas Hardy and Other Essays*, ed. Bruce Steele (1985); *The Plumed Serpent*, ed. L. D. Clark (1987); *Women in Love* eds David Farmer, Lindeth Vasey, and John Worthen (1987); *Love Among the Haystacks and Other Stories*, ed. John Worthen (1987); *Reflections on the Death of A Porcupine and Other Essays*, ed. Michael Herbert (1988); *Aaron's Rod*, ed. Mara Kalnins (1988); *The Rainbow*, ed. Mark Kinkead-Weekes (1989); *Movements in European History*, ed. Philip Crumpton (1989); *The Boy in the Bush*, ed. Paul Eggert (1990); *England, My England*, ed. Bruce Steele (1990).

First editions of L.'s principal works, on both sides of the Atlantic, are: *The White Peacock* (Heinemann; New York: Duffield, 1911); *The Trespasser* (Duckworth; New York: Kennerly, 1912); *Sons and Lovers* (Duckworth; New York: Kennerly, 1913); *The Widowing of Mrs Holroyd* (New York: Kennerly; Duckworth 1914); *The Prussian Officer* (Duckworth, 1914; New York: Huebsch, 1916); *The Rainbow* (Methuen; New York: Huebsch, 1915); *Twilight in Italy* (Duckworth; New York: Huebsch, 1916); *Touch and Go* (Daniel; New York: Seltzer, 1920); *Women in Love* (New York: privately printed, 1920; Secker; 1921); *The Lost Girl* (Secker, 1920; New York: Seltzer, 1921); *Movements in European History* [by Lawrence H. Davison] (Oxford: Oxford University Press, 1921); *Psychoanalysis and the Unconscious* (New York: Seltzer, 1921; Secker, 1923); *Sea and Sardinia* (New York: Seltzer, 1921; Secker, 1923); *Aaron's Rod* (Secker; New York: Seltzer, 1922); *Fantasia of the Unconscious* (New York: Seltzer, 1922; Secker, 1923); *England, My England* (New York: Seltzer, 1922; Secker, 1924); *The Ladybird* (Secker; New York: Seltzer, 1923); *Studies in Classic American Literature* (New York: Seltzer, 1923; Secker, 1924); *Kangaroo* (Secker; New York: Seltzer, 1923); *Mastro Don Gesualdo*, transl. by L. (New York: Seltzer, 1923; Cape, 1925); *The Boy in the Bush* [with Mollie Skinner], (Secker; New York: Seltzer, 1924); *Little Novels of Sicily*, transl. by L. (New York: Seltzer; Blackwell, 1925); *St Mawr Together with The Princess* (Secker, 1925); *Reflections on the Death of a Porcupine* (Philadelphia: Centaur Press, 1925); *The Plumed Serpent* (Secker; New York: Knopf, 1926); *David* (Secker; New York: Knopf, 1926); *Sun* (Archer, 1926; Paris: Black Sun Press, 1928); *Glad Ghosts* (Ernest Benn Ltd 1926); *Mornings in Mexico* (Secker; New York: Knopf, 1927); *Cavalleria Rusticana*, transl. by L. (Cape; New York: Dial, 1928); *Rawdon's Roof* (Elkin Mathews & Marnot, 1928); *The Woman Who Rode Away and Other Stories* (Secker; New York: Knopf, 1928); *Lady Chatterley's Lover* (Florence: privately printed, 1928; Secker; New

York: Knopf, 1932); *The Story of Doctor Manente*, transl. by L. (Florence: Orioli, 1929); *The Paintings of D. H. Lawrence* (Mandrake Press, 1929); *The Escaped Cock* (Paris: The Black Sun Press, 1929; Secker, 1931); *Assorted Articles* (Secker; New York: Knopf, 1930); *The Virgin and the Gipsy* (Florence: Orioli; Secker; New York: Knopf, 1930); *Love Among the Haystacks* (Nonesuch Press, 1930; New York: Viking, 1933); *Apocalypse* (Florence: Orioli, 1931; Secker; New York: Seltzer, 1932); *Etruscan Places* (Secker; New York: Viking, 1932); *The Lovely Lady* (Secker; New York: Viking, 1933); *The Plays of D. H. Lawrence* (Secker, 1933); *Phoenix: The Posthumous Papers* (Heinemann; New York: Viking, 1936); *Phoenix II* (Heinemann; New York: Viking, 1968).

(iv) LETTERS. Of the projected seven volumes of L.'s correspondence in the Cambridge *The Letters of D. H. Lawrence*, eds James T. Boulton *et al.*, vols i. to vi. have been published (1979–91). Earlier important collections of the correspondence are: *The Letters of D. H. Lawrence*, ed. Aldous Huxley (Heinemann; New York: Viking, 1932); *The Collected Letters of D. H. Lawrence*, 2 vols, ed. Harry T. Moore (London: Heinemann; New York: Viking, 1962); *The Quest for Rananim: D. H. Lawrence's Letters to S. S. Koteliansky 1914–30*, ed. George J. Zytaruk (Montreal: McGill-Queen's University Press, 1970); *Letters to Thomas and Adele Seltzer*, ed. Gerald M. Lacy (Santa Barbara: Black Sparrow Press, 1976).

SECONDARY WORKS

(i) BIOGRAPHIES. As with the authoritative edition of L.'s works, the standard biography will be the three-volume Cambridge, of which vol. I has been published: *D. H. Lawrence: The Early Years: 1885–1912* by John Worthen (1991). Vol. II, 1912–22, will be by Mark Kinkead-Weekes; vol. III, 1922–30, by David Ellis. Other biographies include: Aldington, Richard, *Portrait of a Genius, But . . .* (Heinemann, 1950); Brewster, Earl and Achsah, *D. H. Lawrence: Reminiscences and Correspondence* (Secker, 1934); Carswell, Catherine, *The Savage Pilgrimage* (Secker; New York: Harcourt, 1932); Chambers, Jessie, *D. H. Lawrence: A Personal Record*, by E. T. (Cape, 1935); Corke, Helen, *D. H. Lawrence: The Croydon Years* (Austin: The University of Texas Press, 1957); Delavenay, Emile, *D. H. Lawrence, The Man and His Work: The Formative Years, 1885–1919* (Carbondale & Edwardsville: Southern Illinois University Press, 1972); Lawrence, Ada, and Gelder, G. S., *Young Lorenzo: Early Life of D. H. Lawrence* (Florence: Orioli, 1931); Lawrence, Frieda, *'Not I, but the Wind . . .'* (Santa Fe: Rydal Press; New York: Viking, 1934; Heinemann, 1935); Lawrence, Frieda, *The Memoirs and Correspondence* (Heinemann,

1961; New York: Knopf, 1964); Luhan, Mabel Dodge, *Lorenzo in Taos* (New York: Knopf, 1932); Moore, Harry T., *The Life and Works of D. H. Lawrence* (Allen & Unwin; New York: Twayne, 1951); Moore, Harry T., *The Intelligent Heart* (New York: Farrar, 1954; Heinemann, 1955); Moore, Harry T., *The Priest of Love* (rev. edn, Heinemann, 1974); Murry, John Middleton, *Reminiscences of D. H. Lawrence* (Cape, 1933); Nehls, Edward, *D. H. Lawrence: A Composite Biography*, 3 vols (Madison: University of Wisconsin Press, 1957–9); Sagar, Keith, *D. H. Lawrence: Life into Art* (Harmondsworth: Penguin, 1985).

(ii) CRITICAL WORKS ON THE POEMS. Alvarez, Alfred, 'D. H. Lawrence: The Single State of Mind' in *A D. H. Lawrence Miscellany*, ed. Harry T. Moore (Carbondale: Southern Illinois University Press; Heinemann, 1961); Auden, W. H., 'Some Notes on D. H. Lawrence', *The Nation* (April 26, 1947), pp. 482–4; Auden, W. H., 'D. H. Lawrence' in *The Dyer's Hand and Other Essays* (Faber; New York: Random, 1948); Baker, James R., 'Lawrence as a Prophetic Poet', *The Journal of Modern Literature* (March 1974), pp. 1219–38; Banerjee, A., (ed.), *D. H. Lawrence's Poetry: Demon Liberated* (Macmillan, 1990); Bartlett, Phyllis, 'Lawrence's Collected Poems: The Demon Takes Over' *PMLA* 66 (1951), pp. 583–93; Beal, Anthony, *D. H. Lawrence* (New York; Grove, 1961); Blackmuir, R. P., 'D. H. Lawrence and Expressive Form', *The Double Agent* (New York: Arrow, 1935) and *Language as Gesture: Essays in Poetry* (Allen & Unwin, 1954); Bloom, Harold, 'Lawrence, Blackmuir, Eliot and the Tortoise' in *A D. H. Lawrence Miscellany*, ed. Harry T. Moore (Carbondale: Southern Illinois University Press, 1961); Clark, L. D., *Dark Night of the Body* (Austin: University of Texas Press, 1964); Colmer, John, 'Lawrence and Blake' in *D. H. Lawrence and Tradition*, ed. J. Meyers (Athlone Press, 1985); Davie, Donald, *Thomas Hardy and British Poetry* (Oxford: Oxford University Press, 1972); Draper, R. P., *D. H. Lawrence: The Critical Heritage* (New York: Twayne, 1964; Routledge, 1970); Draper, R. P., 'The Poetry of D. H. Lawrence' in *D. H. Lawrence: New Studies*, ed. Chris Heywood (Macmillan, 1987); Draper, R. P., 'Lawrence's Last Poems' in *Lyrical Tragedy* (Heinemann, 1989); Ellis, David, 'Verse or worse: the place of "pansies" in Lawrence's poetry' in David Ellis and Howard Mills, *D. H. Lawrence's Non-Fiction* (Cambridge: Cambridge University Press, 1988); Ellmann, Richard, 'Barbed Wire and Coming Through' in *The Achievement of D. H. Lawrence*, eds F. J. Hoffman and Harry T. Moore (Norman: University of Oklahoma Press, 1953); Ferrier, Carole, and Tiedje, Egon, 'D. H. Lawrence's Pre-1920 Poetry: The Textual Approach: An Exchange', *The D. H. Lawrence Review* 5 (1972), pp. 149–57; French, Roberts W., 'Whitman and the Poetics of Lawrence' in *D. H. Lawrence and Tradition*, ed. J. Meyers (Athlone Press, 1985); Gilbert, Sandra, *Acts of Attention: The Poems of D. H. Lawrence* (Ithaca & New York: Cornell University Press, 1972); Gilbert, Sandra, 'Hell on Earth: Birds, Beasts and Flowers as Subversive Narrative', *The D. H. Lawrence Review* 12 (1979), pp. 256–73; Hassell, Christopher, 'Black Flowers: A New Light on the Poetics of D. H. Lawrence' in *A D. H. Lawrence Miscellany*, ed. Harry T. Moore (Carbondale: Southern Illinois University Press, 1959); Hough, Graham, *The Dark Sun* (Duckworth, 1956); Jones, R. T., 'D. H. Lawrence's Poetry: Art and the Apprehension of Fact' in *D. H. Lawrence: A Critical Study of the Major Novels and Other Writings*, ed. A. H. Gomme (New York: Barnes, 1978); Kalnins, Mara, 'Symbolic Seeing: Lawrence and Heraclitus' in *D. H. Lawrence: Centenary Essays*, ed. Mara Kalnins (Bristol: Bristol Classical Press, 1986); Langbaum, Robert, *The Modern Spirit: Essays on the Continuity of Nineteenth and Twentieth Century Literature* (Oxford: Oxford University Press, 1970); Langbaum, Robert, *The Mysteries of Identity: A Theme in Modern Literature* (Oxford: Oxford University Press, 1977); Mace, H. R. 'The Genesis of D. H. Lawrence's Poetic Form' in *Critical Essays on D. H. Lawrence*, ed. Jackson and Jackson (Boston: G. K. Hall, 1988); Mandell, Gail P., *The Phoenix Paradox* (Carbondale: Southern Illinois University Press, *c.*1984); Marshall, Tom, *The Psychic Mariner: A Reading of the Poems of D. H. Lawrence* (New York: Viking, 1970); Monroe, Harriet, 'Review of *The Collected Poems*' in *Poetry* xxxv (February, 1930), pp. 273–9; Nahal, Chaman, 'The Colour Ambience in Lawrence's Early and Later Poetry' in *The D. H. Lawrence Review* 8 (1975), pp. 147–54; Nin, Anais, *D. H. Lawrence: An Unprofessional Study* (Paris: Titus, 1932); Oates, Joyce Carol, *The Hostile Sun: The Poetry of D. H. Lawrence* (Los Angeles: Black Sparrow Press, 1973); Panichas, George A., *Adventures in Consciousness* (The Hague: Mouton & Co., 1964); Partlow, Robert B., and Moore, Harry T., (eds), *D. H. Lawrence: The Man Who Lived* (Carbondale & Edwardsville: Southern Illinois University Press, 1980); Perkins, David, *A History of Modern Poetry: From the 1890s to Pound, Eliot and Yeats* (Cambridge, Mass: Harvard University Press, 1976); Pinion, F. B., *A D. H. Lawrence Companion* (Macmillan, 1978); Pinto, Vivian de Sola, *D. H. Lawrence: Prophet of the Midlands* (Nottingham: University of Nottingham Press, 1951); Pinto, Vivian de Sola, 'D. H. Lawrence: Letter-Writer and Craftsman in Verse', *Renaissance and Modern Studies* 1 (1957), pp. 5–34; Pinto, Vivian de Sola, 'Introduction: D. H. Lawrence: Poet Without a Mask', in *Complete Poems*, pp. 1–21 (Heinemann; New York: Viking, 1967); Pollnitz, Chris, 'Raptus Virginis: The Dark God in the Poetry of D. H. Lawrence' in *D. H. Lawrence: Centenary Essays*, ed. Mara Kalnins (Bristol: Bristol Classical Press, 1986); Potts, Abbie Findlay, *The Elegiac Mode: Poetic Form in Wordsworth and Other Elegists* (Ithaca: Cornell University Press, 1967); Pritchard, William H., *Seeing Through*

Everything: English Writers, 1918–49 (Oxford: Oxford University Press, 1977); Sagar, Keith, *The Art of D. H. Lawrence* (Cambridge: Cambridge University Press, 1966); Sagar, Keith, *D. H. Lawrence: Life into Art* (Harmondsworth: Penguin, 1985); Sagar, Keith, 'The Genesis of "Bavarian Gentians"', *The D. H. Lawrence Review* 8 (1975), pp. 47–53; Salgado, Gamini, *A Preface to Lawrence* (Longman, 1982); Shapiro, Karl, 'The Unemployed Magician' in *A D. H. Lawrence Miscellany*, ed. Harry T. Moore, pp. 378–95 (Carbondale: Southern Illinois University Press, 1959); Spender, Stephen, *D. H. Lawrence: Novelist, Poet, Prophet* (New York: Harper, 1973); Tedlock, E. W., *D. H. Lawrence: Artist and Rebel* (Albuquerque: University of New Mexico Press, 1963); Trail, George, 'Toward a Lawrencian Poetic', *The D. H. Lawrence Review* 5 (1972), pp. 67–81; Trail, George, 'West by East: The Psycho-Geography of *Birds, Beasts and Flowers*', *The D. H. Lawrence Review* 12 (1979), pp. 241–55; Vickery, John, 'D. H. Lawrence's Poetry: Myth and Matter', *The D. H. Lawrence Review* 7 (1974), pp. 1–18; Youngblood, Sarah, 'Substance and Shadow: The Self in Lawrence's Poetry', *The D. H. Lawrence Review* 1 (1968), pp. 114–28.

(iii) REFERENCE. Ferrier, Carole, 'D. H. Lawrence's Pre-1920 Poetry: A Descriptive Bibliography of Manuscripts, Typescripts, and Proofs', *The D. H. Lawrence Review* 6 (1973), pp. 333–59; Ferrier, Carole, 'D. H. Lawrence's Poetry, 1920–1928: A Descriptive Bibliography of Manuscripts, Typescripts, and Proofs', *The D. H. Lawrence Review* 12 (1979), pp. 289–303; Ferrier, Carole, 'The Earlier Poetry of D. H. Lawrence: A Variorum Text, Comprising All Extant Incunabula and Published Poems up to and Including the Year 1919', 2 vols, PhD Dissertation, University of Auckland, 1971; McDonald, Edward D., *The Writings of D. H. Lawrence* (Philadelphia: Centaur Bookshop, 1931); Sagar, Keith, *D. H. Lawrence: a calendar of his works*, with a checklist of the manuscripts of D. H. Lawrence by Lindeth Vasey (Manchester: Manchester University Press, 1979); Roberts, Warren, *A Bibliography of D. H. Lawrence* (Rupert Hart-Davis, 1963; rev. edn 1982); Tedlock, E. W., *The Frieda Lawrence Collection of D. H. Lawrence Manuscripts: A Descriptive Bibliography* (Albuquerque: University of New Mexico Press, 1948).

RHYMING POEMS

THE WILD COMMON

The quick sparks on the gorse-bushes are leaping
Little jets of sunlight texture imitating flame;
Above them, exultant, the peewits are sweeping:
They have triumphed again o'er the ages, their screamings
proclaim.

Rabbits, handfuls of brown earth, lie
Low-rounded on the mournful turf they have bitten down to the
quick.
Are they asleep? – are they living? – Now see, when I
Lift my arms, the hill bursts and heaves under their spurting kick!

The common flaunts bravely; but below, from the rushes
Crowds of glittering king-cups surge to challenge the blossoming
bushes;
There the lazy streamlet pushes
His bent course mildly; here wakes again, leaps, laughs, and
gushes

Into a deep pond, an old sheep-dip,
Dark, overgrown with willows, cool, with the brook ebbing
through so slow;
Naked on the steep, soft lip
Of the turf I stand watching my own white shadow quivering to
and fro.

What if the gorse-flowers shrivelled, and I were gone?
What if the waters ceased, where were the marigolds then, and the
gudgeon?
What is this thing that I look down upon?
White on the water wimples my shadow, strains like a dog on a
string, to run on.

How it looks back, like a white dog to its master!
I on the bank all substance, my shadow all shadow looking up to
me, looking back!
And the water runs, and runs faster, runs faster,
And the white dog dances and quivers, I am holding his cord quite
slack.

But how splendid it is to be substance, here!
My shadow is neither here nor there; but I, I am royally here!
I am here! I am here! screams the peewit; the may-blobs burst out
in a laugh as they hear!
Here! flick the rabbits. Here! pants the gorse. Here! say the insects
far and near.

Over my skin in the sunshine, the warm, clinging air
Flushed with the songs of seven larks singing at once, goes kissing
me glad.
You are here! You are here! We have found you! Everywhere
We sought you substantial, you touchstone of caresses, you naked
lad!

Oh but the water loves me and folds me,
Plays with me, sways me, lifts me and sinks me, murmurs:
Oh marvellous stuff!
No longer shadow! – and it holds me
Close, and it rolls me, enfolds me, touches me, as if never it could
touch me enough.

Sun, but in substance, yellow water-blobs!
Wings and feathers on the crying, mysterious ages, peewits
wheeling!
All that is right, all that is good, all that is God takes substance!
a rabbit lobs
In confirmation, I hear sevenfold lark-songs pealing.

DOG-TIRED

If she would come to me here
Now the sunken swaths
Are glittering paths
To the sun, and the swallows cut clear
Into the setting sun! if she came to me here!

If she would come to me now,
Before the last-mown harebells are dead;
While that vetch-clump still burns red!

Before all the bats have dropped from the bough
To cool in the night; if she came to me now!

The horses are untackled, the chattering machine
Is still at last. If she would come
We could gather up the dry hay from
The hill-brow, and lie quite still, till the green
Sky ceased to quiver, and lost its active sheen.

I should like to drop
On the hay, with my head on her knee,
And lie dead still, while she
Breathed quiet above me; and the crop
Of stars grew silently.

I should like to lie still
As if I was dead; but feeling
Her hand go stealing
Over my face and my head, until
This ache was shed.

FROM A COLLEGE WINDOW

The glimmer of the limes, sun-heavy, sleeping,
Goes trembling past me up the College wall.
Below, the lawn, in soft blue shade is keeping
The daisy-froth quiescent, softly in thrall.

Beyond the leaves that overhang the street,
Along the flagged, clean pavement summer-white,
Passes the world with shadows at their feet
Going left and right.

Remote, although I hear the beggar's cough,
See the woman's twinkling fingers tend him a coin,
I sit absolved, assured I am better off
Beyond a world I never want to join.

DISCORD IN CHILDHOOD

Outside the house an ash-tree hung its terrible whips,
And at night when the wind rose, the lash of the tree
Shrieked and slashed the wind, as a ship's
Weird rigging in a storm shrieks hideously.

Within the house two voices arose, a slender lash
Whistling she-delirious rage, and the dreadful sound
Of a male thong booming and bruising, until it had drowned
The other voice in a silence of blood, 'neath the noise of the ash.

CHERRY ROBBERS

Under the long dark boughs, like jewels red
  In the hair of an Eastern girl
Hang strings of crimson cherries, as if had bled
  Blood-drops beneath each curl.

Under the glistening cherries, with folded wings
  Three dead birds lie:
Pale-breasted throstles and a blackbird, robberlings
  Stained with red dye.

Against the haystack a girl stands laughing at me,
  Cherries hung round her ears.
Offers me her scarlet fruit: I will see
  If she has any tears.

GIPSY

I, the man with the red scarf,
  Will give thee what I have, this last week's earnings.
Take them and buy thee a silver ring
  And wed me, to ease my yearnings.

For the rest, when thou art wedded
  I'll wet my brow for thee
With sweat, I'll enter a house for thy sake,
  Thou shalt shut doors on me.

THE COLLIER'S WIFE

Somebody's knockin' at th' door
  Mother, come down an' see!
–I's think it's nobbut a beggar;
  Say I'm busy.

It's not a beggar, mother; hark
  How 'ard 'e knocks!
–Eh, tha'rt a mard-arsed kid,
  'E'll gie thee socks!

Shout an' ax what 'e wants,
  I canna come down.
–'E says, is it Arthur Holliday's?
  –Say Yes, tha clown.

'E says: Tell your mother as 'er mester's
  Got hurt i' th' pit–
What? Oh my Sirs, 'e never says that,
  That's not it!

Come out o' th' way an' let me see!
  Eh, there's no peace!
An' stop thy scraightin', childt,
  Do shut thy face!

'Your mester's 'ad a accident
  An' they ta'ein' 'im i' th' ambulance
Ter Nottingham.' –Eh dear o' me,
  If 'e's not a man for mischance!

Wheer's 'e hurt this time, lad?
  –I dunna know,
They on'y towd me it wor bad–
  It would be so!

Out o' my way, childt! dear o' me, wheer
  'Ave I put 'is clean stockin's an' shirt?
Goodness knows if they'll be able
  To take off 'is pit-dirt!

An' what a moan 'e'll make! there niver
  Was such a man for a fuss
If anything ailed 'im; at any rate
  I shan't 'ave 'im to nuss.

I do 'ope as it's not so very bad!
  Eh, what a shame it seems
As some should ha'e hardly a smite o' trouble
  An' others 'as reams!

It's a shame as 'e should be knocked about
  Like this, I'm sure it is!
'E's 'ad twenty accidents, if 'e's 'ad one;
  Owt bad, an' it's his!

There's one thing, we s'll 'ave a peaceful 'ouse f'r a bit,
  Thank heaven for a peaceful house!
An' there's compensation, sin' it's accident,
  An' club-money – I won't growse.

An' a fork an' a spoon 'e'll want – an' what else?
  I s'll never catch that train!
What a traipse it is, if a man gets hurt!
  I sh'd think 'e'll get right again.

MONOLOGUE OF A MOTHER

This is the last of all, then, this is the last!
I must fold my hands, and turn my face to the fire,
And watch my dead days fusing together in dross,
Shape after shape, and scene after scene of my past
Clotting to one dead mass in the sinking fire
Where ash on the dying coals grows swiftly, like heavy moss.

Strange he is, my son, for whom I have waited like a lover;
Strange to me, like a captive in a foreign country, haunting
The confines, gazing out beyond, where the winds go free;
White and gaunt, with wistful eyes that hover
Always on the distance, as if his soul were chaunting
A monotonous weird of departure away from me.

Like a thin white bird blown out of the northern seas,
Like a bird from the far north blown with a broken wing
Into our sooty garden, he drags and beats
Along the fence perpetually, seeking release
From me, from the hand of my love which creeps up, needing
His happiness, whilst he in displeasure retreats.

I must look away from him, for my faded eyes
Like a cringing dog at his heels offend him now,
Like a toothless hound pursuing him with my will;
Till he chafes at my crouching persistence, and a sharp spark flies
In my soul from under the sudden frown of his brow
As he blenches and turns away, and my heart stands still.

This is the last, it will not be any more.
All my life I have borne the burden of myself,
All the long years of sitting in my husband's house;
Never have I said to myself as he closed the door:
'Now I am caught! You are hopelessly lost, O Self!
You are frightened with joy, my heart, like a frightened mouse.'

Three times have I offered myself, three times rejected.
It will not be any more. No more, my son, my son! –
Never to know the glad freedom of obedience, since long ago
The angel of childhood kissed me and went! I expected
This last one to claim me; – and now, my son, O my son,
I must sit alone and wait, and never know
The loss of myself, till death comes, who cannot fail.

Death, in whose service is nothing of gladness, takes me;
For the lips and the eyes of God are behind a veil.
And the thought of the lipless voice of the Father shakes me
With dread, and fills my heart with the tears of desire,
And my heart rebels with anguish, as night draws nigher.

THE BEST OF SCHOOL

The blinds are drawn because of the sun,
And the boys and the room in a colourless gloom
Of underwater float: bright ripples run
Across the walls as the blinds are blown
To let the sunlight in; and I,
As I sit on the shores of the class, alone,
Watch the boys in their summer blouses
As they write, their round heads busily bowed:
And one after another rouses
His face to look at me,
To ponder very quietly,
As seeing, he does not see.

And then he turns again, with a little, glad
Thrill of his work he turns again from me,
Having found what he wanted, having got what was to be had.

And very sweet it is, while the sunlight waves
In the ripening morning, to sit alone with the class
And feel the stream of awakening ripple and pass
From me to the boys, whose brightening souls it laves
For this little hour.

This morning, sweet it is
To feel the lads' looks light on me,
Then back in a swift, bright flutter to work;
Each one darting away with his
Discovery, like birds that steal and flee.

Touch after touch I feel on me
As their eyes glance at me for the grain
Of rigour they taste delightedly.

As tendrils reach out yearningly,
Slowly rotate till they touch the tree
That they cleave unto, and up which they climb
Up to their lives – so they to me.

I feel them cling and cleave to me
As vines going eagerly up; they twine
My life with other leaves, my time
Is hidden in theirs, their thrills are mine.

DREAMS OLD AND NASCENT

OLD

I have opened the windows to warm my hands on the sill
Where the sunlight soaks in the stone: the afternoon
Is full of dreams, my love; the boys are all still
In a wistful dream of Lorna Doone.

The clink of the shunting engines is sharp and fine
Like savage music striking far off; and there
On the great blue palace at Sydenham, lights stir and shine
Where the glass is domed on the silent air.

There lies the world, my darling, full of wonder and wistfulness,
    and strange
Recognitions and greetings of half-acquaint things, as I greet the
    cloud
Of glass palace aloft there, among misty, indefinite things that
    range
At the back of my life's experience, where dreams from the old
    lives crowd.

Over the nearness of Norwood Hill, through the mellow veil
Of the afternoon glows still the old romance of David and Dora,
With the old, sweet, soothing tears, and laughter that shakes the
    sail
Of the ship of the soul over seas where dreamed dreams lure the
    unoceaned explorer.

All the bygone, hushèd years
Streaming back where the mists distil
To forgetfulness: soft-sailing waters where fears
No longer hurt, where the silk sails fill

With that unfelt breeze that ebbs over the seas where the storm
Of living has passed, ebbing on
Through the stirred iridescence that swims in the warm
Wake of a tumult now spent and gone,
Drifts my boat, wistfully lapsing after
The silence of vanishing tears, and the echoes of laughter.

LETTER FROM TOWN: THE ALMOND-TREE

You promised to send me some violets. Did you forget?
  White ones and blue ones from under the orchard hedge?
  Sweet dark purple, and white ones mixed for a pledge
Of our early love that hardly has opened yet.

Here there's an almond-tree – you have never seen
  Such a one in the north – it flowers on the street, and I stand
  Every day by the fence to look up at the flowers that expand
At rest in the blue, and wonder at what they mean.

Under the almond-tree, the happy lands
  Provence, Japan, and Italy repose;
  And passing feet are chatter and clapping of those
Who play around us, country girls clapping their hands.

You, my love, the foremost, in a flowered gown,
  All your unbearable tenderness, you with the laughter
  Startled upon your eyes now so wide with hereafter,
You with loose hands of abandonment hanging down.

END OF ANOTHER HOME HOLIDAY

When shall I see the half-moon sink again
Behind the black sycamore at the end of the garden?
When will the scent of the dim white phlox
Creep up the wall to me, and in at my open window?

Why is it, the long, slow stroke of the midnight bell
  (Will it never finish the twelve?)
Falls again and again on my heart with a heavy reproach?

The moon-mist is over the village, out of the mist speaks the bell,
And all the little roofs of the village bow low, pitiful, beseeching,
    resigned.
– Speak, you my home! what is it I don't do well?

Ah home, suddenly I love you
As I hear the sharp clean trot of a pony down the road,
Succeeding sharp little sounds dropping into silence
Clear upon the long-drawn hoarseness of a train across the valley.

*

The light has gone out, from under my mother's door.
  That she should love me so! –
  She, so lonely, greying now!
  And I leaving her,
  Bent on my pursuits!

    Love is the great Asker.
    The sun and the rain do not ask the secret
    Of the time when the grain struggles down in the dark.
    The moon walks her lonely way without anguish,
    Because no-one grieves over her departure.

Forever, ever by my shoulder pitiful love will linger,
Crouching as little houses crouch under the mist when I turn.
Forever, out of the mist, the church lifts up a reproachful finger,
Pointing my eyes in wretched defiance where love hides her face to
    mourn.

  Oh! but the rain creeps down to wet the grain
  That struggles alone in the dark,
  And asking nothing, patiently steals back again!
  The moon sets forth o' nights
  To walk the lonely, dusky heights
  Serenely, with steps unswerving;
  Pursued by no sigh of bereavement,
  No tears of love unnerving
  Her constant tread:

While ever at my side,
Frail and sad, with grey, bowed head,
The beggar-woman, the yearning-eyed
Inexorable love goes lagging.

The wild young heifer, glancing distraught,
With a strange new knocking of life at her side
Runs seeking a loneliness.
The little grain draws down the earth, to hide.
Nay, even the slumberous egg, as it labours under the shell
Patiently to divide and self-divide,
Asks to be hidden, and wishes nothing to tell.

But when I draw the scanty cloak of silence over my eyes
Piteous love comes peering under the hood;
Touches the clasp with trembling fingers, and tries
To put her ear to the painful sob of my blood;
While her tears soak through to my breast,
Where they burn and cauterise.

*

The moon lies back and reddens.
In the valley a corncrake calls
Monotonously,
With a plaintive, unalterable voice, that deadens
My confident activity;
With a hoarse, insistent request that falls
Unweariedly, unweariedly,
Asking something more of me,
Yet more of me.

BABY RUNNING BAREFOOT

When the white feet of the baby beat across the grass
The little white feet nod like white flowers in a wind,
They poise and run like puffs of wind that pass
Over water where the weeds are thinned.

And the sight of their white playing in the grass
Is winsome as a robin's song, so fluttering;
Or like two butterflies that settle on a glass
Cup for a moment, soft little wing-beats uttering.

And I wish that the baby would tack across here to me
Like a wind-shadow running on a pond, so she could stand
With two little bare white feet upon my knee
And I could feel her feet in either hand

Cool as syringa buds in morning hours,
Or firm and silken as young peony flowers.

AWARE

Slowly the moon is rising out of the ruddy haze,
Divesting herself of her golden shift, and so
Emerging white and exquisite; and I in amaze
See in the sky before me, a woman I did not know
I loved, but there she goes, and her beauty hurts my heart;
I follow her down the night, begging her not to depart.

COROT

The trees rise taller and taller, lifted
On a subtle rush of cool grey flame
That issuing out of the east has sifted
  The spirit from each leaf's frame.

For the trailing, leisurely rapture of life
Drifts dimly forward, easily hidden
By bright leaves uttered aloud; and strife
  Of shapes by a hard wind ridden,

The grey, plasm-limpid, pellucid advance
Of the luminous purpose of Life shines out
Where lofty trees athwart-stream chance
  To shake flakes of its shadow about.

The subtle, steady rush of the whole
Grey foam-mist of advancing Time
As it silently sweeps to its somewhere, its goal,
  Is seen in the gossamer's rime.

Is heard in the windless whisper of leaves,
In the silent labours of men in the field,
In the downward-dropping of flimsy sheaves
  Of cloud the rain-skies yield.

In the tapping haste of a fallen leaf,
In the flapping of red-roof smoke, and the small
Footstepping tap of men beneath
  Dim trees so huge and tall.

For what can all sharp-rimmed substance but catch
In a backward ripple, the wave-length, reveal
For a moment the mighty direction, snatch
  A spark beneath the wheel!

Since Life sweeps whirling, dim and vast,
Creating the channelled vein of man
And leaf for its passage; a shadow cast
  And gone before we can scan.

Ah listen, for silence is not lonely!
Imitate the magnificent trees
That speak no word of their rapture, but only
  Breathe largely the luminous breeze.

A BABY ASLEEP AFTER PAIN

  As a drenched, drowned bee
Hangs numb and heavy from a bending flower,
  So clings to me
My baby, her brown hair brushed with wet tears
  And laid against her cheek;
Her soft white legs hanging heavily over my arm
  Swing to my walking movement, weak

With after-pain. My sleeping baby hangs upon my life
  Like a burden she hangs on me;
She who has always seemed so light,
  Now wet with tears and pain hangs heavily,
  Even her floating hair sinks heavily
    Reaching downwards;
As the wings of a drenched, drowned bee
  Are a heaviness, and a weariness.

LAST LESSON OF THE AFTERNOON

When will the bell ring, and end this weariness?
How long have they tugged the leash, and strained apart,
My pack of unruly hounds! I cannot start
Them again on a quarry of knowledge they hate to hunt,
I can haul them and urge them no more.

No longer now can I endure the brunt
Of the books that lie out on the desks; a full threescore
Of several insults of blotted pages, and scrawl
Of slovenly work that they have offered me.
I am sick, and what on earth is the good of it all?
What good to them or me, I cannot see!

So, shall I take
My last dear fuel of life to heap on my soul
And kindle my will to a flame that shall consume
Their dross of indifference; and take the toll
Of their insults in punishment? – I will not! –

I will not waste my soul and my strength for this.
What do I care for all that they do amiss!
What is the point of this teaching of mine, and of this
Learning of theirs? It all goes down the same abyss.

What does it matter to me, if they can write
A description of a dog, or if they can't?
What is the point? To us both, it is all my aunt!
And yet I'm supposed to care, with all my might.

I do not, and will not; they won't and they don't; and that's all!
I shall keep my strength for myself; they can keep theirs as well.
Why should we beat our heads against the wall
Of each other? I shall sit and wait for the bell.

DISCIPLINE

It is stormy, and raindrops cling like silver bees to the panes,
The thin sycamore in the playground is swinging with flattened leaves;
The heads of the boys move dimly through a yellow gloom that stains
The class; over them all the dark net of my discipline weaves.

It is no good, dear, gentleness and forbearance; I endured too long.
I have pushed my hands in the dark soil, under the flower of my soul
And the gentle leaves, and have felt where the roots are strong
Fixed in the darkness, grappling for the deep soil's crowded control.

And there in the dark, my darling, where the roots are entangled and fight
Each one for its hold on the concrete darkness, I know that there
In the night where we first have being, before we rise on the light,
We are not lovers, my darling, we fight and we do not spare.

And in the original dark the roots cannot keep, cannot know
Any communion whatever, but they bind themselves on to the dark,
And drawing the darkness together, crush from it a twilight, a slow
Dim self that rises slowly to leaves and the flower's gay spark.

I came to the boys with love, dear, and only they turned on me;
With gentleness came I, with my heart 'twixt my hands like a bowl,
Like a loving-cup, like a grail, but they spilt it triumphantly
And tried to break the vessel, and violate my soul.

And perhaps they were right, for the young are busy deep down at
the roots,
And love would only weaken their under-earth grip, make
shallow
Their hold on reality, enfeeble their rising shoots
With too much tincture of me, instead of the dark's deep fallow.

I thought that love would do all things, but now I know I am
wrong.
There are depths below depths, my darling, where love does not
belong.
Where the fight that is fight for being is fought throughout the
long
Young years, and the old must not win, not even if they love and
are strong.

I must not win their souls, no never, I only must win
The brief material control of the hour, leave them free of me.
Learn they must to obey, for all harmony is discipline,
And only in harmony with others the single soul can be free.

Let them live, the boys, and learn not to trespass; I had to learn
Not to trespass on them with love, they must learn not to trespass
in the young
Cruel self; the fight is not for existence, the fight is to burn
At last into blossom of being, each one his own flower outflung.

They are here to learn but one lesson, that they shall not thwart
each other
Nor be thwarted, in life's slow struggle to unfold the flower of the
self.
They draw their sap from the Godhead, not from me, but they
must not smother
The sun from their neighbour either, nor be smothered in turn by
pelf.

I will teach them the beginning of the lesson at the roots, and then
no more.
I throw from out of the darkness myself like a flower into sight
Of the day, but it's nothing to do with the boys, so let them ignore
What's beyond them, and fight with me in discipline's little fight.

But whoever would pluck apart my flowering will burn their
hands,
For flowers are tender folk, and roots can only hide.
But sometimes the opening petals are fire, and the scarlet brands
Of the blossom are roses to look at, but flames when they're tried.

But now I am trodden to earth, and my fires are low;
Now I am broken down like a plant in winter, and all
Myself but a knowledge of roots, of roots in the dark, that throw
A net on the undersoil, that lies passive, and quickened with gall.

Yet wait awhile, for henceforth I will love when a blossom calls
To my blossom in perfume and seed-dust, and only then; I will
give
My love where it is wanted. Yet wait awhile! My fall
Is complete for the moment, yet wait, and you'll see that my
flower will live.

THE BRIDE

My love looks like a girl to-night,
But she is old.
The plaits that lie along her pillow
Are not gold,
But threaded with filigree silver,
And uncanny cold.

She looks like a young maiden, since her brow
Is smooth and fair;
Her cheeks are very smooth, her eyes are closed,
She sleeps a rare,
Still, winsome sleep, so still, and so composed.

Nay, but she sleeps like a bride, and dreams her dreams
Of perfect things.
She lies at last, the darling, in the shape of her dream,
And her dead mouth sings
By its shape, like thrushes in clear evenings.

THE VIRGIN MOTHER

My little love, my darling,
You were a doorway to me;
You let me out of the confines
Into this strange countrie
Where people are crowded like thistles,
Yet are shapely and comely to see.

My little love, my dearest,
Twice you have issued me,
Once from your womb, sweet mother,
Once from your soul, to be
Free of all hearts, my darling,
Of each heart's entrance free.

And so, my love, my mother,
I shall always be true to you.
Twice I am born, my dearest:
To life, and to death, in you;
And this is the life hereafter
Wherein I am true.

I kiss you good-bye, my darling,
Our ways are different now;
You are a seed in the night-time,
I am a man, to plough
The difficult glebe of the future
For seed to endow.

I kiss you good-bye, my dearest,
It is finished between us here.
Oh, if I were calm as you are,
Sweet and still on your bier!
Oh God, if I had not to leave you
Alone, my dear!

Is the last word now uttered?
Is the farewell said?
Spare me the strength to leave you
Now you are dead.
I must go, but my soul lies helpless
Beside your bed.

BLUENESS

Out of the darkness, fretted sometimes in its sleeping,
Jets of sparks in fountains of blue come leaping
To sight, revealing a secret, numberless secrets keeping.

Sometimes the darkness trapped within a wheel
Runs into speed like a dream, the blue of the steel
Showing the rocking darkness now a-reel.

And out of the invisible, streams of bright blue drops
Rain from the showery heavens, and bright blue crops
Of flowers surge from below to their ladder-tops.

And all the manifold blue, amazing eyes,
The rainbow arching over in the skies,
New sparks of wonder opening in surprise:

All these pure things come foam and spray of the sea
Of Darkness abundant, which shaken mysteriously
Breaks into dazzle of living, as dolphins leap from the sea
Of midnight and shake it to fire, till the flame of the shadow we
see.

PIANO

Softly, in the dusk, a woman is singing to me;
Taking me back down the vista of years, till I see
A child sitting under the piano, in the boom of the tingling strings
And pressing the small, poised feet of a mother who smiles as she
sings.

In spite of myself, the insidious mastery of song
Betrays me back, till the heart of me weeps to belong
To the old Sunday evenings at home, with winter outside
And hymns in the cosy parlour, the tinkling piano our guide.

So now it is vain for the singer to burst into clamour
With the great black piano appassionato. The glamour
Of childish days is upon me, my manhood is cast
Down in the flood of remembrance, I weep like a child for the
past.

SEVEN SEALS

Since this is the last night I keep you home,
Come, I will consecrate you for the journey.

Rather I had you would not go. Nay come,
I will not again reproach you. Lie back
And let me love you a long time ere you go.
For you are sullen-hearted still, and lack
The will to love me. But even so
I will set a seal upon you from my lip,
Will set a guard of honour at each door,
Seal up each channel out of which might slip
Your love for me.

I kiss your mouth. Ah, love,
Could I but seal its ruddy, shining spring
Of passion, parch it up, destroy, remove
Its softly-stirring crimson welling-up
Of kisses! Oh, help me, God! Here at the source
I'd lie for ever drinking and drawing in
Your fountains, as heaven drinks from out their course
The floods.

I close your ears with kisses
And seal your nostrils; and round your neck you'll wear –
Nay, let me work – a delicate chain of kisses.
Like beads they go around, and not one misses
To touch its fellow on either side.

And there
Full mid-between the champaign of your breast
I place a great and burning seal of love

Like a dark rose, a mystery of rest
On the slow bubbling of your rhythmic heart.

Nay, I persist, and very faith shall keep
You integral to me. Each door, each mystic port
Of egress from you I will seal and steep
In perfect chrism.
Now it is done. The mort
Will sound in heaven before it is undone.
But let me finish what I have begun
And shirt you now invulnerable in the mail
Of iron kisses, kisses linked like steel.
Put greaves upon your thighs and knees, and frail
Webbing of steel on your feet. So you shall feel
Ensheathed invulnerable with me, with seven
Great seals upon your outgoings, and woven
Chain of my mystic will wrapped perfectly
Upon you, wrapped in indomitable me.

DREAMS OLD AND NASCENT

NASCENT

The world is a painted memory, where coloured shapes
Of old, spent lives linger blurred and warm;
An endless tapestry the past has woven, drapes
The halls of my mind, compelling my life to conform.

I have lived delighted in the halls of the past
Where dead men's lives glow gently, and iron hurts
No more, and money stinks not, and death at last
Is only sad men taking off their shirts.

But now I think I have seen it all, and now
I feel thick walls of stone behind the arras.
I am shut in, a prisoner, I know not how.
And past lives hamper me, clog and embarrass.

They have no hands, they have no bodies, all
These shapes that now are dreams and once were men.
And so my heart begins to cry and call
But to get out from this dim, dreadful den.

*

The surface of dreams is broken, the arras is torn,
There's a breach in the walls of the past, lets the daylight through.
Fluent figures of men go down the upborne
Track of the railway, alive, and with something to do.

Along the railway, active figures of men!
Each with a secret which stirs in his limbs, as they move
Out of the distance nearer, coming to prove
With a touch the dead and the living, while time counts ten.

In the subtle lift of the thighs as they come unmarching
Beats the new fresh air of life. They come for strife,
For the ripping of arras, and smashing of walls, and the fight for
    life;
With axe in hand, and the hammer, and the pick-axe overarching.

Oh come, and break this prison, this house of yesterday!
The arras is all illusion, oh come and tear it away!
The walls are thick, and the inner rooms are such, they dismay
The heart, all crowded with slaves, most working, some few at
    play.

*

The old dreams are beautiful, beloved, soft-toned and sure,
But worn out, they hide no more the walls they stand before.
Walled in, walled in, the whole world is a vast impure
Interior, a house of dreams where the dreamers writhe and snore.

Oh come, and wake us up from the ghastly dream of to-day.
We asphyxiate in a sleep of dreams, rebreathing the impure air.
For the house is shut and sealed, and the breath of the hosts is grey
As they dream corrupted dreams, all poisoned with care.

The ghastly dream of labour, and the stench of steel and of oil.
The writhing of myriads of workmen, all dreaming they are going
to be rich
And giving off dreadful effluvia in a ghastly effort of toil
Unfinished for ever, but gasping for money, as they dream and
they itch.

The ghastly dream of riches, of masses of money to spend,
Of walking over the faces of men, like cobble-stones!
Of riding, and being envied, such envy as has no end!
Of making a triumph of envy, the rich and successful ones.

*

The whole wide world is interior now, and we're all shut up.
The air is all close and poisonous, it has drugged our souls, so we
sleep
A sleep that is writhing stupor, weighed down, so we can't wake
up.
The rich and the poor alike dreaming and writhing, all in one
heap.

Oh come, oh, men along the railway! Oh come as men
And break the walls of possession of all the wide world!
Give us air, we cry. Oh, let us but breathe again!
Let us breathe fresh air and wake from foul dreams in which we
are furled.

To feel fresh air in our throats, to have fresh breath in our breasts,
To make new words with our lips, to escape the foul dream
Of having and getting and owning, the struggle which wrests
Money from out of the earth or the beast or the man, as they
labour in steam.

*

Oh, men with the axe and the pick-axe, break the walls of the
filthy dream
And release us, poor ones and rich ones, let us breathe and touch
One another in wonder of wakening, let us wake to the gleam
Of real daylight upon us, released from the foul dream's hutch.

For the proper dream-stuff is molten, and moving mysteriously,
And the bodies of men and women are molten matter of dreams
That stirs with a stir which is cosmic, as ever, invisibly
The heart of the live world pulses, and the blood of the live world
teems.

And what is life, but the swelling and shaping the dream in the
flesh!
And our bodies molten drops of dream-blood that swirl and swell
In a tissue, as all the molten cells in the living mesh
Of a rose-tree move to roses and thorns and a delicate smell.

UNRHYMING POEMS

Look! We Have Come Through!

Birds, Beasts and Flowers

LOOK! WE HAVE COME THROUGH!

LOOK! WE HAVE COME THROUGH!

FOREWORD

These poems should not be considered separately, as so many single pieces. They are intended as an essential story, or history, or confession, unfolding one from the other in organic development, the whole revealing the intrinsic experience of a man during the crisis of manhood, when he marries and comes into himself. The period covered is, roughly, the sixth lustre of a man's life.

ARGUMENT

After much struggling and loss in love and in the world of men, the protagonist throws in his lot with a woman who is already married. Together they go into another country, she perforce leaving her children behind. The conflict of love and hate goes on between the man and the woman, and between these two and the world around them, till it reaches some sort of conclusion, they transcend into some condition of blessedness.

BEI HENNEF

The little river twittering in the twilight,
The wan, wondering look of the pale sky,
  This is almost bliss.

And everything shut up and gone to sleep,
All the troubles and anxieties and pain
  Gone under the twilight.

Only the twilight now, and the soft 'Sh!' of the river
  That will last for ever.

And at last I know my love for you is here;
I can see it all, it is whole like the twilight,
It is large, so large, I could not see it before,
Because of the little lights and flickers and interruptions,
  Troubles, anxieties and pains.

  You are the call and I am the answer,
  You are the wish, and I the fulfilment,
  You are the night, and I the day.
    What else? it is perfect enough.
    It is perfectly complete,
    You and I,
    What more – ?

Strange, how we suffer in spite of this!

Hennef am Rhein.

FIRST MORNING

The night was a failure
  but why not – ?

In the darkness
  with the pale dawn seething at the window
  through the black frame
  I could not be free,

not free myself from the past, those others –
and our love was a confusion,
there was a horror,
you recoiled away from me.

Now, in the morning
As we sit in the sunshine on the seat by the little shrine,
And look at the mountain-walls,
Walls of blue shadow,
And see so near at our feet in the meadow
Myriads of dandelion pappus
Bubbles ravelled in the dark green grass
Held still beneath the sunshine –
It is enough, you are near –
The mountains are balanced,
The dandelion seeds stay half-submerged in the grass;
You and I together
We hold them proud and blithe
On our love.
They stand upright on our love,
Everything starts from us,
We are the source.

Beuerberg.

MUTILATION

A thick mist-sheet lies over the broken wheat.
I walk up to my neck in mist, holding my mouth up.
Across there, a discoloured moon burns itself out.

I hold the night in horror;
I dare not turn round.

To-night I have left her alone.
They would have it I have left her for ever.

Oh my God, how it aches
Where she is cut off from me!

Perhaps she will go back to England.
Perhaps she will go back,
Perhaps we are parted for ever.

If I go on walking through the whole breadth of Germany
I come to the North Sea, or the Baltic.

Over there is Russia – Austria, Switzerland, France, in a circle!
I here in the undermist on the Bavarian road.

It aches in me.
What is England or France, far off,
But a name she might take?
I don't mind this continent stretching, the sea far away;
It aches in me for her
Like the agony of limbs cut off and aching;
Not even longing,
It is only agony.

A cripple!
Oh God, to be mutilated!
To be a cripple!

And if I never see her again?

I think, if they told me so
I could convulse the heavens with my horror.
I think I could alter the frame of things in my agony.
I think I could break the System with my heart.
I think, in my convulsion, the skies would break.

She too suffers.
But who could compel her, if she chose me against them all?
She has not chosen me finally, she suspends her choice.
Night folk, Tuatha De Danaan, dark Gods, govern her sleep,
Magnificent ghosts of the darkness, carry off her decision in sleep,
Leave her no choice, make her lapse me-ward, make her,
Oh Gods of the living Darkness, powers of Night.

Wolfratshausen.

HUMILIATION

I have been so innerly proud, and so long alone,
Do not leave me, or I shall break.
Do not leave me.

What should I do if you were gone again
So soon?
What should I look for?
Where should I go?
What should I be, I myself,
'I'?
What would it mean, this
I?

Do not leave me.

What should I think of death?
If I died, it would not be you:
It would be simply the same
Lack of you.
The same want, life or death,
Unfulfilment,
The same insanity of space,
You not there for me.

Think, I daren't die
For fear of the lack in death.
And I daren't live.

Unless there were a morphine or a drug.

I would bear the pain.
But always, strong, unremitting
It would make me not me.

The thing with my body that would go on living
Would not be me.
Neither life nor death could help.

Think, I couldn't look towards death
Nor towards the future:
Only not look.
Only myself
Stand still and bind and blind myself.

God, that I have no choice!
That my own fulfilment is up against me
Timelessly!
The burden of self-accomplishment!
The charge of fulfilment!
And God, that she is *necessary*!
Necessary, and I have no choice!

Do not leave me.

A YOUNG WIFE

The pain of loving you
Is almost more than I can bear.

I walk in fear of you.
The darkness starts up where
You stand, and the night comes through
Your eyes when you look at me.

Ah never before did I see
The shadows that live in the sun!

Now every tall glad tree
Turns round its back to the sun
And looks down on the ground, to see
The shadow it used to shun.

At the foot of each glowing thing
A night lies looking up.

Oh, and I want to sing
And dance, but I can't lift up
My eyes from the shadows: dark
They lie spilt round the cup.

What is it? – Hark
The faint fine seethe in the air!

Like the seething sound in a shell!
It is death still seething where
The wild-flower shakes its bell
And the skylark twinkles blue –

The pain of loving you
Is almost more than I can bear.

GREEN

The dawn was apple-green,
  The sky was green wine held up in the sun,
The moon was a golden petal between.

She opened her eyes, and green
  They shone, clear like flowers undone
For the first time, now for the first time seen.

Icking.

GLOIRE DE DIJON

When she rises in the morning
I linger to watch her;
She spreads the bath-cloth underneath the window
And the sunbeams catch her
Glistening white on the shoulders,
While down her sides the mellow
Golden shadow glows as

She stoops to the sponge, and her swung breasts
Sway like full-blown yellow
Gloire de Dijon roses.

She drips herself with water, and her shoulders
Glisten as silver, they crumple up
Like wet and falling roses, and I listen
For the sluicing of their rain-dishevelled petals.
In the window full of sunlight
Concentrates her golden shadow
Fold on fold, until it glows as
Mellow as the glory roses.

Icking.

ROSES ON THE BREAKFAST TABLE

Just a few of the roses we gathered from the Isar
Are fallen, and their mauve-red petals on the cloth
Float like boats on a river, while other
Roses are ready to fall, reluctant and loth.

She laughs at me across the table, saying
I am beautiful. I look at the rumpled young roses
And suddenly realise, in them as in me,
How lovely is the self this day discloses.

I AM LIKE A ROSE

I am myself at last; now I achieve
My very self. I, with the wonder mellow,
Full of fine warmth, I issue forth in clear
And single me, perfected from my fellow.

Here I am all myself. No rose-bush heaving
Its limpid sap to culmination has brought
Itself more sheer and naked out of the green
In stark-clear roses, than I to myself am brought.

A DOE AT EVENING

As I went through the marshes
a doe sprang out of the corn
and flashed up the hill-side
leaving her fawn.

On the sky-line
she moved round to watch,
she pricked a fine black blotch
on the sky.

I looked at her
and felt her watching;
I became a strange being.
Still, I had my right to be there with her.

Her nimble shadow trotting
along the sky-line, she
put back her fine, level-balanced head.
And I knew her.

Ah yes, being male, is not my head hard-balanced,
antlered?
Are not my haunches light?
Has she not fled on the same wind with me?
Does not my fear cover her fear?

Irschenhausen.

SONG OF A MAN WHO IS NOT LOVED

The space of the world is immense, before me and around me;
If I turn quickly, I am terrified, feeling space surround me;
Like a man in a boat on very clear, deep water, space frightens
and confounds me.

I see myself isolated in the universe, and wonder
What effect I can have. My hands wave under
The heavens like specks of dust that are floating asunder.

I hold myself up, and feel a big wind blowing
Me like a gadfly into the dusk, without my knowing
Whither or why or even how I am going.

So much there is outside me, so infinitely
Small am I, what matter if minutely
I beat my way, to be lost immediately?

How shall I flatter myself that I can do
Anything in such immensity? I am too
Little to count in the wind that drifts me through.

Glashütte.

GIORNO DEI MORTI

Along the avenue of cypresses,
All in their scarlet cloaks and surplices
Of linen, go the chanting choristers,
The priests in gold and black, the villagers. . . .

And all along the path to the cemetery
The round dark heads of men crowd silently,
And black-scarved faces of womenfolk, wistfully
Watch at the banner of death, and the mystery.

And at the foot of a grave a father stands
With sunken head, and forgotten, folded hands;
And at the foot of a grave a mother kneels
With pale shut face, nor either hears nor feels

The coming of the chanting choristers
Between the avenue of cypresses,
The silence of the many villagers,
The candle-flames beside the surplices.

NEW YEAR'S EVE

There are only two things now,
The great black night scooped out
And this fireglow.

This fireglow, the core,
And we the two ripe pips
That are held in store.

Listen, the darkness rings
As it circulates round our fire.
Take off your things.

Your shoulders, your bruised throat!
Your breasts, your nakedness!
This fiery coat!

As the darkness flickers and dips,
As the firelight falls and leaps
From your feet to your lips!

SONG OF A MAN WHO HAS COME THROUGH

Not I, not I, but the wind that blows through me!
A fine wind is blowing the new direction of Time.
If only I let it bear me, carry me, if only it carry me!
If only I am sensitive, subtle, oh, delicate, a winged gift!
If only, most lovely of all, I yield myself and am borrowed
By the fine, fine wind that takes its course through the chaos of the
world
Like a fine, an exquisite chisel, a wedge-blade inserted;
If only I am keen and hard like the sheer tip of a wedge
Driven by invisible blows,
The rock will split, we shall come at the wonder, we shall find the
Hesperides.

Oh, for the wonder that bubbles into my soul,
I would be a good fountain, a good well-head
Would blur no whisper, spoil no expression.

What is the knocking?
What is the knocking at the door in the night?
It is somebody wants to do us harm.

No, no, it is the three strange angels.
Admit them, admit them.

'SHE SAID AS WELL TO ME'

She said as well to me: 'Why are you ashamed?
That little bit of your chest that shows between
the gap of your shirt, why cover it up?
Why shouldn't your legs and your good strong thighs
be rough and hairy? – I'm glad they are like that.
You are shy, you silly, you silly shy thing.
Men are the shyest creatures, they never will come
out of their covers. Like any snake
slipping into its bed of dead leaves, you hurry into your clothes.
And I love you so! Straight and clean and all of a piece is the body
    of a man,
such an instrument, a spade, like a spear, or an oar,
such a joy to me –'
So she laid her hands and pressed them down my sides,
so that I began to wonder over myself, and what I was.

She said to me: 'What an instrument, your body!
single and perfectly distinct from everything else!
What a tool in the hands of the Lord!
Only God could have brought it to its shape.
It feels as if his handgrasp, wearing you
had polished you and hollowed you,
hollowed this groove in your sides, grasped you under the breasts
and brought you to the very quick of your form,
subtler than an old, soft-worn fiddle-bow.

'When I was a child, I loved my father's riding-whip
that he used so often.
I loved to handle it, it seemed like a near part of him.
So I did his pens, and the jasper seal on his desk.
Something seemed to surge through me when I touched them.

'So it is with you, but here
The joy I feel!
God knows what I feel, but it is joy!
Look, you are clean and fine and singled out!
I admire you so, you are beautiful: this clean sweep of your sides,
this firmness, this hard mould!
I would die rather than have it injured with one scar.
I wish I could grip you like the fist of the Lord,
and have you –'

So she said, and I wondered,
feeling trammelled and hurt.
It did not make me free.

Now I say to her: 'No tool, no instrument, no God!
Don't touch me and appreciate me.
It is an infamy.
You would think twice before you touched a weasel on a fence
as it lifts its straight white throat.
Your hand would not be so flig and easy.
Nor the adder we saw asleep with her head on her shoulder,
curled up in the sunshine like a princess;
when she lifted her head in delicate, startled wonder
you did not stretch forward to caress her
though she looked rarely beautiful
and a miracle as she glided delicately away, with such dignity.
And the young bull in the field, with his wrinkled, sad face,
you are afraid if he rises to his feet,
though he is all wistful and pathetic, like a monolith, arrested,
static.

'Is there nothing in me to make you hesitate?
I tell you there is all these.
And why should you overlook them in me? –'

BIRDS, BEASTS AND FLOWERS

Fruits

POMEGRANATE

You tell me I am wrong.
Who are you, who is anybody to tell me I am wrong?
I am not wrong.

In Syracuse, rock left bare by the viciousness of Greek women,
No doubt you have forgotten the pomegranate-trees in flower,
Oh so red, and such a lot of them.

Whereas at Venice,
Abhorrent, green, slippery city
Whose Doges were old, and had ancient eyes,
In the dense foliage of the inner garden
Pomegranates like bright green stone,
And barbed, barbed with a crown.
Oh, crown of spiked green metal
Actually growing!

Now in Tuscany,
Pomegranates to warm your hands at;
And crowns, kingly, generous, tilting crowns
Over the left eyebrow.

And, if you dare, the fissure!

Do you mean to tell me you will see no fissure?
Do you prefer to look on the plain side?

For all that, the setting suns are open.
The end cracks open with the beginning:
Rosy, tender, glittering within the fissure.

Do you mean to tell me there should be no fissure?
No glittering, compact drops of dawn?
Do you mean it is wrong, the gold-filmed skin, integument, shown
ruptured?

For my part, I prefer my heart to be broken.
It is so lovely, dawn-kaleidoscopic within the crack.

San Gervasio in Tuscany.

PEACH

Would you like to throw a stone at me?
Here, take all that's left of my peach.

Blood-red, deep;
Heaven knows how it came to pass.
Somebody's pound of flesh rendered up.

Wrinkled with secrets
And hard with the intention to keep them.

Why, from silvery peach-bloom,
From that shallow-silvery wine-glass on a short stem
This rolling, dropping, heavy globule?

I am thinking, of course, of the peach before I ate it.

Why so velvety, why so voluptuous heavy?
Why hanging with such inordinate weight?
Why so indented?

Why the groove?
Why the lovely, bivalve roundnesses?
Why the ripple down the sphere?
Why the suggestion of incision?

Why was not my peach round and finished like a billiard ball?
It would have been if man had made it.
Though I've eaten it now.

But it wasn't round and finished like a billiard ball.
And because I say so, you would like to throw something at me.

Here, you can have my peach stone.

San Gervasio.

MEDLARS AND SORB-APPLES

I love you, rotten,
Delicious rottenness.

I love to suck you out from your skins
So brown and soft and coming suave,
So morbid, as the Italians say.

What a rare, powerful, reminiscent flavour
Comes out of your falling through the stages of decay:
Stream within stream.

Something of the same flavour as Syracusan muscat wine
Or vulgar Marsala.

Though even the word Marsala will smack of preciosity
Soon in the pussyfoot West.

What is it?
What is it, in the grape turning raisin,
In the medlar, in the sorb-apple,
Wineskins of brown morbidity,
Autumnal excrementa;
What is it that reminds us of white gods?

Gods nude as blanched nut-kernels,
Strangely, half-sinisterly flesh-fragrant
As if with sweat,
And drenched with mystery.

Sorb-apples, medlars with dead crowns.

I say, wonderful are the hellish experiences,
Orphic, delicate
Dionysos of the Underworld.

A kiss, and a spasm of farewell, a moment's orgasm of rupture,
Then along the damp road alone, till the next turning.
And there, a new partner, a new parting, a new unfusing into
    twain,

A new gasp of further isolation,
A new intoxication of loneliness, among decaying, frost-cold leaves.

Going down the strange lanes of hell, more and more intensely alone,
The fibres of the heart parting one after the other
And yet the soul continuing, naked-footed, ever more vividly embodied
Like a flame blown whiter and whiter
In a deeper and deeper darkness
Ever more exquisite, distilled in separation.

So, in the strange retorts of medlars and sorb-apples
The distilled essence of hell.
The exquisite odour of leave-taking.
Jamque vale!
Orpheus, and the winding, leaf-clogged, silent lanes of hell.

Each soul departing with its own isolation,
Strangest of all strange companions,
And best.

Medlars, sorb-apples,
More than sweet
Flux of autumn
Sucked out of your empty bladders

And sipped down, perhaps, with a sip of Marsala
So that the rambling, sky-dropped grape can add its savour to yours,
Orphic farewell, and farewell, and farewell
And the *ego sum* of Dionysos
The *sono io* of perfect drunkenness
Intoxication of final loneliness.

San Gervasio.

FIGS

The proper way to eat a fig, in society,
Is to split it in four, holding it by the stump,
And open it, so that it is a glittering, rosy, moist, honied, heavy-
petalled four-petalled flower.

Then you throw away the skin
Which is just like a four-sepalled calyx,
After you have taken off the blossom with your lips.

But the vulgar way
Is just to put your mouth to the crack, and take out the flesh in one
bite.

Every fruit has its secret.

The fig is a very secretive fruit.
As you see it standing growing, you feel at once it is symbolic:
And it seems male.
But when you come to know it better, you agree with the Romans,
it is female.

The Italians vulgarly say, it stands for the female part; the fig-
fruit:
The fissure, the yoni,
The wonderful moist conductivity towards the centre.

Involved,
Inturned,
The flowering all inward and womb-fibrilled;
And but one orifice.

The fig, the horse-shoe, the squash-blossom.
Symbols.

There was a flower that flowered inward, womb-ward;
Now there is a fruit like a ripe womb.

It was always a secret.
That's how it should be, the female should always be secret.

There never was any standing aloft and unfolded on a bough
Like other flowers, in a revelation of petals;
Silver-pink peach, venetian green glass of medlars and sorb-
apples,
Shallow wine-cups on short, bulging stems
Openly pledging heaven:
Here's to the thorn in flower! Here is to Utterance!
The brave, adventurous rosaceæ.

Folded upon itself, and secret unutterable,
And milky-sapped, sap that curdles milk and makes *ricotta*,
Sap that smells strange on your fingers, that even goats won't taste
it;
Folded upon itself, enclosed like any Mohammedan woman,
Its nakedness all within-walls, its flowering forever unseen,
One small way of access only, and this close-curtained from the
light;
Fig, fruit of the female mystery, covert and inward,
Mediterranean fruit, with your covert nakedness,
Where everything happens invisible, flowering and fertilisation,
and fruiting
In the inwardness of your you, that eye will never see
Till it's finished, and you're over-ripe, and you burst to give up
your ghost.

Till the drop of ripeness exudes,
And the year is over.

And then the fig has kept her secret long enough.
So it explodes, and you see through the fissure the scarlet.
And the fig is finished, the year is over.

That's how the fig dies, showing her crimson through the purple
slit
Like a wound, the exposure of her secret, on the open day.
Like a prostitute, the bursten fig, making a show of her secret.

That's how women die too.

The year is fallen over-ripe,
The year of our women.

The year of our women is fallen over-ripe.
The secret is laid bare.
And rottenness soon sets in.
The year of our women is fallen over-ripe.

When Eve once knew *in her mind* that she was naked
She quickly sewed fig-leaves, and sewed the same for the man.
She'd been naked all her days before,
But till then, till that apple of knowledge, she hadn't had the fact on her mind.

She got the fact on her mind, and quickly sewed fig-leaves.
And women have been sewing ever since.
But now they stitch to adorn the bursten fig, not to cover it.
They have their nakedness more than ever on their mind,
And they won't let us forget it.

Now, the secret
Becomes an affirmation through moist, scarlet lips
That laugh at the Lord's indignation.

What then, good Lord! cry the women.
We have kept our secret long enough.
We are a ripe fig.
Let us burst into affirmation.

They forget, ripe figs won't keep.
Ripe figs won't keep.

Honey-white figs of the north, black figs with scarlet inside, of the south.
Ripe figs won't keep, won't keep in any clime.
What then, when women the world over have all bursten into self-assertion?
And bursten figs won't keep?

San Gervasio.

GRAPES

So many fruits come from roses,
From the rose of all roses,
From the unfolded rose,
Rose of all the world.

Admit that apples and strawberries and peaches and pears and
blackberries
Are all Rosaceæ,
Issue of the explicit rose,
The open-countenanced, skyward-smiling rose.

What then of the vine?
Oh, what of the tendrilled vine?

Ours is the universe of the unfolded rose,
The explicit
The candid revelation.

But long ago, oh, long ago
Before the rose began to simper supreme,
Before the rose of all roses, rose of all the world, was even in bud,
Before the glaciers were gathered up in a bunch out of the
unsettled seas and winds,
Or else before they had been let down again, in Noah's flood,
There was another world, a dusky, flowerless, tendrilled world
And creatures webbed and marshy,
And on the margin, men soft-footed and pristine,
Still, and sensitive, and active,
Audile, tactile sensitiveness as of a tendril which orientates and
reaches out,
Reaching out and grasping by an instinct more delicate than the
moon's as she feels for the tides.

Of which world, the vine was the invisible rose,
Before petals spread, before colour made its disturbance, before
eyes saw too much.

In a green, muddy, web-foot, unutterly songless world
The vine was rose of all roses.

There were no poppies or carnations,
Hardly a greenish lily, watery faint.
Green, dim, invisible flourishing of vines
Royally gesticulate.

Look now even now, how it keeps its power of invisibility!
Look how black, how blue-black, how globed in Egyptian
darkness
Dropping among his leaves, hangs the dark grape!
See him there, the swart, so palpably invisible:
Whom shall we ask about him?

The negro might know a little.
When the vine was rose, Gods were dark-skinned.
Bacchus is a dream's dream.
Once God was all negroid, as now he is fair.
But it's so long ago, the ancient Bushman has forgotten more
utterly than we, who have never known.

For we are on the brink of re-remembrance.
Which, I suppose, is why America has gone dry.
Our pale day is sinking into twilight,
And if we sip the wine, we find dreams coming upon us
Out of the imminent night.
Nay, we find ourselves crossing the fern-scented frontiers
Of the world before the floods, where man was dark and
evasive
And the tiny vine-flower rose of all roses, perfumed,
And all in naked communion communicating as now our clothed
vision can never communicate.
Vistas, down dark avenues,
As we sip the wine.

The grape is swart, the avenues dusky and tendrilled, subtly
prehensile,
But we, as we start awake, clutch at our vistas democratic,
boulevards, tram-cars, policemen.
Give us our own back,
Let us go to the soda-fountain, to get sober.

Soberness, sobriety.
It is like the agonised perverseness of a child heavy with sleep, yet
    fighting, fighting to keep awake;
Soberness, sobriety, with heavy eyes propped open.

Dusky are the avenues of wine,
And we must cross the frontiers, though we will not,
Of the lost, fern-scented world:
Take the fern-seed on our lips,
Close the eyes, and go
Down the tendrilled avenues of wine and the otherworld.

San Gervasio.

Trees

CYPRESSES

Tuscan cypresses,
What is it?

Folded in like a dark thought
For which the language is lost,
Tuscan cypresses,
Is there a great secret?
Are our words no good?

The undeliverable secret,
Dead with a dead race and a dead speech, and yet
Darkly monumental in you,
Etruscan cypresses.

Ah, how I admire your fidelity,
Dark cypresses!

Is it the secret of the long-nosed Etruscans?
The long-nosed, sensitive-footed, subtly-smiling Etruscans,
Who made so little noise outside the cypress groves?

Among the sinuous, flame-tall cypresses
That swayed their length of darkness all around
Etruscan-dusky, wavering men of old Etruria:
Naked except for fanciful long shoes,
Going with insidious, half-smiling quietness
And some of Africa's imperturbable sang-froid
About a forgotten business.

What business, then?
Nay, tongues are dead, and words are hollow as hollow seed-
    pods,
Having shed their sound and finished all their echoing
Etruscan syllables,
That had the telling.

Yet more I see you darkly concentrate,
Tuscan cypresses,
On one old thought:

On one old slim imperishable thought, while you remain
Etruscan cypresses;
Dusky, slim marrow-thought of slender, flickering men of
Etruria,
Whom Rome called vicious.

Vicious, dark cypresses:
Vicious, you supple, brooding, softly-swaying pillars of dark
flame.
Monumental to a dead, dead race
Embowered in you!

Were they then vicious, the slender, tender-footed
Long-nosed men of Etruria?
Or was their way only evasive and different, dark, like cypress-
trees in a wind?

They are dead, with all their vices,
And all that is left
Is the shadowy monomania of some cypresses
And tombs.

The smile, the subtle Etruscan smile still lurking
Within the tombs,
Etruscan cypresses.
He laughs longest who laughs last;
Nay, Leonardo only bungled the pure Etruscan smile.

What would I not give
To bring back the rare and orchid-like
Evil-yclept Etruscan?

For as to the evil
We have only Roman word for it,
Which I, being a little weary of Roman virtue,
Don't hang much weight on.

For oh, I know, in the dust where we have buried
The silenced races and all their abominations,
We have buried so much of the delicate magic of life.

There in the deeps
That churn the frankincense and ooze the myrrh,
Cypress shadowy,
Such an aroma of lost human life!

They say the fit survive,
But I invoke the spirits of the lost.
Those that have not survived, the darkly lost,
To bring their meaning back into life again,
Which they have taken away
And wrapt inviolable in soft cypress-trees,
Etruscan cypresses.

Evil, what is evil?
There is only one evil, to deny life
As Rome denied Etruria
And mechanical America Montezuma still.

Fiesole.

BARE ALMOND-TREES

Wet almond-trees, in the rain,
Like iron sticking grimly out of earth;
Black almond trunks, in the rain,
Like iron implements twisted, hideous, out of the earth,
Out of the deep, soft fledge of Sicilian winter-green,
Earth-grass uneatable,
Almond trunks curving blackly, iron-dark, climbing the slopes.

Almond-tree, beneath the terrace rail,
Black, rusted, iron trunk,
You have welded your thin stems finer,
Like steel, like sensitive steel in the air,
Grey, lavender, sensitive steel, curving thinly and brittly up in a
parabola.

What are you doing in the December rain?
Have you a strange electric sensitiveness in your steel tips?
Do you feel the air for electric influences
Like some strange magnetic apparatus?
Do you take in messages, in some strange code,
From heaven's wolfish, wandering electricity, that prowls so
constantly round Etna?
Do you take the whisper of sulphur from the air?

Do you hear the chemical accents of the sun?
Do you telephone the roar of the waters over the earth?
And from all this, do you make calculations?

Sicily, December's Sicily in a mass of rain
With iron branching blackly, rusted like old, twisted implements
And brandishing and stooping over earth's wintry fledge,
    climbing the slopes
Of uneatable soft green!

Taormina.

TROPIC

Sun, dark sun,
Sun of black void heat,
Sun of the torrid mid-day's horrific darkness:

Behold my hair twisting and going black.
Behold my eyes turn tawny yellow
Negroid;
See the milk of northern spume
Coagulating and going black in my veins
Aromatic as frankincense.

Columns dark and soft,
Sunblack men,
Soft shafts, sunbreathing mouths,
Eyes of yellow, golden sand
As frictional, as perilous, explosive as brimstone.

Rock, waves of dark heat;
Waves of dark heat, rock, sway upwards,
Waver perpendicular.

What is the horizontal rolling of water
Compared to the flood of black heat that rolls upwards past
    my eyes?

Taormina.

Flowers

ALMOND BLOSSOM

Even iron can put forth,
Even iron.

This is the iron age,
But let us take heart
Seeing iron break and bud,
Seeing rusty iron puff with clouds of blossom.

The almond-tree,
December's bare iron hooks sticking out of earth.

The almond-tree,
That knows the deadliest poison, like a snake
In supreme bitterness.

Upon the iron, and upon the steel,
Odd flakes as if of snow, odd bits of snow,
Odd crumbs of melting snow.

But you mistake, it is not from the sky;
From out the iron, and from out the steel,
Flying not down from heaven, but storming up,
Strange storming up from the dense under-earth
Along the iron, to the living steel
In rose-hot tips, and flakes of rose-pale snow
Setting supreme annunciation to the world.

Nay, what a heart of delicate super-faith,
Iron-breaking,
The rusty swords of almond-trees.

Trees suffer, like races, down the long ages.
They wander and are exiled, they live in exile through long ages
Like drawn blades never sheathed, hacked and gone black,
The alien trees in alien lands: and yet
The heart of blossom,
The unquenchable heart of blossom!

Look at the many-cicatrised frail vine, none more scarred and
frail,
Yet see him fling himself abroad in fresh abandon
From the small wound-stump.

Even the wilful, obstinate, gummy fig-tree
Can be kept down, but he'll burst like a polyp into prolixity.

And the almond-tree, in exile, in the iron age!

This is the ancient southern earth whence the vases were baked,
amphoras, craters, cantharus, œnochœ, and open-hearted
cylix,
Bristling now with the iron of almond-trees

Iron, but unforgotten,
Iron, dawn-hearted,
Ever-beating dawn-heart, enveloped in iron against the exile,
against the ages.

See it come forth in blossom
From the snow-remembering heart
In long-nighted January,
In the long dark nights of the evening star, and Sirius, and the Etna
snow-wind through the long night.

Sweating his drops of blood through the long-nighted Gethse-
mane
Into blossom, into pride, into honey-triumph, into most exquisite
splendour.
Oh, give me the tree of life in blossom
And the Cross sprouting its superb and fearless flowers!

Something must be reassuring to the almond, in the evening star,
and the snow-wind, and the long, long nights,
Some memory of far, sun-gentler lands,
So that the faith in his heart smiles again
And his blood ripples with that untellable delight of once-more
vindicated faith,
And the Gethsemane blood at the iron pores unfolds, unfolds,
Pearls itself into tenderness of bud

And in a great and sacred forthcoming steps forth, steps out in one
stride
A naked tree of blossom, like a bridegroom bathing in dew,
divested of cover,
Frail-naked, utterly uncovered
To the green night-baying of the dog-star, Etna's snow-edged
wind
And January's loud-seeming sun.

Think of it, from the iron fastness
Suddenly to dare to come out naked, in perfection of blossom,
beyond the sword-rust.
Think, to stand there in full-unfolded nudity, smiling,
With all the snow-wind, and the sun-glare, and the dog-star
baying epithalamion.

Oh, honey-bodied beautiful one
Come forth from iron,
Red your heart is.
Fragile-tender, fragile-tender life-body,
More fearless than iron all the time,
And so much prouder, so disdainful of reluctances.

In the distance like hoar-frost, like silvery ghosts communing on a
green hill,
Hoar-frost-like and mysterious.

In the garden raying out
With a body like spray, dawn-tender, and looking about
With such insuperable, subtly-smiling assurance,
Sword-blade-born.

Unpromised,
No bounds being set.
Flaked out and come unpromised,
The tree being life-divine,
Fearing nothing, life-blissful at the core
Within iron and earth.

Knots of pink, fish-silvery
In heaven, in blue, blue heaven,

Soundless, bliss-full, wide-rayed, honey-bodied,
Red at the core,
Red at the core,
Knotted in heaven upon the fine light.

Open,
Open,
Five times wide open,
Six times wide open,
And given, and perfect;
And red at the core with the last sore-heartedness,
Sore-hearted-looking.

Fontana Vecchia.

SICILIAN CYCLAMENS

When he pushed his bush of black hair off his brow:
When she lifted her mop from her eyes, and screwed it in a knob
behind
– O act of fearful temerity!
When they felt their foreheads bare, naked to heaven, their eyes
revealed:
When they felt the light of heaven brandished like a knife at their
defenceless eyes,
And the sea like a blade at their face,
Mediterranean savages:
When they came out, face-revealed, under heaven, from the
shaggy undergrowth of their own hair
For the first time,
They saw tiny rose cyclamens between their toes, growing
Where the slow toads sat brooding on the past.

Slow toads, and cyclamen leaves
Stickily glistening with eternal shadow
Keeping to earth.
Cyclamen leaves
Toad-filmy, earth-iridescent
Beautiful

Frost-filigreed
Spumed with mud
Snail-nacreous
Low down.

The shaking aspect of the sea
And man's defenceless bare face
And cyclamens putting their ears back.

Long, pensive, slim-muzzled greyhound buds
Dreamy, not yet present,
Drawn out of earth
At his toes.

Dawn-rose
Sub-delighted, stone-engendered
Cyclamens, young cyclamens
Arching
Waking, pricking their ears
Like delicate very-young greyhound bitches
Half-yawning at the open, inexperienced
Vista of day,
Folding back their soundless petalled ears.

Greyhound bitches
Bending their rosy muzzles pensive down,
And breathing soft, unwilling to wake to the new day
Yet sub-delighted.

Ah Mediterranean morning, when our world began!
Far-off Mediterranean mornings,
Pelasgic faces uncovered,
And unbudding cyclamens.

The hare suddenly goes uphill
Laying back her long ears with unwinking bliss.

And up the pallid, sea-blenched Mediterranean stone-slopes
Rose cyclamen, ecstatic fore-runner!
Cyclamens, ruddy-muzzled cyclamens
In little bunches like bunches of wild hares

Muzzles together, ears-aprick,
Whispering witchcraft
Like women at a well, the dawn-fountain.

Greece, and the world's morning
Where all the Parthenon marbles still fostered the roots of the
cyclamen.
Violets
Pagan, rosy-muzzled violets
Autumnal
Dawn-pink,
Dawn-pale
Among squat toad-leaves sprinkling the unborn
Erechtheion marbles.

Taormina.

The Evangelistic Beasts

ST MATTHEW

They are not all beasts.
One is a man, for example, and one is a bird.

I, Matthew, am a man.

'And I, if I be lifted up, will draw all men unto me' –

That is Jesus.
But then Jesus was not quite a man.
He was the Son of Man
Filius Meus, O remorseless logic
Out of His own mouth.

I, Matthew, being a man
Cannot be lifted up, the Paraclete
To draw all men unto me,
Seeing I am on a par with all men.

I, on the other hand,
Am drawn to the Uplifted, as all men are drawn,
To the Son of Man
Filius Meus.

Wilt thou lift me up, Son of Man?
How my heart beats!
I am man.

I am man, and therefore my heart beats, and throws the dark
blood from side to side
All the time I am lifted up.
Yes, even during my uplifting.

And if it ceased?
If it ceased, I should be no longer man
As I am, if my heart in uplifting ceased to beat, to toss the dark
blood from side to side, causing my myriad secret streams.

After the cessation
I might be a soul in bliss, an angel, approximating to the Uplifted;
But that is another matter;
I am Matthew, the man,
And I am not that other angelic matter.

So I will be lifted up, Saviour,
But put me down again in time, Master,
Before my heart stops beating, and I become what I am not.
Put me down again on the earth, Jesus, on the brown soil
Where flowers sprout in the acrid humus, and fade into humus
again.
Where beasts drop their unlicked young, and pasture, and drop
their droppings among the turf.
Where the adder darts horizontal.
Down on the damp, unceasing ground, where my feet belong
And even my heart, Lord, forever, after all uplifting:
The crumbling, damp, fresh land, life horizontal and ceaseless.

Matthew I am, the man.
And I take the wings of the morning, to Thee, Crucified, Glorified.
But while flowers club their petals at evening
And rabbits make pills among the short grass
And long snakes quickly glide into the dark hole in the wall,
hearing man approach,
I must be put down, Lord, in the afternoon,
And at evening I must leave off my wings of the spirit
As I leave off my braces,

And I must resume my nakedness like a fish, sinking down the
dark reversion of night
Like a fish seeking the bottom, Jesus,
ΙΧΘΥΣ
Face downwards
Veering slowly
Down between the steep slopes of darkness, fucus-dark, sea-
weed-fringed valleys of the waters under the sea,
Over the edge of the soundless cataract
Into the fathomless, bottomless pit
Where my soul falls in the last throes of bottomless convulsion,
and is fallen

Utterly beyond Thee, Dove of the Spirit;
Beyond everything, except itself.

Nay, Son of Man, I have been lifted up.
To Thee I rose like a rocket ending in mid-heaven.
But even thou, Son of Man, canst not quaff out the dregs of
terrestrial manhood!
They fall back from Thee.

They fall back, and like a dripping of quicksilver taking the
downward track,
Break into drops, burn into drops of blood, and dropping,
dropping take wing
Membraned, blood-veined wings.
On fans of unsuspected tissue, like bats
They thread and thrill and flicker ever downward
To the dark zenith of Thine antipodes
Jesus Uplifted.

Bat-winged heart of man,
Reversed flame
Shuddering a strange way down the bottomless pit
To the great depths of its reversèd zenith.

Afterwards, afterwards
Morning comes, and I shake the dews of night from the wings of
my spirit
And mount like a lark, Beloved.

But remember, Saviour,
That my heart which like a lark at heaven's gate singing, hovers
morning-bright to Thee,
Throws still the dark blood back and forth
In the avenues where the bat hangs sleeping, upside-down
And to me undeniable, Jesus.

Listen, Paraclete.
I can no more deny the bat-wings of my fathom-flickering spirit of
darkness
Than the wings of the Morning and Thee, Thou Glorified.

I am Matthew, the Man:
It is understood.
And Thou art Jesus, Son of Man
Drawing all men unto Thee, but bound to release them when the hour strikes.

I have been, and I have returned.
I have mounted up on the wings of the morning, and I have dredged down to the zenith's reversal.
Which is my way, being man.
Gods may stay in mid-heaven, the Son of Man has climbed to the Whitsun zenith,
But I, Matthew, being a man
Am a traveller back and forth.

So be it.

ST MARK

There was a lion in Judah
Which whelped, and was Mark.

But winged.
A lion with wings.
At least at Venice.
Even as late as Daniele Manin.

Why should he have wings?
Is he to be a bird also?
Or a spirit?
Or a winged thought?
Or a soaring consciousness?

Evidently he is all that,
The lion of the spirit.

Ah, Lamb of God,
Would a wingless lion lie down before Thee, as this winged lion lies?

The lion of the spirit.

Once he lay in the mouth of a cave
And sunned his whiskers,
And lashed his tail slowly, slowly
Thinking of voluptuousness
Even of blood.

But later, in the sun of the afternoon,
Having tasted all there was to taste, and having slept his fill
He fell to frowning, as he lay with his head on his paws
And the sun coming in through the narrowest fibril of a slit in his
eyes.

So, nine-tenths asleep, motionless, bored, and statically angry,
He saw in a shaft of light a lamb on a pinnacle, balancing a flag on
its paw,
And he was thoroughly startled.

Going out to investigate
He found the lamb beyond him, on the inaccessible pinnacle of
light.
So he put his paw to his nose, and pondered.

'Guard my sheep,' came the silvery voice from the pinnacle,
'And I will give thee the wings of the morning.'
So the lion of the senses thought it was worth it.

Hence he became a curly sheep-dog with dangerous propensities,
As Carpaccio will tell you:
Ramping round, guarding the flock of mankind,
Sharpening his teeth on the wolves,
Ramping up through the air like a kestrel
And lashing his tail above the world
And enjoying the sensation of heaven and righteousness and
voluptuous wrath.

There is a new sweetness in his voluptuously licking his paw
Now that it is a weapon of heaven.
There is a new ecstasy in his roar of desirous love
Now that it sounds self-conscious through the unlimited sky.

He is well aware of himself
And he cherishes voluptuous delights, and thinks about them
And ceases to be a blood-thirsty king of beasts
And becomes the faithful sheep-dog of the Shepherd, thinking of
his voluptuous pleasures of chasing the sheep to the fold
And increasing the flock, and perhaps giving a real nip here and
there, a real pinch, but always well meant.

And somewhere there is a lioness,
The she-mate.
Whelps play between the paws of the lion,
The she-mate purrs,
Their castle is impregnable, their cave,
The sun comes in their lair, they are well-off,
A well-to-do family.

Then the proud lion stalks abroad alone,
And roars to announce himself to the wolves
And also to encourage the red-cross Lamb
And also to ensure a goodly increase in the world.

Look at him, with his paw on the world
At Venice and elsewhere.
Going blind at last.

ST LUKE

A wall, a bastion,
A living forehead with its slow whorl of hair
And a bull's large, sombre, glancing eye
And glistening, adhesive muzzle
With cavernous nostrils where the winds run hot
Snorting defiance
Or greedily snuffling behind the cows.

Horns,
The golden horns of power,
Power to kill, power to create
Such as Moses had, and God,
Head-power.

Shall great wings flame from his shoulder sockets
Assyrian-wise?
It would be no wonder.

Knowing the thunder of his heart,
The massive thunder of his dew-lapped chest
Deep and reverberating,
It would be no wonder if great wings, like flame, fanned out from the furnace-cracks of his shoulder-sockets.

Thud! Thud! Thud!
And the roar of black bull's blood in the mighty passages of his chest.
Ah, the dewlap swings pendulous with excess.
The great, roaring weight above
Like a furnace dripping a molten drip

The urge, the massive, burning ache
Of the bull's breast.
The open furnace-doors of his nostrils.

For what does he ache, and groan?

Is his breast a wall?

Nay, once it was also a fortress wall, and the weight of a vast battery.
But now it is a burning hearthstone only,
Massive old altar of his own burnt offering.

It was always an altar of burnt offering
His own black blood poured out like a sheet of flame over his fecundating herd
As he gave himself forth.

But also it was a fiery fortress frowning shaggily on the world
And announcing battle ready.

Since the Lamb bewitched him with that red-struck flag
His fortress is dismantled
His fires of wrath are banked down
His horns turn away from the enemy.

He serves the Son of Man.

And hear him bellow, after many years, the bull that serves the
Son of Man.
Moaning, booing, roaring hollow
Constrained to pour forth all his fire down the narrow sluice of
procreation
Through such narrow loins, too narrow

Is he not over-charged by the dammed-up pressure of his own
massive black blood
Luke, the Bull, the father of substance, the Providence Bull, after
two thousand years?
Is he not over-full of offering, a vast, vast offer of himself
Which must be poured through so small a vent?

Too small a vent.

Let him remember his horns, then.
Seal up his forehead once more to a bastion,
Let it know nothing.
Let him charge like a mighty catapult on the red-cross flag, let him
roar out challenge on the world
And throwing himself upon it, throw off the madness of his blood.
Let it be war.

And so it is war.
The bull of the proletariat has got his head down.

ST JOHN

John, oh John,
Thou honourable bird,
Sun-peering eagle.

Taking a bird's-eye view
Even of Calvary and Resurrection
Not to speak of Babylon's whoredom.

High over the mild effulgence of the dove
Hung all the time, did we but know it, the all-knowing shadow
Of John's great gold-barred eagle.

John knew all about it
Even the very beginning.

'In the beginning was the Word
And the Word was God
And the Word was with God.'

Having been to school
John knew the whole proposition.
As for innocent Jesus
He was one of Nature's phenomena, no doubt.

Oh that mind-soaring eagle of an Evangelist
Staring creation out of countenance
And telling it off
As an eagle staring down on the Sun!

The Logos, the Logos!
'In the beginning was the Word.'

Is there not a great Mind pre-ordaining?
Does not a supreme Intellect ideally procreate the Universe?
Is not each soul a vivid thought in the great consciousness stream
of God?

Put salt on his tail
The sly bird of John.

Proud intellect, high-soaring Mind
Like a king eagle, bird of the most High, sweeping the round of
heaven

And casting the cycles of creation
On two wings, like a pair of compasses;
Jesus' pale and lambent dove, cooing in the lower boughs
On sufferance.

In the beginning was the Word, of course.
And the word was the first offspring of the almighty Johannine
mind,
Chick of the intellectual eagle.

Yet put salt on the tail of the Johannine bird
Put salt on its tail
John's eagle.

Shoo it down out of the empyrean
Of the all-seeing, all-fore-ordaining ideal.
Make it roost on bird-spattered, rocky Patmos
And let it moult there, among the stones of the bitter sea.

For the almighty eagle of the fore-ordaining Mind
Is looking rather shabby and island-bound these days:
Moulting, and rather naked about the rump, and down in the
beak,
Rather dirty, on dung-whitened Patmos.

From which we are led to assume
That the old bird is weary, and almost willing
That a new chick should chip the extensive shell
Of the mundane egg.

The poor old golden eagle of the word-fledged spirit
Moulting and moping and waiting, willing at last
For the fire to burn it up, feathers and all,
So that a new conception of the beginning and end
Can rise from the ashes.

Ah Phœnix, Phœnix,
John's Eagle!
You are only known to us now as the badge of an insurance
Company.

Phœnix, Phœnix,
The nest is in flames,
Feathers are singeing,
Ash flutters flocculent, like down on a blue, wan fledgeling.

San Gervasio.

Creatures

THE MOSQUITO

When did you start your tricks,
Monsieur?

What do you stand on such high legs for?
Why this length of shredded shank,
You exaltation?

Is it so that you shall lift your centre of gravity upwards
And weigh no more than air as you alight upon me,
Stand upon me weightless, you phantom?

I heard a woman call you the Winged Victory
In sluggish Venice.
You turn your head towards your tail, and smile.

How can you put so much devilry
Into that translucent phantom shred
Of a frail corpus?

Queer, with your thin wings and your streaming legs,
How you sail like a heron, or a dull clot of air,
A nothingness.

Yet what an aura surrounds you;
Your evil little aura, prowling, and casting a numbness on my
    mind.

That is your trick, your bit of filthy magic:
Invisibility, and the anæsthetic power
To deaden my attention in your direction.

But I know your game now, streaky sorcerer.

Queer, how you stalk and prowl the air
In circles and evasions, enveloping me,
Ghoul on wings
Winged Victory.

Settle, and stand on long thin shanks
Eyeing me sideways, and cunningly conscious that I am aware,
You speck.

I hate the way you lurch off sideways into air
Having read my thoughts against you.

Come then, let us play at unawares,
And see who wins in this sly game of bluff.
Man or mosquito.

You don't know that I exist, and I don't know that you exist.
Now then!

It is your trump,
It is your hateful little trump,
You pointed fiend,
Which shakes my sudden blood to hatred of you:
It is your small, high, hateful bugle in my ear.

Why do you do it?
Surely it is bad policy.

They say you can't help it.

If that is so, then I believe a little in Providence protecting the
innocent.
But it sounds so amazingly like a slogan,
A yell of triumph as you snatch my scalp.

Blood, red blood
Super-magical
Forbidden liquor.

I behold you stand
For a second enspasmed in oblivion,
Obscenely ecstasied
Sucking live blood,
My blood.

Such silence, such suspended transport,
Such gorging,
Such obscenity of trespass.

You stagger
As well as you may.
Only your accursed hairy frailty,
Your own imponderable weightlessness
Saves you, wafts you away on the very draught my anger makes in
its snatching.

Away with a pæan of derision,
You winged blood-drop.

Can I not overtake you?
Are you one too many for me,
Winged Victory?
Am I not mosquito enough to out-mosquito you?

Queer, what a big stain my sucked blood makes
Beside the infinitesimal faint smear of you!
Queer, what a dim dark smudge you have disappeared into!

Siracusa.

FISH

Fish, oh Fish,
So little matters!

Whether the waters rise and cover the earth
Or whether the waters wilt in the hollow places,
All one to you.

Aqueous, subaqueous,
Submerged
And wave-thrilled.

As the waters roll
Roll you.
The waters wash,
You wash in oneness
And never emerge.

Never know,
Never grasp.

Your life a sluice of sensation along your sides,
A flush at the flails of your fins, down the whorl of your tail,
And water wetly on fire in the grates of your gills;
Fixed water-eyes.

Even snakes lie together.

But oh, fish, that rock in water,
You lie only with the waters;
One touch.

No fingers, no hands and feet, no lips;
No tender muzzles,
No wistful bellies,
No loins of desire,
None.

You and the naked element,
Sway-wave.
Curvetting bits of tin in the evening light.

Who is it ejects his sperm to the naked flood?
In the wave-mother?
Who swims enwombed?
Who lies with the waters of his silent passion, womb-element?
– Fish in the waters under the earth.

What price *his* bread upon the waters?

Himself all silvery himself
In the element,
No more.

Nothing more.

Himself,
And the element.
Food, of course!
Water-eager eyes,
Mouth-gate open
And strong spine urging, driving;
And desirous belly gulping.

Fear also!
He knows fear!
Water-eyes craning,
A rush that almost screams,

Almost fish-voice
As the pike comes . . .
Then gay fear, that turns the tail sprightly, from a shadow.

Food, and fear, and joie de vivre,
Without love.

The other way about:
Joie de vivre, and fear, and food,
All without love.

Quelle joie de vivre
Dans l'eau!
Slowly to gape through the waters,
Alone with the element;
To sink, and rise, and go to sleep with the waters;
To speak endless inaudible wavelets into the wave;
To breathe from the flood at the gills,
Fish-blood slowly running next to the flood, extracting fish-fire;
To have the element under one, like a lover;
And to spring away with a curvetting click in the air,
Provocative.
Dropping back with a slap on the face of the flood.
And merging oneself!

To be a fish!

So utterly without misgiving
To be a fish
In the waters.

Loveless, and so lively!
Born before God was love,
Or life knew loving.
Beautifully beforehand with it all.

Admitted, they swarm in companies,
Fishes.
They drive in shoals.
But soundless, and out of contact.
They exchange no word, no spasm, not even anger.
Not one touch.
Many suspended together, forever apart,
Each one alone with the waters, upon one wave with the rest.

A magnetism in the water between them only.

I saw a water-serpent swim across the Anapo,
And I said to my heart, *look, look at him!*
With his head up, steering like a bird!
He's a rare one, but he belongs . . .

But sitting in a boat on the Zeller lake
And watching the fishes in the breathing waters
Lift and swim and go their way –

I said to my heart, *who are these?*
And my heart couldn't own them . . .

A slim young pike, with smart fins
And grey-striped suit, a young cub of a pike
Slouching along away below, half out of sight,
Like a lout on an obscure pavement . . .

Aha, there's somebody in the know!

But watching closer
That motionless deadly motion,
That unnatural barrel body, that long ghoul nose, . . .
I left off hailing him.

I had made a mistake, I didn't know him,
This grey, monotonous soul in the water,
This intense individual in shadow,
Fish-alive.

I didn't know his God,
I didn't know his God.

Which is perhaps the last admission that life has to wring out of
us.

I saw, dimly,
Once a big pike rush,
And small fish fly like splinters.
And I said to my heart, *there are limits*
To you, my heart;
And to the one God.
Fish are beyond me.

Other Gods
Beyond my range . . . gods beyond my God . . .

They are beyond me, are fishes.
I stand at the pale of my being
And look beyond, and see
Fish, in the outwards,
As one stands on a bank and looks in.

I have waited with a long rod
And suddenly pulled a gold-and-greenish, lucent fish from below,
And had him fly like a halo round my head,
Lunging in the air on the line.

Unhooked his gorping, water-horny mouth,
And seen his horror-tilted eye,
His red-gold, water-precious, mirror-flat bright eye;
And felt him beat in my hand, with his mucous, leaping life-throb.

And my heart accused itself
Thinking: *I am not the measure of creation.*
This is beyond me, this fish.
His God stands outside my God.

And the gold-and-green pure lacquer-mucus comes off in my
hand,
And the red-gold mirror-eye stares and dies,
And the water-suave contour dims.

But not before I have had to know
He was born in front of my sunrise,
Before my day.

He outstarts me.
And I, a many-fingered horror of daylight to him,
Have made him die.

Fishes
With their gold, red eyes, and green-pure gleam, and under-gold,
And their pre-world loneliness,
And more-than-lovelessness,
And white meat;
They move in other circles.

Outsiders.
Water-wayfarers.
Things of one element.
Aqueous,
Each by itself.

Cats, and the Neapolitans,
Sulphur sun-beasts,
Thirst for fish as for more-than-water;
Water-alive
To quench their over-sulphureous lusts.

But I, I only wonder
And don't know.
I don't know fishes.

In the beginning
Jesus was called The Fish. . . .
And in the end.

Zell-am-See.

BAT

At evening, sitting on this terrace,
When the sun from the west, beyond Pisa, beyond the mountains
of Carrara
Departs, and the world is taken by surprise . . .

When the tired flower of Florence is in gloom beneath the glowing
Brown hills surrounding . . .

When under the arches of the Ponte Vecchio
A green light enters against stream, flush from the west,
Against the current of obscure Arno . . .

Look up, and you see things flying
Between the day and the night;
Swallows with spools of dark thread sewing the shadows
together.

A circle swoop, and a quick parabola under the bridge arches
Where light pushes through;
A sudden turning upon itself of a thing in the air.
A dip to the water.

And you think:
'The swallows are flying so late!'

Swallows?

Dark air-life looping
Yet missing the pure loop . . .
A twitch, a twitter, an elastic shudder in flight
And serrated wings against the sky,

Like a glove, a black glove thrown up at the light,
And falling back.

Never swallows!
Bats!
The swallows are gone.

At a wavering instant the swallows give way to bats
By the Ponte Vecchio . . .
Changing guard.

Bats, and an uneasy creeping in one's scalp
As the bats swoop overhead!
Flying madly.

Pipistrello!
Black piper on an infinitesimal pipe.
Little lumps that fly in air and have voices indefinite, wildly
 vindictive;

Wings like bits of umbrella.

Bats!

Creatures that hang themselves up like an old rag, to sleep;
And disgustingly upside down.
Hanging upside down like rows of disgusting old rags
And grinning in their sleep.
Bats!

In China the bat is symbol of happiness.

Not for me!

MAN AND BAT

When I went into my room, at mid-morning,
Say ten o'clock . . .
My room, a crash-box over that great stone rattle
The Via de' Bardi. . . .

When I went into my room at mid-morning,
Why? . . . a bird!

A bird
Flying round the room in insane circles.

In insane circles!
. . . *A bat!*

A digusting bat
At mid-morning! . . .

Out! Go Out!

Round and round and round
With a twitchy, nervous, intolerable flight,
And a neurasthenic lunge,
And an impure frenzy;
A bat, big as a swallow.

Out, out of my room!

The venetian shutters I push wide
To the free, calm upper air;
Loop back the curtains. . . .

Now out, out from my room!

So to drive him out, flicking with my white handkerchief: *Go!*
But he will not.

Round and round and round
In an impure haste,
Fumbling, a beast in air,
And stumbling, lunging and touching the walls, the bell-wires
About my room!

Always refusing to go out into the air
Above that crash-gulf of the Via de' Bardi,
Yet blind with frenzy, with cluttered fear.

At last he swerved into the window bay,
But blew back, as if an incoming wind blew him in again.
A strong inrushing wind.

And round and round and round!
Blundering more insane, and leaping, in throbs, to clutch at a
corner,
At a wire, at a bell-rope:
On and on, watched relentless by me, round and round in my
room,
Round and round and dithering with tiredness and haste and
increasing delirium
Flicker-splashing round my room.

I would not let him rest;
Not one instant cleave, cling like a blot with his breast to the wall
In an obscure corner.
Not an instant!

I flicked him on,
Trying to drive him through the window.

Again he swerved into the window bay
And I ran forward, to frighten him forth.
But he rose, and from a terror worse than me he flew past me
Back into my room, and round, round, round in my room
Clutch, cleave, stagger,
Dropping about the air
Getting tired.

Something seemed to blow him back from the window
Every time he swerved at it;
Back on a strange parabola, then round, round, dizzy in my room.

He *could* not go out,
I also realised. . . .
It was the light of day which he could not enter,
Any more than I could enter the white-hot door of a blast furnace.

He could not plunge into the daylight that streamed at the
 window.
It was asking too much of his nature.

Worse even than the hideous terror of me with my handkerchief
Saying: *Out, go out!* . . .
Was the horror of white daylight in the window!

So I switched on the electric light, thinking: *Now*
The outside will seem brown. . . .

But no.
The outside did not seem brown.
And he did not mind the yellow electric light.

Silent!
He was having a silent rest.
But never!
Not in my room.

Round and round and round
Near the ceiling as if in a web,
Staggering;
Plunging, falling out of the web,
Broken in heaviness,
Lunging blindly,
Heavier;
And clutching, clutching for one second's pause,
Always, as if for one drop of rest,
One little drop.

And I!
Never, I say. . . .
Go out!

Flying slower,
Seeming to stumble, to fall in air.
Blind-weary.

Yet never able to pass the whiteness of light into freedom . . .
A bird would have dashed through, come what might.

Fall, sink, lurch, and round and round
Flicker, flicker-heavy;
Even wings heavy:
And cleave in a high corner for a second, like a clot, also a prayer.

But no.
Out, you beast.

Till he fell in a corner, palpitating, spent.
And there, a clot, he squatted and looked at me.
With sticking-out, bead-berry eyes, black,
And improper derisive ears,
And shut wings,
And brown, furry body.

Brown, nut-brown, fine fur!
But it might as well have been hair on a spider; thing
With long, black-paper ears.

So, a dilemma!
He squatted there like something unclean.

No, he must not squat, nor hang, obscene, in my room!

Yet nothing on earth will give him courage to pass the sweet fire of
day.

What then?
Hit him and kill him and throw him away?

Nay,
I didn't create him.
Let the God that created him be responsible for his death . . .
Only, in the bright day, I will not have this clot in my room.

Let the God who is maker of bats watch with them in their
unclean corners. . . .
I admit a God in every crevice,
But not bats in my room;
Nor the God of bats, while the sun shines.

So out, out, you brute! . . .
And he lunged, flight-heavy, away from me, sideways, *a sghembo!*
And round and round and round my room, a clot with wings,
Impure even in weariness.

Wings dark skinny and flapping the air,
Lost their flicker.
Spent.

He fell again with a little thud
Near the curtain on the floor.
And there lay.

Ah death, death
You are no solution!
Bats must be bats.

Only life has a way out.
And the human soul is fated to wide-eyed responsibility
In life.

So I picked him up in a flannel jacket,
Well covered, lest he should bite me.
For I would have had to kill him if he'd bitten me, the impure
    one . . .
And he hardly stirred in my hand, muffled up.

Hastily, I shook him out of the window.

And away he went!
Fear craven in his tail.
Great haste, and straight, almost bird straight above the Via
    de' Bardi.
Above that crash-gulf of exploding whips,
Towards the Borgo San Jacopo.

And now, at evening, as he flickers over the river
Dipping with petty triumphant flight, and tittering over the sun's
    departure,

I believe he chirps, pipistrello, seeing me here on this terrace
    writing:
There he sits, the long loud one!
But I am greater than he . . .
I escaped him. . . .

Florence.

Reptiles

SNAKE

A snake came to my water-trough
On a hot, hot day, and I in pyjamas for the heat,
To drink there.

In the deep, strange-scented shade of the great dark carob-tree
I came down the steps with my pitcher
And must wait, must stand and wait, for there he was at the
    trough before me.

He reached down from a fissure in the earth-wall in the gloom
And trailed his yellow-brown slackness soft-bellied down, over
    the edge of the stone trough
And rested his throat upon the stone bottom,
And where the water had dripped from the tap, in a small
    clearness,
He sipped with his straight mouth,
Softly drank through his straight gums, into his slack long body,
Silently.

Someone was before me at my water-trough,
And I, like a second comer, waiting.

He lifted his head from his drinking, as cattle do,
And looked at me vaguely, as drinking cattle do,
And flickered his two-forked tongue from his lips, and mused a
    moment,
And stooped and drank a little more,
Being earth-brown, earth-golden from the burning bowels of the
    earth
On the day of Sicilian July, with Etna smoking.

The voice of my education said to me
He must be killed,
For in Sicily the black, black snakes are innocent, the gold are
    venomous.

And voices in me said, If you were a man
You would take a stick and break him now, and finish him off.

But must I confess how I liked him,
How glad I was he had come like a guest in quiet, to drink at my
water-trough
And depart peaceful, pacified, and thankless,
Into the burning bowels of this earth?

Was it cowardice, that I dared not kill him?
Was it perversity, that I longed to talk to him?
Was it humility, to feel so honoured?
I felt so honoured.

And yet those voices:
If you were not afraid, you would kill him!

And truly I was afraid, I was most afraid,
But even so, honoured still more
That he should seek my hospitality
From out the dark door of the secret earth.

He drank enough
And lifted his head, dreamily, as one who has drunken,
And flickered his tongue like a forked night on the air, so black,
Seeming to lick his lips,
And looked around like a god, unseeing, into the air,
And slowly turned his head,
And slowly, very slowly, as if thrice adream,
Proceeded to draw his slow length curving round
And climb again the broken bank of my wall-face.

And as he put his head into that dreadful hole,
And as he slowly drew up, snake-easing his shoulders, and entered
farther,
A sort of horror, a sort of protest against his withdrawing into
that horrid black hole,
Deliberately going into the blackness, and slowly drawing himself
after,
Overcame me now his back was turned.

I looked round, I put down my pitcher,
I picked up a clumsy log
And threw it at the water-trough with a clatter.

I think it did not hit him,
But suddenly that part of him that was left behind convulsed in
    undignified haste,
Writhed like lightning, and was gone
Into the black hole, the earth-lipped fissure in the wall-front,
At which, in the intense still noon, I stared with fascination.

And immediately I regretted it.
I thought how paltry, how vulgar, what a mean act!
I despised myself and the voices of my accursed human education.

And I thought of the albatross,
And I wished he would come back, my snake.

For he seemed to me again like a king,
Like a king in exile, uncrowned in the underworld,
Now due to be crowned again.

And so, I missed my chance with one of the lords
Of life.
And I have something to expiate;
A pettiness.

Taormina.

Tortoises

BABY TORTOISE

You know what it is to be born alone,
Baby tortoise!

The first day to heave your feet little by little from the shell,
Not yet awake,
And remain lapsed on earth,
Not quite alive.

A tiny, fragile, half-animate bean.

To open your tiny beak-mouth, that looks as if it would never
open,
Like some iron door;
To lift the upper hawk-beak from the lower base
And reach your skinny little neck
And take your first bite at some dim bit of herbage,
Alone, small insect,
Tiny bright-eye,
Slow one.

To take your first solitary bite
And move on your slow, solitary hunt.
Your bright, dark little eye,
Your eye of a dark disturbed night,
Under its slow lid, tiny baby tortoise,
So indomitable.

No one ever heard you complain.

You draw your head forward, slowly, from your little wimple
And set forward, slow-dragging, on your four-pinned toes,
Rowing slowly forward.
Whither away, small bird?

Rather like a baby working its limbs,
Except that you make slow, ageless progress
And a baby makes none.

The touch of sun excites you,
And the long ages, and the lingering chill
Make you pause to yawn,
Opening your impervious mouth,
Suddenly beak-shaped, and very wide, like some suddenly gaping
    pincers;
Soft red tongue, and hard thin gums,
Then close the wedge of your little mountain front,
Your face, baby tortoise.

Do you wonder at the world, as slowly you turn your head in its
    wimple
And look with laconic, black eyes?
Or is sleep coming over you again,
The non-life?

You are so hard to wake.

Are you able to wonder?
Or is it just your indomitable will and pride of the first life
Looking round
And slowly pitching itself against the inertia
Which had seemed invincible?

The vast inanimate,
And the fine brilliance of your so tiny eye,
Challenger.

Nay, tiny shell-bird,
What a huge vast inanimate it is, that you must row against,
What an incalculable inertia.

Challenger,
Little Ulysses, fore-runner,
No bigger than my thumb-nail,
Buon viaggio.

All animate creation on your shoulder,
Set forth, little Titan, under your battle-shield.

The ponderous, preponderate,
Inanimate universe;
And you are slowly moving, pioneer, you alone.

How vivid your travelling seems now, in the troubled sunshine,
Stoic, Ulyssean atom;
Suddenly hasty, reckless, on high toes.

Voiceless little bird,
Resting your head half out of your wimple
In the slow dignity of your eternal pause.
Alone, with no sense of being alone,
And hence six times more solitary;
Fulfilled of the slow passion of pitching through immemorial ages
Your little round house in the midst of chaos.

Over the garden earth,
Small bird,
Over the edge of all things.

Traveller,
With your tail tucked a little on one side
Like a gentleman in a long-skirted coat.

All life carried on your shoulder,
Invincible fore-runner.

TORTOISE SHELL

The Cross, the Cross
Goes deeper in than we know,
Deeper into life;
Right into the marrow
And through the bone.

Along the back of the baby tortoise
The scales are locked in an arch like a bridge,
Scale-lapping, like a lobster's sections
Or a bee's.

Then crossways down his sides
Tiger-stripes and wasp-bands.

Five, and five again, and five again,
And round the edges twenty-five little ones,
The sections of the baby tortoise shell.

Four, and a keystone;
Four, and a keystone;
Four, and a keystone;
Then twenty-four, and a tiny little keystone.

It needed Pythagoras to see life playing with counters on the living back
Of the baby tortoise;
Life establishing the first eternal mathematical tablet,
Not in stone, like the Judean Lord, or bronze, but in life-clouded, life-rosy tortoise shell.

The first little mathematical gentleman
Stepping, wee mite, in his loose trousers
Under all the eternal dome of mathematical law.

Fives, and tens,
Threes and fours and twelves,
All the *volte face* of decimals,
The whirligig of dozens and the pinnacle of seven.

Turn him on his back,
The kicking little beetle,
And there again, on his shell-tender, earth-touching belly,
The long cleavage of division, upright of the eternal cross
And on either side count five,
On each side, two above, on each side, two below
The dark bar horizontal.

The Cross!
It goes right through him, the sprottling insect,
Through his cross-wise cloven psyche,
Through his five-fold complex-nature.

So turn him over on his toes again;
Four pin-point toes, and a problematical thumb-piece,
Four rowing limbs, and one wedge-balancing head,
Four and one makes five, which is the clue to all mathematics.

The Lord wrote it all down on the little slate
Of the baby tortoise.
Outward and visible indication of the plan within,
The complex, manifold involvedness of an individual creature
Plotted out
On this small bird, this rudiment,
This little dome, this pediment
Of all creation,
This slow one.

TORTOISE FAMILY CONNECTIONS

On he goes, the little one,
Bud of the universe,
Pediment of life.

Setting off somewhere, apparently.
Whither away, brisk egg?

His mother deposited him on the soil as if he were no more than
droppings,
And now he scuffles tinily past her as if she were an old rusty tin.

A mere obstacle,
He veers round the slow great mound of her –
Tortoises always foresee obstacles.

It is no use my saying to him in an emotional voice:
'This is your Mother, she laid you when you were an egg.'

He does not even trouble to answer: 'Woman, what have I to do
with thee?'
He wearily looks the other way,
And she even more wearily looks another way still,

Each with the utmost apathy,
Incognisant,
Unaware.
Nothing.

As for papa,
He snaps when I offer him his offspring,
Just as he snaps when I poke a bit of stick at him,
Because he is irascible this morning, an irascible tortoise
Being touched with love, and devoid of fatherliness.

Father and mother,
And three little brothers,
And all rambling aimless, like little perambulating pebbles
scattered in the garden,
Not knowing each other from bits of earth or old tins.

Except that papa and mama are old acquaintances, of course,
Though family feeling there is none, not even the beginnings.

Fatherless, motherless, brotherless, sisterless,
Little tortoise.

Row on then, small pebble,
Over the clods of the autumn, wind-chilled sunshine,
Young gaiety.

Does he look for a companion?

No, no, don't think it.
He doesn't know he is alone;
Isolation is his birthright,
This atom.

To row forward, and reach himself tall on spiny toes,
To travel, to burrow into a little loose earth, afraid of the night,
To crop a little substance,
To move, and to be quite sure that he is moving:
Basta!
To be a tortoise!
Think of it, in a garden of inert clods

A brisk, brindled little tortoise, all to himself –
Adam!

In a garden of pebbles and insects
To roam, and feel the slow heart beat
Tortoise-wise, the first bell sounding
From the warm blood, in the dark-creation morning.

Moving, and being himself,
Slow, and unquestioned,
And inordinately there, O stoic!
Wandering in the slow triumph of his own existence,
Ringing the soundless bell of his presence in chaos,
And biting the frail grass arrogantly,
Decidedly arrogantly.

LUI ET ELLE

She is large and matronly
And rather dirty,
A little sardonic-looking, as if domesticity had driven her to it.

Though what she does, except lay four eggs at random in the
    garden once a year
And put up with her husband,
I don't know.

She likes to eat.
She hurries up, striding reared on long uncanny legs
When food is going.
Oh yes, she can make haste when she likes.

She snaps the soft bread from my hand in great mouthfuls,
Opening her rather pretty wedge of an iron, pristine face
Into an enormously wide-beaked mouth
Like sudden curved scissors,
And gulping at more than she can swallow, and working her
    thick, soft tongue,
And having the bread hanging over her chin.

O Mistress, Mistress,
Reptile mistress,
Your eye is very dark, very bright,
And it never softens
Although you watch.

She knows,
She knows well enough to come for food,
Yet she sees me not;
Her bright eye sees, but not me, not anything,
Sightful, sightless, seeing and visionless,
Reptile mistress.

Taking bread in her curved, gaping, toothless mouth,
She has no qualm when she catches my finger in her steel
    overlapping gums,
But she hangs on, and my shout and my shrinking are nothing to
    her.
She does not even know she is nipping me with her curved beak.
Snake-like she draws at my finger, while I drag it in horror away.

Mistress, reptile mistress,
You are almost too large, I am almost frightened.

He is much smaller,
Dapper beside her,
And ridiculously small.

Her laconic eye has an earthy, materialistic look,
His, poor darling, is almost fiery.

His wimple, his blunt-prowed face,
His low forehead, his skinny neck, his long, scaled, striving legs,
So striving, striving,
Are all more delicate than she,
And he has a cruel scar on his shell.

Poor darling, biting at her feet,
Running beside her like a dog, biting her earthy, splay feet,
Nipping her ankles,

Which she drags apathetic away, though without retreating into
her shell.

Agelessly silent,
And with a grim, reptile determination,
Cold, voiceless age-after-age behind him, serpents' long obstinacy
Of horizontal persistence.

Little old man
Scuffling beside her, bending down, catching his opportunity,
Parting his steel-trap face, so suddenly, and seizing her scaly
ankle,
And hanging grimly on,
Letting go at last as she drags away,
And closing his steel-trap face.

His steel-trap, stoic, ageless, handsome face.
Alas, what a fool he looks in this scuffle.

And how he feels it!
The lonely rambler, the stoic, dignified stalker through chaos,
The immune, the animate,
Enveloped in isolation,
Fore-runner.
Now look at him!

Alas, the spear is through the side of his isolation.
His adolescence saw him crucified into sex,
Doomed, in the long crucifixion of desire, to seek his consumma-
tion beyond himself.
Divided into passionate duality,
He, so finished and immune, now broken into desirous
fragmentariness,
Doomed to make an intolerable fool of himself
In his effort toward completion again.

Poor little earthy house-inhabiting Osiris,
The mysterious bull tore him at adolescence into pieces,
And he must struggle after reconstruction, ignominiously.

And so behold him following the tail
Of that mud-hovel of his slowly rambling spouse,
Like some unhappy bull at the tail of a cow,
But with more than bovine, grim, earth-dank persistence.

Suddenly seizing the ugly ankle as she stretches out to walk,
Roaming over the sods,
Or, if it happen to show, at her pointed, heavy tail
Beneath the low-dropping back-board of her shell.

Their two shells like domed boats bumping,
Hers huge, his small;
Their splay feet rambling and rowing like paddles,
And stumbling mixed up in one another,
In the race of love –
Two tortoises,
She huge, he small.

She seems earthily apathetic,
And he has a reptile's awful persistence.

I heard a woman pitying her, pitying the Mère Tortue.
While I, I pity Monsieur.
'He pesters her and torments her,' said the woman.
How much more is *he* pestered and tormented, say I.

What can he do?
He is dumb, he is visionless,
Conceptionless.
His black, sad-lidded eye sees but beholds not
As her earthen mound moves on,
But he catches the folds of vulnerable, leathery skin,
Nail-studded, that shake beneath her shell,
And drags at these with his beak,
Drags and drags and bites,
While she pulls herself free, and rows her dull mound along.

TORTOISE GALLANTRY

Making his advances
He does not look at her, nor sniff at her,
No, not even sniff at her, his nose is blank.

Only he senses the vulnerable folds of skin
That work beneath her while she sprawls along
In her ungainly peace,
Her folds of skin that work and row
Beneath the earth-soiled hovel in which she moves.

And so he strains beneath her housey walls
And catches her trouser-legs in his beak
Suddenly, or her skinny limb,
And strange and grimly drags at her
Like a dog,
Only agelessly silent, with a reptile's awful persistency.

Grim, gruesome gallantry, to which he is doomed.
Dragged out of an eternity of silent isolation
And doomed to partiality, partial being,
Ache, and want of being,
Want,
Self-exposure, hard humiliation, need to add himself on to her.

Born to walk alone,
Fore-runner,
Now suddenly distracted into this mazy side-track,
This awkward, harrowing pursuit,
This grim necessity from within.

Does she know
As she moves eternally slowly away?
Or is he driven against her with a bang, like a bird flying in the
dark against a window,
All knowledgeless?

The awful concussion,
And the still more awful need to persist, to follow, follow,
continue,

Driven, after æons of pristine, fore-god-like singleness and
oneness,
At the end of some mysterious, red-hot iron,
Driven away from himself into her tracks,
Forced to crash against her.

Stiff, gallant, irascible, crook-legged reptile,
Little gentleman,
Sorry plight,
We ought to look the other way.

Save that, having come with you so far,
We will go on to the end.

TORTOISE SHOUT

I thought he was dumb,
I said he was dumb,
Yet I've heard him cry.

First faint scream,
Out of life's unfathomable dawn,
Far off, so far, like a madness, under the horizon's dawning rim,
Far, far off, far scream.

Tortoise *in extremis*.

Why were we crucified into sex?
Why were we not left rounded off, and finished in ourselves,
As we began,
As he certainly began, so perfectly alone?

A far, was-it-audible scream,
Or did it sound on the plasm direct?

Worse than the cry of the new-born,
A scream,
A yell,
A shout,

A pæan,
A death-agony,
A birth-cry,
A submission,
All tiny, tiny, far away, reptile under the first dawn.

War-cry, triumph, acute-delight, death-scream reptilian,
Why was the veil torn?
The silken shriek of the soul's torn membrane?
The male soul's membrane
Torn with a shriek half music, half horror.

Crucifixion.
Male tortoise, cleaving behind the hovel-wall of that dense
female,
Mounted and tense, spread-eagle, out-reaching out of the shell
In tortoise-nakedness,
Long neck, and long vulnerable limbs extruded, spread-eagle over
her house-roof,
And the deep, secret, all-penetrating tail curved beneath her walls,
Reaching and gripping tense, more reaching anguish in uttermost
tension
Till suddenly, in the spasm of coition, tupping like a jerking leap,
and oh!
Opening its clenched face from his outstretched neck
And giving that fragile yell, that scream,
Super-audible,
From his pink, cleft, old-man's mouth,
Giving up the ghost,
Or screaming in Pentecost, receiving the ghost.

His scream, and his moment's subsidence,
The moment of eternal silence,
Yet unreleased, and after the moment, the sudden, startling jerk of
coition, and at once
The inexpressible faint yell –
And so on, till the last plasm of my body was melted back
To the primeval rudiments of life, and the secret.

So he tups, and screams
Time after time that frail, torn scream

After each jerk, the longish interval,
The tortoise eternity,
Age-long, reptilian persistence,
Heart-throb, slow heart-throb, persistent for the next spasm.

I remember, when I was a boy,
I heard the scream of a frog, which was caught with his foot in the
mouth of an up-starting snake;
I remember when I first heard bull-frogs break into sound in the
spring;
I remember hearing a wild goose out of the throat of night
Cry loudly, beyond the lake of waters;
I remember the first time, out of a bush in the darkness, a
nightingale's piercing cries and gurgles startled the depths of
my soul;
I remember the scream of a rabbit as I went through a wood at
midnight;
I remember the heifer in her heat, blorting and blorting through
the hours, persistent and irrepressible;
I remember my first terror hearing the howl of weird, amorous
cats;
I remember the scream of a terrified, injured horse, the sheet-
lightning,
And running away from the sound of a woman in labour,
something like an owl whooing,
And listening inwardly to the first bleat of a lamb,
The first wail of an infant,
And my mother singing to herself,
And the first tenor singing of the passionate throat of a young
collier, who has long since drunk himself to death,
The first elements of foreign speech
On wild dark lips.

And more than all these,
And less than all these,
This last,
Strange, faint coition yell
Of the male tortoise at extremity,
Tiny from under the very edge of the farthest far-off horizon of
life.

The cross,
The wheel on which our silence first is broken,
Sex, which breaks up our integrity, our single inviolability, our
deep silence,
Tearing a cry from us.

Sex, which breaks us into voice, sets us calling across the deeps,
calling, calling for the complement,
Singing, and calling, and singing again, being answered, having
found.

Torn, to become whole again, after long seeking for what is lost,
The same cry from the tortoise as from Christ, the Osiris-cry of
abandonment,
That which is whole, torn asunder,
That which is in part, finding its whole again throughout the
universe.

Birds

TURKEY-COCK

You ruffled black blossom,
You glossy dark wind.

Your sort of gorgeousness,
Dark and lustrous
And skinny repulsive
And poppy-glossy,
Is the gorgeousness that evokes my most puzzled admiration.

Your aboriginality
Deep, unexplained,
Like a Red Indian darkly unfinished and aloof,
Seems like the black and glossy seeds of countless centuries.

Your wattles are the colour of steel-slag which has been red-hot
And is going cold,
Cooling to a powdery, pale-oxydised sky-blue.

Why do you have wattles, and a naked, wattled head?
Why do you arch your naked-set eye with a more-than-
    comprehensible arrogance?

The vulture is bald, so is the condor, obscenely,
But only you have thrown this amazing mantilla of oxydised
    sky-blue
And hot red over you.

This queer dross shawl of blue and vermilion,
Whereas the peacock has a diadem.

I wonder why.
Perhaps it is a sort of uncanny decoration, a veil of loose skin.
Perhaps it is your assertion, in all this ostentation, of raw
    contradictoriness.
Your wattles drip down like a shawl to your breast

And the point of your mantilla drops across your nose, unpleasantly.

Or perhaps it is something unfinished
A bit of slag still adhering, after your firing in the furnace of creation.

Or perhaps there is something in your wattles of a bull's dew-lap
Which slips down like a pendulum to balance the throbbing mass of a generous breast,

The over-drip of a great passion hanging in the balance.
Only yours would be a raw, unsmelted passion, that will not quite fuse from the dross.

You contract yourself,
You arch yourself as an archer's bow
Which quivers indrawn as you clench your spine
Until your veiled head almost touches backward
To the root-rising of your erected tail.
And one intense and backward-curving frisson
Seizes you as you clench yourself together
Like some fierce magnet bringing its poles together.

Burning, pale positive pole of your wattled head!
And from the darkness of that opposite one
The upstart of your round-barred, sun-round tail!

Whilst between the two, along the tense arch of your back
Blows the magnetic current in fierce blasts,
Ruffling black, shining feathers like lifted mail,
Shuddering storm wind, or a water rushing through.

Your brittle, super-sensual arrogance
Tosses the crape of red across your brow and down your breast
As you draw yourself upon yourself in insistence.

It is a declaration of such tension in will
As time has not dared to avouch, nor eternity been able to unbend
Do what it may.
A raw American will, that has never been tempered by life;
You brittle, will-tense bird with a foolish eye.

The peacock lifts his rods of bronze
And struts blue-brilliant out of the far East.
But watch a turkey prancing low on earth
Drumming his vaulted wings, as savages drum
Their rhythms on long-drawn, hollow, sinister drums.
The ponderous, sombre sound of the great drum of Huichilobos
In pyramid Mexico, during sacrifice.

Drum, and the turkey onrush
Sudden, demonic dauntlessness, full abreast,
All the bronze gloss of all his myriad petals
Each one apart and instant.
Delicate frail crescent of the gentle outline of white
At each feather-tip
So delicate:
Yet the bronze wind-bell suddenly clashing
And the eye overweening into madness.

Turkey-cock, turkey-cock,
Are you the bird of the next dawn?

Has the peacock had his day, does he call in vain, screecher, for
the sun to rise?
The eagle, the dove, and the barnyard rooster, do they call in vain,
trying to wake the morrow?
And do you await us, wattled father, Westward?
Will your yell do it?

Take up the trail of the vanished American
Where it disappeared at the foot of the crucifix.
Take up the primordial Indian obstinacy,
The more than human, dense insistence of will,
And disdain, and blankness, and onrush, and prise open the new
day with them?

The East a dead letter, and Europe moribund. . . . Is that so?
And those sombre, dead, feather-lustrous Aztecs, Amerindians,
In all the sinister splendour of their red blood-sacrifices,
Do they stand under the dawn, half-godly, half-demon, awaiting
the cry of the turkey-cock?

Or must you go through the fire once more, till you're smelted
pure,
Slag-wattled turkey-cock,
Dross-jabot?

Fiesole.

HUMMING-BIRD

I can imagine, in some otherworld
Primeval-dumb, far back
In that most awful stillness, that only gasped and hummed,
Humming-birds raced down the avenues.

Before anything had a soul,
While life was a heave of Matter, half inanimate,
This little bit chipped off in brilliance
And went whizzing through the slow, vast, succulent stems.

I believe there were no flowers then,
In the world where the humming-bird flashed ahead of creation.
I believe he pierced the slow vegetable veins with his long beak.

Probably he was big
As mosses, and little lizards, they say, were once big.
Probably he was a jabbing, terrifying monster.

We look at him through the wrong end of the long telescope of
Time,
Luckily for us.

Española.

THE BLUE JAY

The blue jay with a crest on his head
Comes round the cabin in the snow.
He runs in the snow like a bit of blue metal,
Turning his back on everything.

From the pine-tree that towers and hisses like a pillar of shaggy
cloud
Immense above the cabin
Comes a strident laugh as we approach, this little black dog and I.
So halts the little black bitch on four spread paws in the snow
And looks up inquiringly into the pillar of cloud,
With a tinge of misgiving.
Ca-a-a! comes the scrape of ridicule out of the tree.

What voice of the Lord is that, from the tree of smoke?

Oh, Bibbles, little black bitch in the snow,
With a pinch of snow in the groove of your silly snub nose,
What do you look at *me* for?
What do you look at me for, with such misgiving?

It's the blue jay laughing at us.
It's the blue jay jeering at us, Bibs.

Every day since the snow is here
The blue jay paces round the cabin, very busy, picking up bits,
Turning his back on us all,
And bobbing his thick dark crest about the snow, as if darkly
saying:
I ignore those folk who look out.

You acid-blue metallic bird,
You thick bird with a strong crest,
Who are you?
Whose boss are you, with all your bully way?
You copper-sulphate blue bird!

Lobo.

Animals

THE ASS

The long-drawn bray of the ass
In the Sicilian twilight –

All mares are dead!
All mares are dead!
Oh-h!
Oh-h-h!
Oh-h-h-h-h–h!!
I can't bear it, I can't bear it.
I can't!
Oh, I can't!
Oh –
There's one left!
There's one left!
One!
There's one . . . left. . . .

So ending on a grunt of agonised relief.

This is the authentic Arabic interpretation of the braying of the ass.
And Arabs should know.

And yet, as his brass-resonant howling yell resounds through the Sicilian twilight
I am not sure –

His big, furry head,
His big, regretful eyes,
His diminished, drooping hindquarters,
His small toes.

Such a dear!
Such an ass!
With such a knot inside him!
He regrets something that he remembers.
That's obvious.

The Steppes of Tartary,
And the wind in his teeth for a bit,
And *noli me tangere*.

Ah then, when he tore the wind with his teeth,
And trod wolves underfoot,
And over-rode his mares as if he were savagely leaping an
obstacle, to set his teeth in the sun. . . .

Somehow, alas, he fell in love,
And was sold into slavery.

He fell into the rut of love,
Poor ass, like man, always in rut,
The pair of them alike in that.

All his soul in his gallant member
And his head gone heavy with the knowledge of desire
And humiliation.

The ass was the first of all animals to fall finally into love,
From obstacle-leaping pride,
Mare obstacle,
Into love, mare-goal, and the knowledge of love.

Hence Jesus rode him in the Triumphant Entry.
Hence his beautiful eyes.
Hence his ponderous head, brooding over desire, and downfall,
Jesus, and a pack-saddle,

Hence he uncovers his big ass-teeth and howls in that agony that is
half insatiable desire and half unquenchable humiliation.
Hence the black cross on his shoulders.

The Arabs were only half right, though they hinted the whole;
Everlasting lament in everlasting desire.

See him standing with his head down, near the Porta Cappuccini,
Asinello, Ciuco,
Somaro;

With the half-veiled, beautiful eyes, and the pensive face not asleep,
Motionless, like a bit of rock.

Has he seen the Gorgon's head, and turned to stone?
Alas, Love did it.
Now he's a jackass, a pack-ass, a donkey, somaro, burro, with a boss piling loads on his back.
Tied by the nose at the Porta Cappuccini.
And tied in a knot, inside, dead-locked between two desires:
To overleap like a male all mares as obstacles
In a leap at the sun;
And to leap in one last heart-bursting leap like a male at the goal of a mare.
And there end.
Well, you can't have it both roads.

Hee! Hee! Ehee! Ehow! Ehaw!! Oh! Oh! Oh-h-h!!
The wave of agony bursts in the stone that he was,
Bares his long ass's teeth, flattens his long ass's ears, straightens his donkey neck,
And howls his pandemonium on the indignant air.

Yes, it's a quandary.
Jesus rode on him, the first burden on the first beast of burden.
Love on a submissive ass.
So the tale began.

But the ass never forgets.

The horse, being nothing but a nag, will forget.
And men, being mostly geldings and knacker-boned hacks, have almost all forgot.
But the ass is a primal creature, and never forgets.

The Steppes of Tartary,
And Jesus on a meek ass-colt: mares: Mary escaping to Egypt: Joseph's cudgel.

Hee! Hee! Ehee! Ehow-ow!-ow!-aw!-aw!-aw!
All mares are dead!

Or else I am dead!
One of us, or the pair of us,
I don't know-ow!-ow!
Which!
Not sure-ure-ure
Quite which!
Which!

Taormina.

HE-GOAT

See his black nose snubbed back, pressed over like a whale's
    blow-holes,
As if his nostrils were going to curve back to the root of his tail.

As he charges slow among the herd
And rows among the females like a ship pertinaciously,
Heavy with a rancid cargo, through the lesser ships –
Old father
Sniffing forever ahead of him, at the rear of the goats, that they lift
    the little door,
And rowing on, unarrived, no matter how often he enter:
Like a big ship pushing her bowsprit over the little ships
Then swerving and steering afresh
And never, never arriving at journey's end, at the rear of the
    female ships.

Yellow eyes incomprehensible with thin slits
To round-eyed us.

Yet if you had whorled horns of bronze in a frontal dark wall
At the end of a back-bone ridge, like a straight *sierra roqueña*,
And nerves urging forward to the wall, you'd have eyes like his,
Especially if, being given a needle's eye of egress elsewhere
You tried to look back to it, and couldn't.

Sometimes he turns with a start, to fight, to challenge, to suddenly
butt.
And then you see the God that he is, in a cloud of black hair
And storm-lightning-slitted eye.
Splendidly planting his feet, one rocky foot striking the ground
with a sudden rock-hammer announcement.

I am here!
And suddenly lowering his head, the whorls of bone and of horn
Slowly revolving towards unexploded explosion,
As from the stem of his bristling, lightning-conductor tail
In a rush up the shrieking duct of his vertebral way
Runs a rage drawn in from the ether divinely through him
Towards a shock and a crash and a smiting of horns ahead.

That is a grand old lust of his, to gather the great
Rage of the sullen-stagnating atmosphere of goats
And bring it hurtling to a head, with crash of horns against the
horns
Of the opposite enemy goat,
Thus hammering the mettle of goats into proof, and smiting out
The godhead of goats from the shock.

Things of iron are beaten on the anvil,
And he-goat is anvil to he-goat, and hammer to he-goat
In the business of beating the mettle of goats to a godhead.

But they've taken his enemy from him
And left him only his libidinousness,
His nostrils turning back, to sniff at even himself
And his slitted eyes seeking the needle's eye,
His own, unthreaded, forever.

So it is, when they take the enemy from us,
And we can't fight.

He is not fatherly, like the bull, massive Providence of hot blood;
The goat is an egoist, aware of himself, devilish aware of himself,
And full of malice prepense, and overweening, determined to
stand on the highest peak
Like the devil, and look on the world as his own.

And as for love:
With a needle of long red flint he stabs in the dark
At the living rock he is up against;
While she with her goaty mouth stands smiling the while as he
strikes, since sure
He will never *quite* strike home, on the target-quick, for her quick
Is just beyond range of the arrow he shoots
From his leap at the zenith in her, so it falls just short of the mark,
far enough.
It is over before it is finished.
She, smiling with goaty munch-mouth, Mona Lisa, arranges it so.

Orgasm after orgasm after orgasm
And he smells so rank and his nose goes back,
And never an enemy brow-metalled to thresh it out with in the
open field;
Never a mountain peak, to be king of the castle.
Only those eternal females to overleap and surpass, and never
succeed.

The involved voluptuousness of the soft-footed cat
Who is like a fur folding a fur,
The cat who laps blood, and knows
The soft welling of blood invincible even beyond bone or metal of
bone.

The soft, the secret, the unfathomable blood
The cat has lapped;
And known it subtler than frisson-shaken nerves,
Stronger than multiplicity of bone on bone,
And darker than even the arrows of violentest will
Can pierce, for that is where will gives out, like a sinking stone
that can sink no further.

But he-goat,
Black procreant male of the selfish will and libidinous desire,
God in black cloud with curving horns of bronze,
Find an enemy, Egoist, and clash the cymbals in face-to-face
defiance,
And let the lightning out of your smothered dusk.

Forget the female herd for a bit,
And fight to be boss of the world.

Fight, old Satan with a selfish will, fight for your selfish will;
Fight to be the devil on the tip of the peak
Overlooking the world for his own.

But bah, how can he, poor domesticated beast!

Taormina.

SHE-GOAT

Goats go past the back of the house like dry leaves in the dawn,
And up the hill like a river, if you watch.

At dusk they patter back like a bough being dragged on the
ground,
Raising dusk and acridity of goats, and bleating.

Our old goat we tie up at night in the shed at the back of the
broken Greek tomb in the garden,
And when the herd goes by at dawn she begins to bleat for me to
come down and untie her.

Merr-err-err! Merr-er-err! Mer! Mé!
– Wait, wait a bit, I'll come when I've lit the fire.
Merrr!
– Exactly.
Mé! Mer! Merrrrrr!!!
– Tace, tu, crapa, bestia!
Merr-ererrr ererrrr! Merrrr!

She is such an alert listener, with her ears wide, to know am I
coming!
Such a canny listener, from a distance, looking upwards, lending
first one ear, then another.

There she is, perched on her manger, looking over the boards into the day
Like a belle at her window.
And immediately she sees me she blinks, stares, doesn't know me, turns her head and ignores me vulgarly with a wooden blank on her face.

What do I care for her, the ugly female, standing up there with her long tangled sides like an old rug thrown over a fence.
But she puts her nose down shrewdly enough when the knot is untied,
And jumps staccato to earth, a sharp, dry jump, still ignoring me,
Pretending to look round the stall.

Come on, you, crapa! I'm not your servant!

She turns her head away with an obtuse, female sort of deafness, bête.
And then invariably she crouches her rear and makes water.
That being her way of answer, if I speak to her. – Self-conscious!
Le bestie non parlano, poverine!

She was bought at Giardini fair, on the sands, for six hundred lire.

An obstinate old witch, almost jerking the rope from my hands to eat the acanthus, or bite at the almond buds, and make me wait.
Yet the moment I hate her she trips mild and smug like a woman going to mass.
The moment I really detest her.

Queer it is, suddenly, in the garden
To catch sight of her standing like some huge, ghoulish grey bird in the air, on the bough of the leaning almond-tree,
Straight as a board on the bough, looking down like some hairy horrid God the Father in a William Blake imagination.
Come down, crapa, out of that almond-tree!

Instead of which she strangely rears on her perch in the air, vast beast,
And strangely paws the air, delicate,

And reaches her black-striped face up like a snake, far up,
Subtly, to the twigs overhead, far up, vast beast,
And snaps them sharp, with a little twist of her anaconda head;
All her great hairy-shaggy belly open against the morning.

At seasons she curls back her tail like a green leaf in the fire,
Or like a lifted hand, hailing at her wrong end.
And having exposed the pink place of her nakedness, fixedly,
She trots on blithe toes,
And if you look at her, she looks back with a cold, sardonic stare.
Sardonic, sardonyx, rock of cold fire.
See me? She says, *That's me!*

That's her.

Then she leaps the rocks like a quick rock,
Her backbone sharp as a rock,
Sheer will.

Along which ridge of libidinous magnetism
Defiant, curling the leaf of her tail as if she were curling her lip
behind her at all life,
Libidinous desire runs back and forth, asserting itself in that little
lifted bare hand.

Yet she has such adorable spurty kids, like spurts of black ink.
And in a month again is as if she had never had them.

And when the billy goat mounts her
She is brittle as brimstone.
While his slitted eyes squint back to the roots of his ears.

Taormina.

KANGAROO

In the northern hemisphere
Life seems to leap at the air, or skim under the wind
Like stags on rocky ground, or pawing horses, or springy scut-
tailed rabbits.

Or else rush horizontal to charge at the sky's horizon,
Like bulls or bisons or wild pigs.

Or slip like water slippery towards its ends,
As foxes, stoats, and wolves, and prairie dogs.

Only mice, and moles, and rats, and badgers, and beavers, and
perhaps bears
Seem belly-plumbed to the earth's mid-navel.
Or frogs that when they leap come flop, and flop to the centre of
the earth.

But the yellow antipodal Kangaroo, when she sits up,
Who can unseat her, like a liquid drop that is heavy, and just
touches earth.

The downward drip
The down-urge.
So much denser than cold-blooded frogs.

Delicate mother Kangaroo
Sitting up there rabbit-wise, but huge, plumb-weighted,
And lifting her beautiful slender face, oh! so much more gently
and finely lined than a rabbit's, or than a hare's,
Lifting her face to nibble at a round white peppermint drop, which
she loves, sensitive mother Kangaroo.

Her sensitive, long, pure-bred face.
Her full antipodal eyes, so dark,
So big and quiet and remote, having watched so many empty
dawns in silent Australia.

Her little loose hands, and drooping Victorian shoulders.
And then her great weight below the waist, her vast pale belly
With a thin young yellow little paw hanging out, and straggle of a
long thin ear, like ribbon,
Like a funny trimming to the middle of her belly, thin little dangle
of an immature paw, and one thin ear.

Her belly, her big haunches
And, in addition, the great muscular python-stretch of her tail.

There, she shan't have any more peppermint drops.
So she wistfully, sensitively sniffs the air, and then turns, goes off
in slow sad leaps

On the long flat skis of her legs,
Steered and propelled by that steel-strong snake of a tail.

Stops again, half turns, inquisitive to look back.
While something stirs quickly in her belly, and a lean little face
comes out, as from a window,
Peaked and a bit dismayed.
Only to disappear again quickly away from the sight of the world,
to snuggle down in the warmth,
Leaving the trail of a different paw hanging out.

Still she watches with eternal, cocked wistfulness!
How full her eyes are, like the full, fathomless, shining eyes of an
Australian black-boy
Who has been lost so many centuries on the margins of existence!

She watches with insatiable wistfulness.
Untold centuries of watching for something to come,
For a new signal from life, in that silent lost land of the South.

Where nothing bites but insects and snakes and the sun, small life.
Where no bull roared, no cow ever lowed, no stag cried, no
leopard screeched, no lion coughed, no dog barked,
But all was silent save for parrots occasionally, in the haunted
blue bush.

Wistfully watching, with wonderful liquid eyes.
And all her weight, all her blood, dripping sack-wise down
towards the earth's centre,
And the live little-one taking in its paw at the door of her belly.

Leap then, and come down on the line that draws to the earth's
deep, heavy centre.

Sydney.

MOUNTAIN LION

Climbing through the January snow, into the Lobo canyon
Dark grow the spruce-trees, blue is the balsam, water sounds still
 unfrozen, and the trail is still evident.

Men!
Two men!
Men! The only animal in the world to fear!

They hesitate.
We hesitate.
They have a gun.
We have no gun.

Then we all advance, to meet.

Two Mexicans, strangers, emerging out of the dark and snow and
 inwardness of the Lobo valley.
What are they doing here on this vanishing trail?

What is he carrying?
Something yellow.
A deer?

Qué tiene, amigo?
León –

He smiles, foolishly, as if he were caught doing wrong.
And we smile, foolishly, as if we didn't know.
He is quite gentle and dark-faced.

It is a mountain lion,
A long, long slim cat, yellow like a lioness.
Dead.

He trapped her this morning, he says, smiling foolishly.

Lift up her face,
Her round, bright face, bright as frost.
Her round, fine-fashioned head, with two dead ears;
And stripes in the brilliant frost of her face, sharp, fine dark rays,
Dark, keen, fine rays in the brilliant frost of her face.
Beautiful dead eyes.

Hermoso es!

They go out towards the open;
We go on into the gloom of Lobo.
And above the trees I found her lair,
A hole in the blood-orange brilliant rocks that stick up, a little
cave.
And bones, and twigs, and a perilous ascent.

So, she will never leap up that way again, with the yellow flash of a
mountain lion's long shoot!
And her bright striped frost-face will never watch any more, out
of the shadow of the cave in the blood-orange rock,
Above the trees of the Lobo dark valley-mouth!

Instead, I look out.
And out to the dim of the desert, like a dream, never real;
To the snow of the Sangre de Cristo mountains, the ice of the
mountains of Picoris,
And near across at the opposite steep of snow, green trees
motionless standing in snow, like a Christmas toy.

And I think in this empty world there was room for me and a
mountain lion.
And I think in the world beyond, how easily we might spare a
million or two of humans
And never miss them.
Yet what a gap in the world, the missing white frost-face of that
slim yellow mountain lion!

Lobo.

THE RED WOLF

Over the heart of the west, the Taos desert,
Circles an eagle,
And it's dark between me and him.

The sun, as he waits a moment, huge and liquid
Standing without feet on the rim of the far-off mesa
Says: *Look for a last long time then! Look! Look well! I am going.*
So he pauses and is beholden, and straightway is gone.

And the Indian, in a white sheet
Wrapped to the eyes, the sheet bound close on his brows,
Stands saying: *See, I'm invisible!*
Behold how you can't behold me!
The invisible in its shroud!

Now that the sun has gone, and the aspen leaves
And the cotton-wood leaves are fallen, as good as fallen,
And the ponies are in corral,
And it's night.

Why, more has gone than all these;
And something has come.
A red wolf stands on the shadow's dark red rim.

Day has gone to dust on the sage-grey desert
Like a white Christus fallen to dust from a cross;
To dust, to ash, on the twilit floor of the desert.

And a black crucifix like a dead tree spreading wings,
Maybe a black eagle with its wings out
Left lonely in the night
In a sort of worship.

And coming down upon us, out of the dark concave
Of the eagle's wings,
And the coffin-like slit where the Indian's eyes are,
And the absence of cotton-wood leaves, or of aspen,
Even the absence of dark-crossed donkeys:
Come tall old demons, smiling

The Indian smile,
Saying: *How do you do, you pale-face?*

I am very well, old demon.
How are you?

Call me Harry if you will,
Call me Old Harry, says he.
Or the abbreviation of Nicolas,
Nick, Old Nick, maybe.

Well, you're a dark old demon,
And I'm a pale-face like a homeless dog
That has followed the sun from the dawn through the east,
Trotting east and east and east till the sun himself went home,
And left me homeless here in the dark at your door.
How do you think we'll get on,
Old demon, you and I?

You and I, you pale-face,
Pale-face you and I
Don't get on.

Mightn't we try?

Where's your God, you white one?
Where's your white God?

He fell to dust as the twilight fell,
Was fume as I trod
The last step out of the east.

Then you're a lost white dog of a pale-face,
And the day's now dead. . . .

Touch me carefully, old father,
My beard is red.

Thin red wolf of a pale-face,
Thin red wolf, go home.

I have no home, old father,
That's why I come.

We take no hungry stray from the pale-face . . .

Father, you are not asked.
I am come. I am here. The red-dawn-wolf
Sniffs round your place.
Lifts up his voice and howls to the walls of the pueblo.
Announcing he's here.

The dogs of the dark pueblo
Have long fangs . . .

Has the red wolf trotted east and east and east
From the far, far other end of the day
To fear a few fangs?

Across the pueblo river
That dark old demon and I
Thus say a few words to each other

And wolf, he calls me, and red.
I call him no names.
He says, however, he is Star-Road.
I say, he can go back the same gait.

As for me . . .
Since I trotted at the tail of the sun as far as ever the creature went
west,
And lost him here,
I'm going to sit down on my tail right here
And wait for him to come back with a new story.
I'm the red wolf, says the dark old father.
All right, the red-dawn-wolf I am.

Taos.

Ghosts

AUTUMN AT TAOS

Over the rounded sides of the Rockies, the aspens of autumn,
The aspens of autumn,
Like yellow hair of a tigress brindled with pines.

Down on my hearth-rug of desert, sage of the mesa,
An ash-grey pelt
Of wolf all hairy and level, a wolf's wild pelt.

Trot-trot to the mottled foot-hills, cedar-mottled and piñon;
Did you ever see an otter?
Silvery-sided, fish-fanged, fierce-faced, whiskered, mottled.

When I trot my little pony through the aspen-trees of the canyon,
Behold me trotting at ease betwixt the slopes of the golden
Great and glistening-feathered legs of the hawk of Horus;
The golden hawk of Horus
Astride above me.

But under the pines
I go slowly
As under the hairy belly of a great black bear.

Glad to emerge and look back
On the yellow, pointed aspen-trees laid one on another like
    feathers,
Feather over feather on the breast of the great and golden
Hawk as I say of Horus.

Pleased to be out in the sage and the pine fish-dotted foot-hills,
Past the otter's whiskers,
On to the fur of the wolf-pelt that strews the plain.

And then to look back to the rounded sides of the squatting
    Rockies,
Tigress brindled with aspen,
Jaguar-splashed, puma-yellow, leopard-livid slopes of America.

Make big eyes, little pony,
At all these skins of wild beasts;
They won't hurt you.

Fangs and claws and talons and beaks and hawk-eyes
Are nerveless just now.
So be easy.

Taos.

PANSIES

ELEPHANTS IN THE CIRCUS

Elephants in the circus
have æons of weariness round their eyes.
Yet they sit up
and show vast bellies to the children.

ELEPHANTS PLODDING

Plod! Plod!
And what ages of time
the worn arches of their spines support!

ON THE DRUM

The huge old female on the drum
shuffles gingerly round
and smiles; the vastness of her elephant antiquity
is amused.

TWO PERFORMING ELEPHANTS

He stands with his forefeet on the drum
and the other, the old one, the pallid hoary female
must creep her great bulk beneath the bridge of him.

On her knees, in utmost caution
all agog, and curling up her trunk
she edges through without upsetting him.
Triumph! the ancient, pig-tailed monster!

When her trick is to climb over him
with what shadow-like slow carefulness
she skims him, sensitive
as shadows from the ages gone and perished
in touching him, and planting her round feet.

While the wispy, modern children, half-afraid
watch silent. The looming of the hoary, far-gone ages
is too much for them.

BOWLS

Take away all this crystal and silver
and give me soft-skinned wood
that lives erect through long nights, physically
to put to my lips.

HOW BEASTLY THE BOURGEOIS IS –

How beastly the bourgeois is
especially the male of the species –

Presentable, eminently presentable –
shall I make you a present of him?

Isn't he handsome? isn't he healthy? Isn't he a fine specimen?
doesn't he look the fresh clean englishman, outside?
Isn't it god's own image? tramping his thirty miles a day
after partridges, or a little rubber ball?
wouldn't you like to be like that, well off, and quite the thing?

Oh, but wait!
Let him meet a new emotion, let him be faced with another man's need,
let him come home to a bit of moral difficulty, let life face him with a new demand on his understanding
and then watch him go soggy, like a wet meringue.
Watch him turn into a mess, either a fool or a bully.
Just watch the display of him, confronted with a new demand on his intelligence.
a new life-demand.

How beastly the bourgeois is
especially the male of the species –

Nicely groomed, like a mushroom
standing there so sleek and erect and eyeable –
and like a fungus, living on the remains of bygone life
sucking his life out of the dead leaves of greater life than his own.

And even so, he's stale, he's been there too long.
Touch him, and you'll find he's all gone inside
just like an old mushroom, all wormy inside, and hollow
under a smooth skin and an upright appearance.

Full of seething, wormy, hollow feelings
rather nasty –
How beastly the bourgeois is!

Standing in their thousands, these appearances, in damp England
what a pity they can't all be kicked over
like sickening toadstools, and left to melt back, swiftly
into the soil of England.

NATURAL COMPLEXION

But you see, said the handsome young man with the chamois
gloves
to the woman rather older than himself,
if you don't use rouge and a lip-stick, in Paris
they'll take you for a woman of the people.

So spoke the british gentleman
pulling on his chamois gloves
and using his most melodious would-be-oxford voice.

And the woman said: Dear me!
how rough that would be on you, darling!
Only, if you insist on pulling on those chamois gloves
I swear I'll pull off my knickers, right in the Rue de la Paix.

THE OXFORD VOICE

When you hear it languishing
and hooing and cooing and sidling through the front teeth,
        the oxford voice
            or worse still
        the would-be oxford voice
you don't even laugh any more, you can't.

For every blooming bird is an oxford cuckoo nowadays,
you can't sit on a bus nor in the tube
but it breathes gently and languishingly in the back of your neck.

And oh, so seductively superior, so seductively
        self-effacingly
        deprecatingly
            superior. –
We wouldn't insist on it for a moment
        but we are
            we are
        you admit we are
            superior. –

LEDA

Come not with kisses
not with caresses
of hands and lips and murmurings;
come with a hiss of wings
and sea-touch tip of a beak
and treading of wet, webbed, wave-working feet
into the marsh-soft belly.

WHEN I WENT TO THE CIRCUS –

When I went to the circus that had pitched on the waste lot
it was full of uneasy people
frightened of the bare earth and the temporary canvas

and the smell of horses and other beasts
instead of merely the smell of man.

Monkeys rode rather grey and wizened
on curly plump piebald ponies
and the children uttered a little cry –
and dogs jumped through hoops and turned somersaults
and then the geese scuttled in in a little flock
and round the ring they went to the sound of the whip
then doubled, and back, with a funny up-flutter of wings –
and the children suddenly shouted out.
Then came the hush again, like a hush of fear.

The tight-rope lady, pink and blonde and nude-looking, with a few gold spangles
footed cautiously out on the rope, turned prettily, spun round
bowed, and lifted her foot in her hand, smiled, swung her parasol
to another balance, tripped round, poised, and slowly sank
her handsome thighs down, down, till she slept her splendid body on the rope.
When she rose, tilting her parasol, and smiled at the cautious people
they cheered, but nervously.

The trapeze man, slim and beautiful and like a fish in the air
swung great curves through the upper space, and came down like a star
– And the people applauded, with hollow, frightened applause.

The elephants, huge and grey, loomed their curved bulk through the dusk
and sat up, taking strange postures, showing the pink soles of their feet
and curling their precious live trunks like ammonites
and moving always with soft slow precision
as when a great ship moves to anchor.
The people watched and wondered, and seemed to resent the mystery that lies in beasts.

Horse, gay horses, swirling round and plaiting
in a long line, their heads laid over each other's necks;

they were happy, they enjoyed it;
all the creatures seemed to enjoy the game
in the circus, with their circus people.

But the audience, compelled to wonder
compelled to admire the bright rhythms of moving bodies
compelled to see the delicate skill of flickering human bodies
flesh flamey and a little heroic, even in a tumbling clown,
they were not really happy.
There was no gushing response, as there is at the film.

When modern people see the carnal body dauntless and flickering gay
playing among the elements neatly, beyond competition
and displaying no personality,
modern people are depressed.

Modern people feel themselves at a disadvantage.
They know they have no bodies that could play among the elements.
They have only their personalities, that are best seen flat, on the film,
flat personalities in two dimensions, imponderable and touchless.

And they grudge the circus people the swooping gay weight of limbs
that flower in mere movement,
and they grudge them the immediate, physical understanding they have with their circus beasts,
and they grudge them their circus-life altogether.

Yet the strange, almost frightened shout of delight that comes now and then from the children
shows that the children vaguely know how cheated they are of their birthright
in the bright wild circus flesh.

THINGS MEN HAVE MADE –

Things men have made with wakened hands, and put soft life into
are awake through years with transferred touch, and go on
glowing
for long years.
And for this reason, some old things are lovely
warm still with the life of forgotten men who made them.

THINGS MADE BY IRON –

Things made by iron and handled by steel
are born dead, they are shrouds, they soak life out of us.
Till after a long time, when they are old and have steeped in our
life
they begin to be soothed and soothing: then we throw them away.

WHATEVER MAN MAKES –

Whatever man makes and makes it live
lives because of the life put into it.
A yard of India muslin is alive with Hindu life.
And a Navajo woman, weaving her rug in the pattern of her
dream
must run the pattern out in a little break at the end
so that her soul can come out, back to her.

But in the odd pattern, like snake-marks on the sand
it leaves its trail.

WORK

There is no point in work
unless it absorbs you
like an absorbing game.

If it doesn't absorb you
if it's never any fun,
don't do it.

When a man goes out into his work
he is alive like a tree in spring,
he is living, not merely working.

When the Hindus weave thin wool into long, long lengths of stuff
with their thin dark hands and their wide dark eyes and their still
souls absorbed
they are like slender trees putting forth leaves, a long white web of
living leaf,
the tissue they weave,
and they clothe themselves in white as a tree clothes itself in its
own foliage.

As with cloth, so with houses, ships, shoes, wagons or cups or
loaves
men might put them forth as a snail its shell, as a bird that leans
its breast against its nest, to make it round,
as the turnip models his round root, as the bush makes flowers
and gooseberries,
putting them forth, not manufacturing them,
and cities might be as once they were, bowers grown out from the
busy bodies of people.

And so it will be again, men will smash the machines.

At last, for the sake of clothing himself in his own leaf-like cloth
tissued from his life,
and dwelling in his own bowery house, like a beaver's nibbled
mansion
and drinking from cups that came off his fingers like flowers off
their five-fold stem,
he will cancel the machines we have got.

WHAT IS HE?

What is he?
– A man, of course.
Yes, but what does he do?
– He lives and is a man.
Oh quite! But he must work. He must have a job of some sort.
– Why?
Because obviously he's not one of the leisured classes.
– I don't know. He has lots of leisure. And he makes quite
    beautiful chairs. –
There you are then! He's a cabinet maker.
– No no!
Anyhow a carpenter and joiner.
– Not at all.
But you said so.
– What did I say?
That he made chairs, and was a joiner and carpenter.
– I said he made chairs, but I did not say he was a carpenter.
All right then, he's just an amateur.
– Perhaps! Would you say a thrush was a professional flautist, or
    just an amateur? –
I'd say it was just a bird.
– And I say he is just a man.
All right! You always did quibble.

THE ELEPHANT IS SLOW TO MATE –

The elephant, the huge old beast,
    is slow to mate;
he finds a female, they show no haste
    they wait

for the sympathy in their vast shy hearts
    slowly, slowly to rouse
as they loiter along the river-beds
    and drink and browse

and dash in panic through the brake
  of forest with the herd,
and sleep in massive silence, and wake
  together, without a word.

So slowly the great hot elephant hearts
  grow full of desire,
and the great beasts mate in secret at last,
  hiding their fire.

Oldest they are and the wisest of beasts
  so they know at last
how to wait for the loneliest of feasts
  for the full repast.

They do not snatch, they do not tear;
  their massive blood
moves as the moon-tides, near, more near,
  till they touch in flood.

SEX AND TRUST

If you want to have sex, you've got to trust
at the core of your heart, the other creature.
The other creature, the other creature
not merely the personal upstart;

but the creature there, that has come to meet you;
trust it you must, you must
or the experience amounts to nothing,
mere evacuation-lust.

THE GAZELLE CALF

The gazelle calf, O my children,
goes behind its mother across the desert,
goes behind its mother on blithe bare foot
requiring no shoes, O my children!

LITTLE FISH

The tiny fish enjoy themselves
in the sea.
Quick little splinters of life,
their little lives are fun to them
in the sea.

THE MOSQUITO KNOWS –

The mosquito knows full well, small as he is
he's a beast of prey.
But after all
he only takes his bellyful,
he doesn't put my blood in the bank.

SELF-PITY

I never saw a wild thing
sorry for itself.
A small bird will drop frozen dead from a bough
without ever having felt sorry for itself.

NEW MOON

The new moon, of no importance
lingers behind as the yellow sun glares and is gone beyond the
sea's edge;
earth smokes blue;
the new moon, in cool height above the blushes,
brings a fresh fragrance of heaven to our senses.

SPRAY

It is a wonder foam is so beautiful.
A wave bursts in anger on a rock, broken up
in wild white sibilant spray
and falls back, drawing in its breath with rage,
with frustration how beautiful!

SEA-WEED

Sea-weed sways and sways and swirls
as if swaying were its form of stillness;
and if it flushes against fierce rock
it slips over it as shadows do, without hurting itself.

FIDELITY

Fidelity and love are two different things, like a flower and a gem.
And love, like a flower, will fade, will change into something else
or it would not be flowery.

O flowers they fade because they are moving swiftly; a little torrent of life
leaps up to the summit of the stem, gleams, turns over round the bend
of the parabola of curved flight,
sinks, and is gone, like a comet curving into the invisible.

O flowers they are all the time travelling
like comets, and they come into our ken
for a day, for two days, and withdraw, slowly vanish again.

And we, we must take them on the wing, and let them go.
Embalmed flowers are not flowers, immortelles are not flowers;
flowers are just a motion, a swift motion, a coloured gesture;
that is their loveliness. And that is love.

But a gem is different. It lasts so much longer than we do
so much much much longer
that it seems to last forever.
Yet we know it is flowing away
as flowers are, and we are, only slower.
The wonderful slow flowing of the sapphire!

All flows, and every flow is related to every other flow.
Flowers and sapphires and us, diversely streaming.

In the old days, when sapphires were breathed upon and brought
forth
during the wild orgasms of chaos
time was much slower, when the rocks came forth.
It took æons to make a sapphire, æons for it to pass away.

And a flower it takes a summer.

And man and woman are like the earth, that brings forth flowers
in summer, and love, but underneath is rock.
Older than flowers, older than ferns, older than foraminiferæ
older than plasm altogether is the soul of a man underneath.

And when, throughout all the wild orgasms of love
slowly a gem forms, in the ancient, once-more-molten rocks
of two human hearts, two ancient rocks, a man's heart and a
woman's,
that is the crystal of peace, the slow hard jewel of trust,
the sapphire of fidelity.
The gem of mutual peace emerging from the wild chaos of love.

NO! MR LAWRENCE!

No, Mr Lawrence, it's not like that!
I don't mind telling you
I know a thing or two about love,
perhaps more than you do.

And what I know is that you make it
too nice, too beautiful.
It's not like that, you know; you fake it.
It's really rather dull.

RED-HERRING

My father was a working man
and a collier was he,
at six in the morning they turned him down
and they turned him up for tea.

My mother was a superior soul
a superior soul was she,
cut out to play a superior rôle
in the god-damn bourgeoisie.

We children were the in-betweens
little non-descripts were we,
indoors we called each other *you*,
outside, it was *tha* and *thee*.

But time has fled, our parents are dead
we've risen in the world all three;
but still we are in-betweens, we tread
between the devil and the deep cold sea.

O I am a member of the bourgeoisie
and a servant-maid brings me my tea –
But I'm always longing for someone to say:
'ark 'ere, lad! atween thee an' me

they're a' a b—d— lot o' —s,
an' I reckon it's nowt but right
we should start an' kick their —ses for 'em
an' tell 'em to —.

MANY MANSIONS

When a bird flips his tail in getting his balance on a tree
he feels much gayer than if somebody had left him a fortune
or than if he'd just built himself a nest with a bathroom –
Why can't people be gay like that?

WEALTH

Peace I have from the core of the atom, from the core of space,
and grace, if I don't lose it, from the same place.
And I look shabby, yet my roots go beyond my knowing,
deep beyond the world of man.
And where my little leaves flutter highest
there are no people, nor ever will be.

Yet my roots are in a woman too.
And my leaves are green with the breath of human experience.

BEAUTIFUL OLD AGE

It ought to be lovely to be old
to be full of the peace that comes of experience
and wrinkled ripe fulfilment.

The wrinkled smile of completeness that follows a life
lived undaunted and unsoured with accepted lies.
If people lived without accepting lies
they would ripen like apples, and be scented like pippins
in their old age.

Soothing, old people should be, like apples
when one is tired of love.
Fragrant like yellowing leaves, and dim with the soft
stillness and satisfaction of autumn.

And a girl should say:
It must be wonderful to live and grow old.
Look at my mother, how rich and still she is! –

And a young man should think: By Jove
my father has faced all weathers, but it's been a life! –

COURAGE

What makes people unsatisfied
is that they accept lies.

If people had courage, and refused lies
and found out what they really felt and really meant
and acted on it,

they would distil the essential oil out of every experience
and like hazel-nuts in autumn, at last
be sweet and sound.

And the young among the old
would be as in the hazel-woods of September
nutting, gathering nuts of ripe experience.

As it is, all that the old can offer
is sour, bitter fruits, cankered by lies.

DESIRE IS DEAD

Desire may be dead
and still a man can be
a meeting place for sun and rain,
wonder outwaiting pain
as in a wintry tree.

WHEN THE RIPE FRUIT FALLS –

When the ripe fruit falls
its sweetness distils and trickles away into the veins of the earth.

When fulfilled people die
the essential oil of their experience enters
the veins of living space, and adds a glisten
to the atom, to the body of immortal chaos.

For space is alive
and it stirs like a swan
whose feathers glisten
silky with oil of distilled experience.

ELEMENTAL

Why don't people leave off being lovable
or thinking they are lovable, or wanting to be lovable,
and be a bit elemental instead?

Since man is made up of the elements
fire, and rain, and air, and live loam
and none of these is lovable
but elemental,
man is lop-sided on the side of the angels.

I wish men would get back their balance among the elements
and be a bit more fiery, as incapable of telling lies
as fire is.
I wish they'd be true to their own variation, as water is,
which goes through all the stages of steam and stream and ice
without losing its head.

I am sick of lovable people,
somehow they are a lie.

FIRE

Fire is dearer to us than love or food,
hot, hurrying, yet it burns if you touch it.

What we ought to do
is not to add our love together, or our good-will, or any of that,
for we're sure to bring in a lot of lies,
but our fire, our elemental fire
so that it rushes up in a huge blaze like a phallus into hollow space
and fecundates the zenith and the nadir
and sends off millions of sparks of new atoms
and singes us, and burns the house down.

I WISH I KNEW A WOMAN –

I wish I knew a woman
who was like a red fire on the hearth
glowing after the day's restless draughts.

So that one could draw near her
in the red stillness of the dusk
and really take delight in her

without having to make the polite effort of loving her
or the mental effort of making her acquaintance.
Without having to take a chill, talking to her.

DIES IRAE

Even the old emotions are finished,
we have worn them out.
And desire is dead.
And the end of all things is inside us.

Our epoch is over,
a cycle of evolution is finished

our activity has lost its meaning,
we are ghosts, we are seed;
for our word is dead
and we know not how to live wordless.

We live in a vast house
full of inordinate activities,
and the noise, and the stench, and the dreariness and lack of
meaning
madden us, but we don't know what to do.

All we can know at this moment
is the fulfilment of nothingness.
Lo, I am nothing!

It is a consummation devoutly to be wished
in this world of mechanical self-assertion.

DIES ILLA

Dies irae, dies illa
solvet saeclum in favilla –

Day of wrath, O day of warning!
Flame devours the world.

It does, even if we don't see it.
For there are all sorts of flame:
slow, creeping cold ones
that burn inwardly
like flickering cancers.

And the slow cold flames
may burn for long years
before they've eaten through the joists and the girders
and the house comes down, with a subsiding crash.

BE STILL!

The only thing to be done, now,
now that the waves of our undoing have begun to strike on us,
is to contain ourselves.

To keep still, and let the wreckage of ourselves go,
let everything go, as the wave smashes us,
yet keep still, and hold
the tiny grain of something that no wave can wash away,
not even the most massive wave of destiny.

Among all the smashed debris of myself
keep quiet, and wait.
For the word is Resurrection.
And even the sea of seas will have to give up its dead.

A SANE REVOLUTION

If you make a revolution, make it for fun,
don't make it in ghastly seriousness,
don't do it in deadly earnest,
do it for fun.

Don't do it because you hate people,
do it just to spit in their eye.

Don't do it for the money,
do it and be damned to the money.

Don't do it for equality,
do it because we've got too much equality
and it would be fun to upset the apple-cart
and see which way the apples would go a-rolling.

Don't do it for the working classes.
Do it so that we can all of us be little aristocracies on our own
and kick our heels like jolly escaped asses.

Don't do it, anyhow, for international Labour.
Labour is the one thing a man has had too much of.
Let's abolish labour, let's have done with labouring!
Work can be fun, and men can enjoy it; then it's not labour.
Let's have it so! Let's make a revolution for fun!

A MAN

All I care about in a man
is that unbroken spark in him
where he is himself
undauntedly.

And all I want is to see the spark flicker
vivid and clean.

But our civilisation, alas,
with lust crushes out the spark
and leaves men living clay.

Because when the spark is crushed in a man
he can't help being a slave, a wage-slave,
a money-slave.

LIZARD

A lizard ran out on a rock and looked up, listening
no doubt to the sounding of the spheres.
And what a dandy fellow! the right toss of a chin for you
and swirl of a tail!

If men were as much men as lizards are lizards
they'd be worth looking at.

RELATIVITY

I like relativity and quantum theories
because I don't understand them
and they make me feel as if space shifted about like a swan that
 can't settle,
refusing to sit still and be measured;
and as if the atom were an impulsive thing
always changing its mind.

SPACE

Space, of course, is alive
that's why it moves about;
and that's what makes it eternally spacious and unstuffy.

And somewhere it has a wild heart
that sends pulses even through me;
and I call it the sun;
and I feel aristocratic, noble, when I feel a pulse go through me
from the wild heart of space, that I call the sun of suns.

DEMOCRACY

I am a democrat in so far as I love the free sun in men
and an aristocrat in so far as I detest narrow-gutted, possessive
 persons.

I love the sun in any man
when I see it between his brows
clear, and fearless, even if tiny.

But when I see these grey successful men
so hideous and corpse-like, utterly sunless,
like gross successful slaves mechanically waddling,
then I am more than radical, I want to work a guillotine.

And when I see working men
pale and mean and insect-like, scuttling along
and living like lice, on poor money
and never looking up,
then I wish, like Tiberius, the multitude had only one head
so that I could lop it off.

I feel that when people have gone utterly sunless
they shouldn't exist.

THINK –!

Imagine what it must have been to have existence
in the wild days when life was sliding whirlwinds, blue-hot
    weights,
in the days called chaos, which left us rocks, and gems!

Think that the sapphire is only alumina, like kitchen pans
crushed utterly, and breathed through and through
with fiery weight and wild life, and coming out
clear and flowery blue!

PEACOCK

Think how a peacock in a forest of high trees
shimmers in a stream of blueness and long-tressed magnificence!
And women even cut their shimmery hair!

TRUST

Oh we've got to trust
one another again
in some essentials.

Not the narrow little
bargaining trust
that says: I'm for you
if you'll be for me.–

But a bigger trust,
a trust of the sun
that does not bother
about moth and rust,
and we see it shining
in one another.

Oh don't you trust me,
don't burden me
with your life and affairs; don't thrust me
into your cares.

But I think you may trust
the sun in me
that glows with just
as much glow as you see
in me, and no more.

But if it warms
your heart's quick core
why then trust it, it forms
one faithfulness more.

And be, oh be
a sun to me,
not a weary, insistent
personality

but a sun that shines
and goes dark, but shines
again and entwines
with the sunshine in me

till we both of us
are more glorious
and more sunny.

NETTLES

INNOCENT ENGLAND

Oh what a pity, Oh! don't you agree
that figs aren't found in the land of the free!

Fig-trees don't grow in my native land;
there's never a fig-leaf near at hand

when you want one; so I did without;
and that is what the row's about.

Virginal, pure policemen came
and hid their faces for very shame,

while they carried the shameless things away
to gaol, to be hid from the light of day.

And Mr Mead, that old, old lily
said: 'Gross! coarse! hideous!' – and I, like a silly,

thought he meant the faces of the police-court officials,
and how right he was, and I signed my initials

to confirm what he said; but alas, he meant
my pictures, and on the proceedings went.

The upshot was, my picture must burn
that English artists might finally learn

when they painted a nude, to put a *cache sexe* on,
a cache sexe, a cache sexe, or else begone!

A fig-leaf; or, if you cannot find it
a wreath of mist, with nothing behind it.

A wreath of mist is the usual thing
in the north, to hide where the turtles sing.

Though they never sing, they never sing,
don't you dare to suggest such a thing

or Mr Mead will be after you.
– But what a pity I never knew

A wreath of English mist would do
as a cache sexe! I'd have put a whole fog.

But once and forever barks the old dog,
so my pictures are in prison, instead of in the Zoo.

MODERN PRAYER

Almighty Mammon, make me rich!
Make me rich quickly, with never a hitch
in my fine prosperity! Kick those in the ditch
who hinder me, Mammon, great son of a bitch!

LEAVES OF GRASS, FLOWERS OF GRASS

Leaves of grass, what about leaves of grass?
Grass blossoms, grass has flowers, flowers of grass
dusty pollen of grass, tall grass in its midsummer maleness
hay-seed and tiny grain of grass, graminiferae
not far from the lily, the considerable lily;

even the blue-grass blossoms;
even the bison knew it;
even the stupidest farmer gathers his hay in bloom, in blossom
just before it seeds.

Only the best matters; even the cow knows it;
grass in blossom, blossoming grass, risen to its height and its
    natural pride
in its own splendour and its own feathery maleness
the grass, the grass.

Leaves of grass, what are leaves of grass, when at its best grass
    blossoms.

LAST POEMS

IMAGE-MAKING LOVE

And now
the best of all
is to be alone, to possess one's soul in silence.

Nakedly to be alone, unseen
is better than anything else in the world,
a relief like death.

Always
at the core of me
burns the small flame of anger, gnawing
from trespassed contacts, from red-hot finger-bruises, on my
inward flesh,
from hot, digging in fingers of love.

Always
in the eyes of those who loved me
I have seen at last the image of him they loved
and took for me
mistook for me.

And always
it was a simulacrum, something
like me, and like a gibe at me.

So now I want, above all things
to preserve my nakedness
from the gibe of image-making love.

DESIRE

Ah, in the past, towards rare individuals
I have felt the pull of desire:
Oh come, come nearer, come into touch!
Come physically nearer, be flesh to my flesh –

But say little, oh say little,
and afterwards, leave me alone.
Keep your aloneness, leave me my aloneness,
I used to say this, in the past, but now no more.
It has always been a failure
They have always insisted on love
and on talking about it
and on the me-and-thee and what we meant to each other.

So now I have no desire any more
Except to be left, in the last resort, alone, quite alone.

ULTIMATE REALITY

A young man said to me:
I am interested in the problem of reality.

I said: Really!
Then I saw him turn to glance, surreptitiously,
in the big mirror, at his own fascinating shadow.

INTIMATES

Don't you care for my love? she said bitterly.

I handed her the mirror, and said:
Please address these questions to the proper person!
Please make all requests to head-quarters!
In all matters of emotional importance
please approach the supreme authority direct!
So I handed her the mirror.

And she would have broken it over my head,
but she caught sight of her own reflection
and that held her spell-bound for two seconds
while I fled.

ANDRAITX. – POMEGRANATE FLOWERS

It is June, it is June
the pomegranates are in flower,
the peasants are bending cutting the bearded wheat.

The pomegranates are in flower
beside the high-road, past the deathly dust,
and even the sea is silent in the sun.

Short gasps of flame in the green of night, way off
the pomegranates are in flower,
small sharp red fires in the night of leaves.

And noon is suddenly dark, is lustrous, is silent and dark
men are unseen, beneath the shading hats;
only, from out the foliage of the secret loins
red flamelets here and there reveal
a man, a woman there.

THERE ARE TOO MANY PEOPLE

There are too many people on earth
insipid, unsalted, rabbity, endlessly hopping.
They nibble the face of the earth to a desert.

THE HEART OF MAN

There is the other universe, of the heart of man
that we know nothing of, that we dare not explore.

A strange grey distance separates
our pale mind still from the pulsing continent
of the heart of man.

Fore-runners have barely landed on the shore
and no man knows, no woman knows
the mystery of the interior
when darker still than Congo or Amazon
flow the heart's rivers of fulness, desire and distress.

THE CHURCH

If I was a member of the Church of Rome
I should advocate reform:
the marriage of priests
the priests to wear rose-colour or magenta in the streets
to teach the Resurrection in the flesh
to start the year on Easter Sunday
to add the mystery of Joy-in-Resurrection to the Mass
to inculcate the new conception of the Risen Man.

THE UPROOTED

People who complain of loneliness must have lost something
lost some living connection with the cosmos, out of themselves,
lost their life-flow
like a plant whose roots are cut.
And they are crying like plants whose roots are cut.
But the presence of other people will not give them new, rooted
    connection
it will only make them forget.
The thing to do is in solitude slowly and painfully put forth new
    roots
into the unknown, and take root by oneself.

DELIGHT OF BEING ALONE

I know no greater delight than the sheer delight of being alone.
It makes me realise the delicious pleasure of the moon
that she has in travelling by herself, throughout time,
or the splendid growing of an ash-tree
alone, on a hill-side in the north, humming in the wind.

FUTURE RELATIONSHIPS

The world is moving, moving still, towards further democracy.
But not a democracy of idea or ideal, nor of property, nor even of
the emotion of brotherhood.
But a democracy of men, a democracy of touch.

FUTURE RELIGION

The future of religion is in the mystery of touch.
The mind is touchless, so is the will, so is the spirit.
First come the death, then the pure aloneness, which is permanent
then the resurrection into touch.

FUTURE STATES

Once men touch one another, then the modern industrial form of
machine civilisation will melt away
and universalism and cosmopolitanism will cease
the great movement of centralising into oneness will stop
and there will be a vivid recoil into separateness
many vivid small states, like a kaleidoscope, all colours
and all the differences given expression.

FUTURE WAR

After our industrial civilisation has broken, and the civilisation of touch has begun
war will cease, there will be no more wars.
The heart of man, in so far as it is budding, is budding warless
and budding towards infinite variety, variegation
and where there is infinite variety, there is no interest in war.
Oneness makes war, and the obsession of oneness.

NON-EXISTENCE

We don't exist unless we are deeply and sensually in touch
with that which can be touched but not known.

ALL-KNOWING

All that we know is nothing, we are merely crammed waste-paper baskets
unless we are in touch with that which laughs at all our knowing.

LUCIFER

Angels are bright still, though the brightest fell.
But tell me, tell me, how do you know
that he lost any of his brightness in falling?
He only fell out of your ken, you orthodox angels,
you dull angels, tarnished with centuries of conventionality.

FALLEN LEAVES

There is the organic connection, like leaves that belong to a tree
and there is the mechanical connection, like leaves that are cast to the earth.

Winds of heaven fan the leaves of the tree like flames and tunes,
but winds of heaven are mills of God to the fallen leaves
grinding them small to humus, on earth's nether mill-stone.

THE DIFFERENCE

People are like leaves, fluttering and gay on the bush of the globe,
or they are like leaves, rustling thick, in crowds on the floor of the earth,
and the thick, fallen crowds crackle and crumble under the milling of the winds,
the winds of change that will not be still
the breath of life.
But the living leaves in the breath of the wind are more lively
they glisten and shake.

THE BREATH OF LIFE

The breath of life and the sharp winds of change are the same thing.
But people who are fallen from the organic connection with the cosmos
feel the winds of change grind them down.

FATALITY

No one, not even God, can put back a leaf on to a tree
once it has fallen off.

And no one, not God nor Christ nor any other
can put back a human life into connection with the living cosmos
once the connection has been broken
and the person has become finally self-centred.

Death alone, through the long processes of disintegration
can melt the detached life back
through the dark Hades at the roots of the tree
into the circulating sap, once more, of the tree of life.

TENDER REVERENCE

To be humble before other men is degrading, I am humble before
no man
and I want no man to be humble before me.

But when I see the life-spirit fluttering and struggling in a man
I want to show always the human tender reverence.

ABSOLUTE REVERENCE

I feel absolute reverence to nobody and to nothing human
neither to persons nor things nor ideas, ideals nor religions nor
institutions,
to these things I feel only respect, and a tinge of reverence
when I see the fluttering of pure life in them.

But to something unseen, unknown, creative
from which I feel I am a derivative
I feel absolute reverence. Say no more!

BELIEF

Forever nameless
Forever unknown
Forever unconceived
Forever unrepresented
yet forever felt in the soul.

BELLS

The Mohammedans say that the sound of bells
especially big ones, is obscene,

That hard clapper striking in a hard mouth
and resounding after with a long hiss of insistence is obscene.

Yet bells call the Christians to God
especially clapper bells, hard tongues wagging in hard mouths,
metal hitting on metal, to enforce our attention,
and bring us to God.

The soft thudding of drums
of finger or fist or soft-skinned sticks upon the stretched
membrane of sound
sends summons in the old hollows of the sun.

And the accumulated splashing of a gong
where tissue plunges into bronze with wide wild circles of sound
and leaves off,
belongs to the bamboo thickets, and the drake in the air flying
past.

And the sound of a blast through the sea-curved core of a shell
when a black priest blows on a conch,
and the dawn-cry from a minaret, God is great
and the calling of the old Red Indian high on the pueblo roof
whose voice flies on, calling like a swan

singing between the sun and the marsh,
on and on, like a dark-faced bird singing alone
singing to the men below, the fellow-tribesmen
who go by without pausing, soft-foot, without listening, yet who
hear:
these are other ways of summons, crying: Listen! Listen! Come
near!

THE TRIUMPH OF THE MACHINE

They talk of the triumph of the machine,
but the machine will never triumph.

Out of the thousands and thousands of centuries of man
the unrolling of ferns, white tongues of the acanthus lapping at the
sun,
for one sad century
machines have triumphed, rolled us hither and thither,
shaking the lark's nest till the eggs have broken.

Shaken the marshes, till the geese have gone
and the wild swans flown away singing the swan-song of us.

Hard, hard on the earth the machines are rolling,
but through some hearts they will never roll.

The lark nests in his heart
and the white swan swims in the marshes of his loins,
and through the wide prairies of his breast a young bull herds his
cows,
lambs frisk among the daisies of his brain.

And at last
all these creatures that cannot die, driven back
into the uttermost corners of the soul
will send up the wild cry of despair.

The trilling lark in a wild despair will trill down from the sky,
the swan will beat the waters in rage, white rage of an enraged
swan,
even the lambs will stretch forth their necks like serpents,
like snakes of hate, against the man in the machine:
even the shaking white poplar will dazzle like splinters of glass
against him.

And against this inward revolt of the native creatures of the soul
mechanical man, in triumph seated upon the seat of his machine
will be powerless, for no engine can reach into the marshes and
depths of a man.

So mechanical man in triumph seated upon the seat of his machine
will be driven mad from himself, and sightless, and on that day
the machines will turn to run into one another
traffic will tangle up in a long-drawn-out crash of collision
and engines will rush at the solid houses, the edifice of our life
will rock in the shock of the mad machine, and the house will
come down.

Then, far beyond the ruin, in the far, in the ultimate, remote places
the swan will lift up again his flattened, smitten head
and look round, and rise, and on the great vaults of his wings
will sweep round and up to greet the sun with a silky glitter of a
new day

and the lark will follow trilling, angerless again,
and the lambs will bite off the heads of the daisies for friskiness.
But over the middle of the earth will be the smoky ruin of iron
the triumph of the machine.

FORTE DEI MARMI

The evening sulks along the shore, the reddening sun
reddens still more on the blatant bodies of these all-but-naked,
sea-bathing city people.

Let me tell you that the sun is alive, and can be angry,
and the sea is alive, and can sulk,
and the air is alive, and can deny us as a woman can.

But the blatant bathers don't know, they know nothing;
the vibration of the motor-car has bruised their insensitive
bottoms
into rubber-like deadness, Dunlop inflated unconcern.

DARK SATANIC MILLS

The dark, satanic mills of Blake
how much darker and more satanic they are now!
But oh, the streams that stream white-faced, in and out
in and out when the hooter hoots, white-faced, with a dreadful
gush
of multitudinous ignominy,
what shall we think of these?
They are millions to my one!

They are millions to my one! But oh
what have they done to you, white-faced millions
mewed and mangled in the mills of man?
What have they done to you, what have they done to you,
what is this awful aspect of man?

Oh Jesus, didn't you see, when you talked of service
this would be the result!
When you said: Retro me, Satanas!
this is what you gave him leave to do
behind your back!

And now, the iron has entered into the soul
and the machine has entangled the brain, and got it fast,
and steel has twisted the loins of man, electricity has exploded the
heart
and out of the lips of people just strange mechanical noises in
place of speech.

What is man, that thou art no longer mindful of him?
and the son of man, that thou pitiest him not?
Are these no longer men, these millions, millions?
What are they then?

WE DIE TOGETHER

Oh, when I think of the industrial millions, when I see some of
them,

a weight comes over me heavier than leaden linings of coffins
and I almost cease to exist, weighed down to extinction
and sunk into depression that almost blots me out.

Then I say to myself: Am I also dead? is that the truth?
Then I know
that with so many dead men in mills
I too am almost dead.
I know the unliving factory-hand, living-dead millions
is unliving me, living-dead me,
I, with them, am living dead, mechanical enslaved at the machine.

And enshrouded in the vast corpse of the industrial millions
embedded in them, I look out on the sunshine of the South.

And though the pomegranate has red flowers outside the window
and oleander is hot with perfume under the afternoon sun
and I am 'Il Signore' and they love me here,
yet I am a mill-hand in Leeds
and the death of the Black Country is upon me
and I am wrapped in the lead of a coffin-lining, the living death of
    my fellow men.

WHAT HAVE THEY DONE TO YOU – ?

What have they done to you, men of the masses, creeping back
    and forth to work?

What have they done to you, the saviours of the people, oh what
    have they saved you from, while they pocketed the money?

Alas, they have saved you from yourself, from your own frail
    dangers
and devoured you with the machine, the vast maw of iron.

They saved you from squalid cottages and poverty of hand to
    mouth
and embedded you in the workmen's dwellings, where your wage
    is the dole of work, and the dole is your wage of nullity.

They took away, oh they took away your man's native instincts
and intuitions
and gave a board-school education, newspapers, and cinema.

They stole your body from you, and left you an animated carcase
to work with, and nothing else:
unless goggling eyes, to goggle at the film
and a board-school brain, stuffed up with the ha' penny press.
Your instincts gone, your intuition gone, your passion dead
Oh carcase with a board-school mind and a ha' penny newspaper
intelligence,
what have they done to you, what have they done to you, oh what
have they done to you?
Oh look at my fellow men, oh look at them
the masses! Oh, what has been done to them?

SOULS TO SAVE

You tell me every man has a soul to save?
I tell you, not one man in a thousand has even a soul to lose.
The automat has no soul to lose
so it can't have one to save.

MEN LIKE GODS

Men wanted to be like gods
so they became like machines
and now even they're not satisfied.

MAN AND MACHINE

Man invented the machine
and now the machine has invented man.
God the Father is a dynamo
and God the Son a talking radio
and God the Holy Ghost is gas that keeps it all going.

And men have perforce to be little dynamos
and little talking radios
and the human spirit is so much gas, to keep it all going.

Man invented the machine
so now the machine has invented man.

OH WONDERFUL MACHINE!

Oh wonderful machine, so self-sufficient, so sufficient unto
 yourself!
You who have no feeling of the moon as she changes her quarters!
You who don't hear the sea's uneasiness!
You to whom the sun is merely something that makes the
 thermometer rise!

O wonderful machine, you who are man's idea of godliness,
you who feel nothing, who know nothing, who run on absolved
from any other connection!
O you godly and smooth machine, spinning on in your own
 Nirvana,
turning the blue wheels of your own heaven
almighty machine
how is it you have to be looked after by some knock-kneed wretch
at two pounds a week?

Oh great god of the machine
what lousy archangels and angels you have to surround yourself
 with!
And you can't possibly do without them!

LOVE THY NEIGHBOUR –

I love my neighbour
but
are these things my neighbours?
these two legged things that walk and talk
and eat and cachinnate, and even seem to smile
seem to smile, ye gods!

Am I told that these things are my neighbours?
All I can say is Nay! nay! nay! nay!

AS THYSELF – !

Supposing I say: dogs are my neighbours
I will love dogs as myself!

Then gradually I approximate to the dogs,
wriggle and wag and slaver, and get the mentality of a dog!
This I call a shocking humiliation.

The same with my robot neighbours.
If I try loving them, I fall into their robot jig-jig-jig
their robot cachinnation comes rattling out of my throat –
and I had better even have approximated to the dog.

Who then, O Jesus, is my neighbour?
If you point me to that fat money-smelling man in a motor-car,
or that hard-boiled young woman beside him
I shall have to refuse entirely to accept either of them.

My neighbour is not the man in the street, and never was:
he jigs along in the imbecile cruelty of the machine
and is implacable.

My neighbour, O my neighbour!
Occasionally I see him, silent, a little wondering
with his ears pricked and his body wincing
threading his way among the robot machine-people.

O my neighbour
sometimes I see her, like a flower, nodding her way and shrinking
from the robot contact on every hand!

How can that be my neighbour
which I shrink from!

LONELY, LONESOME, LONEY – O!

When I hear somebody complain of being lonely
or, in American, lonesome
I really wonder and wonder what they mean.

Do they mean they are a great deal alone?

But what is lovelier than to be alone?
escaping the petrol fumes of human conversation
and the exhaust-smell of people
and be alone!

Be alone, and feel the trees silently growing.
Be alone, and see the moonlight outside, white and busy and
    silent.
Be quite alone, and feel the living cosmos softly rocking
soothing and restoring and healing.

Soothed, restored and healed
when I am alone with the silent great cosmos
and there is no grating of people with their presences gnawing
at the stillness of the air.

TREES IN THE GARDEN

Ah in the thunder air
how still the trees are!

And the lime-tree, lovely and tall, every leaf silent
hardly looses even a last breath of perfume.

And the ghostly, creamy coloured little tree of leaves
white, ivory white among the rambling greens
how evanescent, variegated elder, she hesitates on the green grass
as if, in another moment, she would disappear
with all her grace of foam!

And the larch that is only a column, it goes up too tall to see:
and the balsam-pines that are blue with the grey-blue blueness of
things from the sea,
and the young copper beech, its leaves red-rosy at the ends
how still they are together, they stand so still
in the thunder air, all strangers to one another
as the green grass glows upwards, strangers in the garden.

Lichtental.

STORM IN THE BLACK FOREST

Now it is almost night, from the bronzey soft sky
jugful after jugful of pure white liquid fire, bright white
tipples over and spills down,
and is gone
and gold-bronze flutters beat through the thick upper air.

And as the electric liquid pours out, sometimes
a still brighter white snake wriggles among it, spilled
and tumbling wriggling down the sky:
and then the heavens cackle with uncouth sounds.

And the rain won't come, the rain refuses to come!

This is the electricity that man is supposed to have mastered
chained, subjugated to his use!
supposed to!

WORSHIP

All men are worshippers
unless they have fallen, and become robots.

All men worship the wonder of life
until they collapse into egoism, the mechanical, self-centred
system of the robot.

But even in pristine men, there is the difference:
some men can see life clear and flickering all around,
and some can only see what they are shown.

Some men look straight into the eyes of the gods
and some men can see no gods, they only know
the gods are there because of the gleam on the faces of the men
who see.

Most men, even unfallen, can only live
by the transmitted gleam from the faces of vivider men
who look into the eyes of the gods.
And worship is the joy of the gleam from the eyes of the gods,
and the robot is denial of the same,
even the denial that there *is* any gleam.

DEMOCRACY IS SERVICE

Democracy is service, but not the service of demos.
Democracy is demos serving life
and demos serves life as it gleams on the face of the few,
and the few look into the eyes of the gods, and serve the sheer
gods.

WHAT ARE THE GODS?

What are the gods, then, what are the gods!

The gods are nameless and imageless
yet looking in a great full lime-tree of summer
I suddenly saw deep into the eyes of gods:
it is enough.

THE GODS! THE GODS!

People were bathing and posturing themselves on the beach
and all was dreary, great robot limbs, robot breasts
robot voices, robot even the gay umbrellas.

But a woman, shy and alone, was washing herself under a tap
and the glimmer of the presence of the gods was like lilies,
and like water-lilies.

NAME THE GODS!

I refuse to name the gods, because they have no name.
I refuse to describe the gods, because they have no form nor shape
nor substance.

Ah, but the simple ask for images!
Then for a time at least, they must do without.

But all the time I see the gods:
the man who is moving the tall white corn,
suddenly, as it curves, as it yields, the white wheat
and sinks down with a swift rustle, and a strange, falling flatness,
ah! the gods, the swaying body of god!
ah the fallen stillness of god, autumnus, and it is only July
the pale-gold flesh of Priapus dropping asleep.

THERE ARE NO GODS –

There are no gods, and you can please yourself
have a game of tennis, go out in the car, do some shopping, sit and
talk, talk, talk
with a cigarette browning your fingers.

There are no gods, and you can please yourself –
go and please yourself –

But leave me alone, leave me alone, to myself!
and then in the room, whose is the presence
that makes the air so still and lovely to me?

Who is it that softly touches the sides of my breast
and touches me over the heart
so that my heart beats soothed, soothed, soothed and at peace?

Who is it smooths the bed-sheets like the cool
smooth ocean when the fishes rest on edge
in their own dream?

Who is it that clasps and kneads my naked feet, till they unfold,
till all is well, till all is utterly well? the lotus-lilies of the feet!

I tell you, it is no woman, it is no man, for I am alone.
And I fall asleep with the gods, the gods
that are not, or that are
according to the soul's desire,
like a pool into which we plunge, or do not plunge.

RETORT TO WHITMAN

And whoever walks a mile full of false sympathy
walks to the funeral of the whole human race.

RETORT TO JESUS

And whoever forces himself to love anybody
begets a murderer in his own body.

COMMANDMENTS

When Jesus commanded us to love our neighbour
he forced us to live a great lie, or to disobey:
for we can't love anybody, neighbour or no neighbour, to order,
and faked love has rotted our marrow.

SUNSET

There is a band of dull gold in the west, and say what you like
again and again some god of evening leans out of it
and shares being with me, silkily
all of twilight.

RACE AND BATTLE

The race is not to the swift
but to those that can sit still
and let the waves go over them.

The battle is not to the strong
but to the frail, who know best
how to efface themselves
to save the streaked pansy of the heart from being trampled to mud.

NOTHING TO SAVE

There is nothing to save, now all is lost,
but a tiny core of stillness in the heart
like the eye of a violet.

THE ENGLISH ARE SO NICE!

The English are so nice
so awfully nice
they're the nicest people in the world.

And what's more, they're very nice about being nice
about your being nice as well!
If you're not nice, they soon make you feel it.

Americans and French and Germans and so on
they're all very well
but they're not *really* nice, you know.
They're not nice in *our* sense of the word, are they now?

That's why one doesn't have to take them seriously.
We must be nice to them, of course,
of course, naturally.
But it doesn't really matter what you say to them,
they don't really understand –
you can just say anything to them:
be nice, you know, just nice –
but you must never take them seriously, they wouldn't under-
stand,
just be nice, you know! Oh, fairly nice,
not too nice of course, they take advantage –
but nice enough, just nice enough
to let them feel they're not quite as nice as they might be.

TOURISTS

There is nothing to look at any more.
everything has been seen to death.

PROPERTY AND NO-PROPERTY

The bourgeois asserts that he owns his property by divine right,
and the bolshevist asserts that by human right no man shall own
property
and between the two blades of this pair of shears, property and
no-property
we shall all be cut to bits.

TERRA INCOGNITA

There are vast realms of consciousness still undreamed of
vast ranges of experience, like the humming of unseen harps,
we know nothing of, within us.

Oh when man escaped from the barbed-wire entanglement
of his own ideas and his own mechanical devices
there is a marvellous rich world of contact and sheer fluid beauty
and fearless face-to-face awareness of now-naked life
and me, and you, and other men and women
and grapes, and ghouls, and ghosts and green moonlight
and ruddy-orange limbs stirring the limbo
of the unknown air, and eyes so soft
softer than the space between the stars,
and all things, and nothing, and being and not-being
alternately palpitant,
when at last we escape the barbed wire enclosure
of *Know Thyself*, knowing we can never know,
we can but touch, and wonder, and ponder, and make our effort
and dangle in a last fastidious fine delight
as the fuchsia does, dangling her reckless drop
of purple after so much putting forth
and slow mounting marvel of a little tree.

ALL SORTS OF GODS

There's all sorts of gods, all sorts and every sort,
and every god that humanity has ever known is still a god today
the African queer ones and Scandinavian queer ones,
the Greek beautiful ones, the Phoenician ugly ones, the Aztec
hideous ones
goddesses of love, goddesses of dirt, excrement-eaters or lily
virgins
Jesus, Buddha, Jehovah and Ra, Egypt and Babylon
all the gods, and you see them all if you look, alive and moving
today,
and alive and moving tomorrow, many tomorrows, as yesterdays.

Where do you see them, you say?
You see them in glimpses, in the faces and forms of people, in glimpses.
When men and women, when lads and girls are not thinking,
when they are pure, which means when they are quite clean from self-consciousness
either in anger or tenderness, or desire or sadness or wonder or mere stillness
you may see glimpses of the gods in them.

FOR A MOMENT

For a moment, at evening, tired, as he stepped off the tram-car,
– the young tram-conductor in a blue uniform, to himself forgotten, –
and lifted his face up, with blue eyes looking at the electric rod which he was going to turn round,
for a moment, pure in the yellow evening light, he was Hyacinthus.

In the green garden darkened the shadow of coming rain
and a girl ran swiftly, laughing breathless, taking in her white washing
in rapid armfuls from the line, tossing in the basket,
and so rapidly, and so flashing, fleeing before the rain
for a moment she was Io, Io, who fled from Zeus, or the Danae.

When I was waiting and not thinking, sitting at a table on the hotel terrace
I saw suddenly coming towards me, lit up and uplifted with pleasure
advancing with the slow-swiftness of a ship backing her white sails into port
the woman who looks for me in the world
and for the moment she was Isis, gleaming, having found her Osiris.

For a moment, as he looked at me through his spectacles
pondering, yet eager, the broad and thick-set Italian who works in with me,

for a moment he was the Centaur, the wise yet horse-hoofed
Centaur
in whom I can trust.

THOUGHT

Thought, I love thought.
But not the jiggling and twisting of already existent ideas
I despise that self-important game.
Thought is the welling up of unknown life into consciousness
Thought is the testing of statements on the touchstone of the
conscience
Thought is gazing on to the face of life, and reading what can
be read,
Thought is pondering over experience, and coming to conclusion.
Thought is not a trick, or an exercise, or a set of dodges
Thought is a man in his wholeness wholly attending.

SO LET ME LIVE

So let me live that I may die
eagerly, passing over from the entanglement of life
to the adventure of death, in eagerness
turning to death as I turn to beauty
to the breath, that is, of new beauty unfolding in death.

GLADNESS OF DEATH

Oh death
about you I know nothing, nothing –
about the afterwards
as a matter of fact, we know nothing

yet of death, oh death
also I know so much about you
the knowledge is within me, without being a matter of fact.

And so I know
after the painful, painful experience of dying
there comes an after-gladness, a strange joy
in a great adventure.
Oh the great adventure of death, where Thomas Cook cannot
guide us.

I have always wanted to be as the flowers are
so unhampered in their living and dying,
and in death I believe I shall be as the flowers are.
I shall blossom like a dark pansy, and be delighted
there among the dark sun-rays of death.
I can feel myself unfolding in the dark sunshine of death
to something flowery and fulfilled, and with a strange sweet
perfume.
Men prevent one another from being men
but in the great spaces of death
the winds of the afterwards kiss us into blossom of manhood.

SELF-SACRIFICE

Self-Sacrifice, after all, is a wrong and mistaken idea.
It cannot be anything but wrong to sacrifice
good, healthy, natural feelings, instincts, passions or desires,
just as it cannot be anything but wrong to cut the throats
of doves for Venus, or steers for Hermes,
if it is merely Venus or Hermes you are thinking of.

Venus would rather have live doves than dead, if you want to
make an offering.
If you want to make her an offering, let the doves fly from her
altar.

But what we may sacrifice, if we call it sacrifice, from the self,
are all the obstructions to life, self-importance, self-conceit,
egoistic self-will,
or all the ugly old possessions that make up the impediments of
life,

ugly old furniture, ugly old books, ugly old buildings, ugly old
    'art',
anything that belongs to us, and is ugly and an impediment to the
    free motion of life
sacrifice that to the bright gods, and satisfy the destructive
    instinct.

GOD IS BORN

The history of the cosmos
is the history of the struggle of becoming.
When the dim flux of unformed life
struggled, convulsed back and forth upon itself,
and broke at last into light and dark
came into existence as light,
came into existence as cold shadow
then every atom of the cosmos trembled with delight.
Behold, God is born!
He is bright light!
He is pitch dark and cold!

And in the great struggle of intangible chaos
when, at a certain point, a drop of water began to drip
    downwards
and a breath of vapour began to wreath up
Lo again the shudder of bliss through all the atoms!
Oh, God is born!
Behold, He is born wet!
Look, He hath movement upward! He spirals!

And so, in the great æons, of accomplishment and débacle
from time to time the wild crying of every electron:
Lo! God is born.

When sapphires cooled out of molten chaos:
See, God is born! He is blue, he is deep blue, he is for ever blue!

When gold lay shining threading the cooled-off rock:
God is born! God is born! bright yellow and ductile He is born.

When the little eggy amoeba emerged out of foam and nowhere
then all the electrons held their breath:
Ach! Ach! Now indeed God is born! He twinkles within.

When from a world of mosses and of ferns
at last the narcissus lifted a tuft of five-point stars
and dangled them in the atmosphere,
then every molecule of creation jumped and clapped its hands:
God is born! God is born perfumed and dangling and with a little
 cup!

Throughout the æons, as the lizard swirls his tail finer than water,
as the peacock turns to the sun, and could not be more splendid,
as the leopard smites the small calf with a spangled paw, perfect,
the universe trembles: God is born! God is here!

And when at last man stood on two legs and wondered,
then there was a hush of suspense at the core of every electron:
Behold, now very God is born!
God Himself is born!
And so we see, God is not
until he is born.

And also we see
there is no end to the birth of God.

THE WHITE HORSE

The youth walks up to the white horse, to put its halter on
and the horse looks at him in silence.
They are so silent they are in another world.

FLOWERS AND MEN

Flowers achieve their own floweriness and it is a miracle.
Men don't achieve their own manhood, alas, oh alas! alas!

All I want of you, men and women,
all I want of you
is that you shall achieve your own beauty
as the flowers do.

Oh leave off saying I want you to be savages.
Tell me, is the gentian savage, at the top of its coarse stem?
Oh what in you can answer to this blueness?
[I want you to be as savage] as the gentian and the daffodil.
Tell me! tell me! is there in you a beauty to compare
to the honeysuckle at evening now
pouring out his breath.

PRAYER

Give me the moon at my feet
Put my feet upon the crescent, like a Lord!
O let my ankles be bathed in moonlight, that I may go
sure and moon-shod, cool and bright-footed
towards my goal

For the sun is hostile, now
his face is like the red lion,
. . .

THE ARGONAUTS

They are not dead, they are not dead!
Now that the sun, like a lion, licks his paws
and goes slowly down the hill:
now that the moon, who remembers, and only cares
that we should be lovely in the flesh, with bright, crescent feet,
pauses near the crest of the hill, climbing slowly, like a queen
looking down on the lion as he retreats.

Now the sea is the Argonaut's sea, and in the dawn
Odysseus calls the commands, as he steers past those foamy
islands
wait, wait, don't bring the coffee yet, nor the *pain grillé*.
The dawn is not off the sea, and Odysseus' ships
have not yet passed the islands. I must watch them still.

MIDDLE OF THE WORLD

This sea will never die, neither will it ever grow old
nor cease to be blue, nor in the dawn
cease to lift up its hills
and let the slim black ship of Dionysos come sailing in
with grape-vines up the mast, and dolphins leaping.

What do I care if the smoking ships
of the P & O and the Orient Line and all the other stinkers
cross like clock-work the Minoan distance!
They only cross, the distance never changes.

And now that the moon who gives men glistening bodies
is in her exaltation, and can look down on the sun
I see descending from the ships at dawn
slim naked men from Cnossos, smiling the archaic smile
of those that will without fail come back again,
and kindling little fires upon the shores
and crouching, and speaking the music of lost languages.

And the Minoan Gods, and the Gods of Tiryns
are heard softly laughing and chatting, as ever;
and Dionysos, young, and a stranger
leans listening on the gate, in all respect.

FOR THE HEROES ARE DIPPED IN SCARLET

Before Plato told the great lie of ideals
men slimly went like fishes, and didn't care.

They had long hair, like Samson,
and clean as arrows they sped at the mark
when the bow-cord twanged.

They knew it was no use knowing
their own nothingness:
for they were not nothing.

So now they come back! Hark!
Hark! the low and shattering laughter of bearded men
with the slim waists of warriors, and the long feet
of moon-lit dancers.

Oh, and their faces scarlet, like the dolphin's blood!
Lo! the loveliest is red all over, rippling vermilion
as he ripples upwards!
laughing in his black beard!

They are dancing! they return, as they went, dancing!
For the thing that is done without the glowing as of god,
    vermilion,
were best not done at all.
How glistening red they are!

DEMIURGE

They say that reality exists only in the spirit
that corporal existence is a kind of death
that pure being is bodiless
that the idea of the form precedes the form substantial.

But what nonsense it is!
as if any Mind could have imagined a lobster
dozing the under-deeps, then reaching out a savage and iron claw!

Even the mind of God can only imagine
those things that have become themselves:
bodies and presences, here and now, creatures with a foothold in
    creation
even if it is only a lobster on tip-toe.

[RELIGION]

Religion knows better than philosophy.
Religion knows that Jesus never was Jesus
till he was born from a womb, and ate soup and bread
and grew up, and became, in the wonder of creation, Jesus,
with a body and with needs, and a lovely spirit.

RED GERANIUM AND GODLY MIGNONETTE

Imagine that any mind ever *thought* a red geranium!
As if the redness of a red geranium could be anything but a sensual experience
and as if sensual experience could take place before there were any senses.
We know that even God could not imagine the redness of a red geranium
nor the smell of mignonette
when geraniums were not, and mignonette neither.
And even when they were, even God would have to have a nose
to smell at the mignonette.
You can't imagine the Holy Ghost sniffing at cherry-pie heliotrope.
Or the Most High, during the coal age, cudgelling his mighty brains
even if he had any brains: straining his mighty mind
to think, among the moss and mud of lizards and mastodons
to think out, in the abstract, when all was twilit green and muddy:
'Now there shall be tum-tiddly-um, and tum-tiddly-um,
hey-presto! scarlet geranium!'

We know it couldn't be done.

But imagine, among the mud and the mastodons
god sighing and yearning with tremendous creative yearning, in that dark green mess
oh, for some other beauty, some other beauty
that blossomed at last, red geranium, and mignonette.

THE BODY OF GOD

God is the great urge that has not yet found a body
but urges towards incarnation with the great creative urge.

And becomes at last a clove carnation: lo! that is god!
and becomes at last Helen, or Ninon: any lovely and generous
woman
at her best and her most beautiful, being god, made manifest,
any clear and fearless man being god, very god.

There is no god
apart from poppies and the flying fish,
men singing songs, and women brushing their hair in the sun.
The lovely things are god that has come to pass, like Jesus came.
The rest, the undiscoverable, is the demi-urge.

THE RAINBOW

Even the rainbow has a body
made of the drizzling rain
and is an architecture of glistening atoms
built up, built up
yet you can't lay your hand on it,
nay, nor even your mind.

MAXIMUS

God is older than the sun and moon
and the eye cannot behold him
nor voice describe him.

But a naked man, a stranger, leaned on the gate
with his cloak over his arm, waiting to be asked in.
So I called him: Come in, if you will! –
He came in slowly, and sat down by the hearth.
I said to him: And what is your name? –

He looked at me without answer, but such a loveliness
entered me, I smiled to myself, saying: He is God!
So he said: *Hermes!*
God is older than the sun and moon
and the eye cannot behold him
nor the voice describe him:
and still, this is the god Hermes, sitting by my hearth.

THE MAN OF TYRE

The man of Tyre went down to the sea
pondering, for he was Greek, that God is one and all alone and
ever more shall be so.

And a woman who had been washing clothes in the pool of rock
where a stream came down to the gravel of the sea and sank in,
who had spread white washing on the gravel banked above the
bay,
who had lain her shift on the shore, on the shingle slope,
who had waded to the pale green sea of evening, out to a shoal,
pouring sea-water over herself
now turned, and came slowly back, with her back to the evening
sky.

Oh lovely, lovely with the dark hair piled up, as she went deeper,
deeper down the channel, then rose shallower, shallower,
with the full thighs slowly lifting of the wader wading shorewards
and the shoulders pallid with light from the silent sky behind
both breasts dim and mysterious, with the glamorous kindness of
twilight between them
and the dim blotch of black maidenhair like an indicator,
giving a message to the man –

So in the cane-brake he clasped his hands in delight
that could only be god-given, and murmured:
Lo! God is one god! But here in the twilight
godly and lovely comes Aphrodite out of the sea
towards me!

THEY SAY THE SEA IS LOVELESS

They say the sea is loveless, that in the sea
love cannot live, but only bare, salt splinters
of loveless life.
But from the sea
the dolphins leap round Dionysos' ship
whose masts have purple vines,
and up they come with the purple dark of rainbows
and flip! they go! with the nose-dive of sheer delight;
and the sea is making love to Dionysos
in the bouncing of these small and happy whales.

WHALES WEEP NOT!

They say the sea is cold, but the sea contains
the hottest blood of all, and the wildest, the most urgent.

All the whales in the wider deeps, hot are they, as they urge
on and on, and dive beneath the ice-bergs.
The right whales, the sperm-whales, the hammer-heads, the killers
there they blow, there they blow, hot wild white breath out of the sea!

And they rock, and they rock, through the sensual ageless ages
on the depths of the seven seas,
and through the salt they reel with drunk delight
and in the tropics tremble they with love
and roll with massive, strong desire, like gods.
Then the great bull lies up against his bride
in the blue deep of the sea
as mountain pressing on mountain, in the zest of life:
and out of the inward roaring of the inner red ocean of whale blood
the long tip reaches strong, intense, like the maelstrom-tip, and comes to rest
in the clasp and the soft, wild clutch of a she-whale's fathomless body.

And over the bridge of the whale's strong phallus, linking the wonder of whales
the burning archangels under the sea keep passing, back and forth,
keep passing archangels of bliss
from him to her, from her to him, great Cherubim
that wait on whales in mid-ocean, suspended in the waves of the sea
great heaven of whales in the waters, old hierarchies.
And enormous mother whales lie dreaming suckling their whale-tender young
and dreaming with strange whale eyes wide open in the waters of the beginning and the end.

And bull-whales gather their women and whale-calves in a ring
when danger threatens, on the surface of the ceaseless flood
and range themselves like great fierce Seraphim facing the threat
encircling their huddled monsters of love.
And all this happens in the sea, in the salt
where God is also love, but without words:
and Aphrodite is the wife of whales
most happy, happy she!

and Venus among the fishes skips and is a she-dolphin
she is the gay, delighted porpoise sporting with love and the sea
she is the female tunny-fish, round and happy among the males
and dense with happy blood, dark rainbow bliss in the sea.

INVOCATION TO THE MOON

You beauty, O you beauty
you glistening garmentless beauty!
great lady, great glorious lady
greatest of ladies
crownless and jewelless and garmentless
because naked you are more wonderful than anything we can stroke.

Be good to me, lady, great lady of the nearest
heavenly mansion, and last!
Now I am at your gate, you beauty, you lady of all nakedness!
Now I must enter your mansion, and beg your gift
Moon, O Moon, great lady of the heavenly few.

Far and forgotten is the Villa of Venus the glowing
and behind me now in the gulfs of space lies the golden house of
the sun,
and six have given me gifts, and kissed me god-speed
kisses of four great lords, beautiful, as they held me to their bosom
in farewell,
and kiss of the far-off lingering lady who looks over the distant
fence of the twilight,
and one warm kind kiss of the lion with golden paws.

Now, lady of the Moon, now open the gate of your silvery house
and let me come past the silver bells of your flowers and the
cockle-shells
into your house, garmentless lady of the last great gift:
who will give me back my lost limbs
and my lost white fearless breast
and set me again on moon-remembering feet
a healed, whole man, O Moon!

Lady, lady of the last house down the long, long street of the stars
be good to me now, as I beg you, as you've always been good to
men
who begged of you and gave you homage
and watched for your glistening feet down the garden path!

BUTTERFLY

Butterfly, the wind blows sea-ward, strong beyond the garden
wall!
Butterfly, why do you settle on my shoe, and sip the dirt on my
shoe,
lifting your veined wings, lifting them? big white butterfly!

Already it is October, and the wind blows strong to the sea
from the hills where the snow must have fallen, the wind is
polished with snow.
Here in the garden, with red geraniums, it is warm, it is warm
but the wind blows strong to sea-ward, white butterfly, content
on my shoe!

Will you go, will you go from my warm house?
Will you climb on your big soft wings, black-dotted,
as up an invisible rainbow, an arch
till the wind slides you sheer from the arch-crest
and in a strange level fluttering you go out to sea-ward, white
speck!

Farewell, farewell, lost soul!
you have melted in the crystalline distance,
it is enough! I saw you vanish into air.

BAVARIAN GENTIANS

Not every man has gentians in his house
in Soft September, at slow, Sad Michaelmas.

Bavarian gentians, big and dark, only dark
darkening the day-time torch-like with the smoking blueness of
Pluto's gloom,
ribbed and torch-like, with their blaze of darkness spread blue
down flattening into points, flattened under the sweep of white
day
torch-flower of the blue-smoking darkness. Pluto's dark-blue
daze,
black lamps from the halls of Dis, burning dark blue,
giving off darkness, blue darkness, as Demeter's pale lamps give
off light,
lead me then, lead me the way.

Reach me a gentian, give me a torch!
let me guide myself with the blue, forked torch of this flower

down the darker and darker stairs, where blue is darkened on
blueness
even where Persephone goes, just now, from the frosted Sep-
tember
to the sightless realm where darkness is awake upon the dark
and Persephone herself is but a voice
or a darkness invisible enfolded in the deeper dark
of the arms Plutonic, and pierced with the passion of dense gloom,
among the splendour of torches of darkness, shedding darkness
on the lost bride and her groom.

LUCIFER

Angels are bright still, though the brightest fell.
But tell me, tell me, how do you know
he lost any of his brightness in the falling?
In the dark-blue depths, under layers and layers of darkness
I see him more like the ruby, a gleam from within
of his own magnificence,
coming like the ruby in the invisible dark, glowing
with his own annunciation, towards us.

THE BREATH OF LIFE

The breath of life is in the sharp winds of change
mingled with the breath of destruction.
But if you want to breathe deep, sumptuous life
breathe all alone, in silence, in the dark,
and see nothing.

PAX

All that matters is to be at one with the living God
to be a creature in the house of the God of Life.

Like a cat asleep on a chair
at peace, in peace
and at one with the master of the house, with the mistress,
at home, at home in the house of the living,
sleeping on the hearth, and yawning before the fire.

Sleeping on the hearth of the living world
yawning at home before the fire of life
feeling the presence of the living God
like a great reassurance
a deep calm in the heart
a presence
as of the master sitting at the board
in his own and greater being,
in the house of life.

ONLY MAN

Only man can fall from God
Only man.

No animal, no beast nor creeping thing
no cobra nor hyaena nor scorpion nor hideous white ant
can slip entirely through the fingers of the hands of god
into the abyss of self-knowledge,
knowledge of the self-apart-from god.

For the knowledge of the self-apart-from-God
is an abyss down which the soul can slip
writhing and twisting in all the revolutions
of the unfinished plunge
of self-awareness, now apart from God, falling
fathomless, fathomless, self-consciousness wriggling
writhing deeper and deeper in all the minutae of self-knowledge,
downwards, exhaustive,
yet never, never coming to the bottom, for there is no bottom;
zigzagging down like the fizzle from a finished rocket
the frizzling falling fire that cannot go out, dropping wearily,
neither can it reach the depth

for the depth is bottomless,
so it wriggles its way even further down, further down
at last in sheer horror of not being able to leave off
knowing itself, knowing itself apart from God, falling.

IN THE CITIES

In the cities
there is even no more any weather
the weather in town is always benzine, or else petrol fumes
lubricating oil, exhaust gas.

As over some dense marsh, the fumes
thicken, miasma, the fumes of the automobile
densely thicken in the cities.

In ancient Rome, down the thronged streets
no wheels might run, no insolent chariots.
Only the footsteps, footsteps
of people
and the gentle trotting of the litter-bearers.

In Minos, in Mycenae
in all the cities with lion gates
the dead threaded the air, lingering
lingering in the earth's shadow
and leaning towards the old hearth.

In London, New York, Paris
in the bursten cities
the dead tread heavily through the muddy air
through the mire of fumes
heavily, stepping weary on our hearts.

LORD'S PRAYER

For thine is the kingdom
the power, and the glory –

Hallowed be thy name, then
Thou who art nameless.

Give me, Oh give me
besides my daily bread
my kingdom, my power, and my glory.

All things that turn to thee
have their kingdom, their power, and their glory.
Like the kingdom of the nightingale at twilight
whose power and glory I have often heard and felt.

Like the kingdom of the fox in the dark
yapping in his power and his glory
which is death to the goose.

Like the power and the glory of the goose in the mist
hawking over the lake.

And I, a naked man, calling
calling to thee for my mana,
my kingdom, my power, and my glory.

MANA OF THE SEA

Do you see the sea, breaking itself to bits against the islands
yet remaining unbroken, the level great sea?

Have I caught from it
the tide in my arms
that runs down to the shallows of my wrists, and breaks
abroad in my hands, like waves among the rocks of substance?

Do the rollers of the sea
roll down my thighs
and over the submerged islets of my knees
with power, sea-power
sea-power
to break against the ground
in the flat, recurrent breakers of my two feet?

And is my body ocean, ocean
whose power runs to the shores along my arms
and breaks in the foamy hands, whose power rolls out
to the white-treading waves of two salt feet?

I am the sea, I am the sea!

SALT

Salt is scorched water that the sun has scorched
into substance and flaky whiteness
in the eternal opposition
between the two great ones, Fire, and the Wet

THE FOUR

To our senses, the elements are four
and have ever been, and will ever be
for they are the elements of life, of poetry, and of perception
the four Great Ones, the Four Roots, the First Four
of Fire and the Wet, Earth and the wide Air of the world.

To find the other many elements, you must go to the laboratory
and hunt them down.
But the four we have always with us, they are our world.
Or rather, they have us with them.

WALK WARILY

Walk warily, walk warily, be careful what you say:
because now the Sunderers are hovering round,
the Dividers are close upon us, dogging our every breath
and watching our every step,
and beating their great wings in our panting faces.

The angels are standing back, the angels of the Kiss.
they wait, they give way now
to the Sunderers, to the swift ones
the ones with the sharp black wings
and the shudder of electric anger
and the drumming of pinions of thunder
and hands like salt
and the sudden dripping down of the knife-edge cleavage of the
lightning
cleaving, cleaving.

Lo, we are in the midst of the sunderers
the cleavers, that cleave us forever apart from one another,
and separate heart from heart, and cut away all caresses
with the white triumphance of lightning and electric delight,
the Dividers, the Thunderers, the Swift Ones, blind with speed
who put salt in our mouths
and currents of excitement in our limbs
and hotness, and then more crusted brine in our hearts.

It is the day of the Sunderers
and the angels are standing back.

MYSTIC

They call all experience of the senses *mystic*, when the experience
is considered.
So an apple becomes *mystic* when I taste in it
the summer and the snows, the wild welter of earth
and the insistence of the sun.
All of which things I can surely taste in a good apple.

Though some apples taste preponderantly of water, wet and sour
and some of too much sun, brackish sweet
like lagoon-water, that has been too much sunned.
If I say I taste these things in an apple, I am called *mystic*, which
    means a liar.
The only way to eat an apple is to hog it down like a pig
and taste nothing
that is *real*.

But if I eat an apple, I like to eat it with all my senses awake.
Hogging it down like a pig I call the feeding of corpses.

ANAXAGORAS

When Anaxagoras says: Even the snow is black!
he is taken by the scientists very seriously
because he is enunciating a 'principle', a 'law'
that all things are mixed, and therefore the purest white snow
has in it an element of blackness.

That they call science, and reality.
I call it mental conceit and mystification
and nonsense, for pure snow is white to us
white and white and only white
with a lovely bloom of whiteness upon white
in which the soul delights and the senses
have an experience of bliss.

And life is for delight, and for bliss
and dread, and the dark, rolling ominousness of doom
then the bright dawning of delight again
from off the sheer white snow, or the poised moon.

And in the shadow of the sun the snow is blue, so blue-aloof
with a hint of the frozen bells of the scylla flower
but never the ghost of a glimpse of Anaxagoras' funeral black.

KISSING AND HORRID STRIFE

I have been defeated and dragged down by pain
and worsted by the evil world-soul of to-day.

But still I know that life is for delight
and for bliss
as now when the tiny wavelets of the sea
tip the morning light on edge, and spill it with delight
to show how inexhaustible it is.

And life is for delight, and bliss
like now where the white sun kisses the sea
and plays with the wavelets like a panther playing with its cubs
cuffing them with soft paws,
and blows that are caresses,
kisses of the soft-balled paws, where the talons are.

And life is for dread,
for doom that darkens, and the Sunderers
that sunder us from each other
that strip us and destroy us and break us down
as the tall fox-gloves and the mulleins and mallows
are torn down by dismembering autumn
till not a vestige is left, and bleak winter has no trace
of any such flowers;
and yet the roots below the blackness are intact:
the Thunderers and the Sunderers have their term
their limit, their thus far and no further.

Life is for kissing and for horrid strife.
Life is for the angels and the Sunderers
Life is for the daimons and the demons
those that put honey on our lips, and those that put salt.

But life is not
for the dead vanity of knowing better, nor the blank
cold superiority, nor silly
conceit of being immune,
nor puerility of contradictions
like saying snow is black, or desire is evil.

Life is for kissing and for horrid strife,
the angels and the Sunderers.
And perhaps in unknown Death we perhaps shall know
Oneness and poised immunity.
But why then should we die while we can live?
And while we live
the kissing and communing cannot cease
nor yet the striving and the horrid strife.

WHEN SATAN FELL

When Satan fell, he only fell
because the Lord Almighty rose a bit too high,
a bit beyond himself.

So Satan only fell to keep a balance.
'Are you so lofty, O my God?
Are you so pure and lofty, up aloft?
Then I will fall, and plant the paths to hell
with vines and poppies and fig-trees
so that lost souls may eat grapes
and the moist fig
and put scarlet buds in their hair on the way to hell,
on the way to dark perdition.'

And hell and heaven are the scales of the balance of life
which swing against each other.

THE WANDERING COSMOS

Oh, do not tell me the heavens as well are a wheel.
For every revolution of the earth around the sun
is a footstep onwards, onwards, we know not whither
and we do not care,
but a step onwards in untravelled space,
for the earth, like the sun, is a wanderer.

Their going round each time is a step
onwards, we know not whither,
but onwards, onwards, for the heavens are wandering
the moon and the earth, the sun, Saturn and Betelgeuse, Vega and
    Sirius and Altair
they wander their strange and different ways in heaven
past Venus and Uranus and the signs.

For life is a wandering, we know not whither, but going.

Only the wheel goes round, but it never wanders.
It stays on its hub.

DEATH IS NOT EVIL, EVIL IS MECHANICAL

Only the human being, absolved from kissing and strife
goes on and on and on, without wandering
fixed upon the hub of the ego
going, yet never wandering, fixed, yet in motion,
the kind of hell that is real, grey and awful
sinless and stainless going round and round
the kind of hell grey Dante never saw
but of which he had a bit inside him.

Know thyself, and that thou art mortal.
But know thyself, denying that thou art mortal:
a thing of kisses and strife
a lit-up shaft of rain
a calling column of blood
a rose tree bronzey with thorns
a mixture of yea and nay
a rainbow of love and hate
a wind that blows back and forth
a creature of beautiful peace, like a river
a creature of conflict, like a cataract:
know thyself, in denial of all these things.

And thou shalt begin to spin round on the hub of the obscene ego
a grey void thing that goes without wandering
a machine that in itself is nothing
a centre of the evil world-soul.

STRIFE

When strife is a thing of two
each knows the other in struggle
and the conflict is a communion
a twoness.

But when strife is a thing of one
a single ego striving for its own ends
and beating down resistances
then strife is evil, because it is not strife.

THE SHIP OF DEATH

I

Now it is autumn and the falling fruit
and the long journey towards oblivion.

The apples falling like great drops of dew
to bruise themselves an exit from themselves.

And it is time to go, to bid farewell
to one's own self, and find an exit
from the fallen self.

II

Have you built your ship of death, O have you?
O build your ship of death, for you will need it.

The grim frost is at hand, when the apples will fall
thick, almost thundrous, on the hardened earth.

And death is on the air like a smell of ashes!
Ah! can't you smell it?
And in the bruised body, the frightened soul
finds itself shrinking, wincing from the cold
that blows upon it through the orifices.

III

And can a man his own quietus make
with a bare bodkin?

With daggers, bodkins, bullets, man can make
a bruise or break of exit for his life;
but is that a quietus, O tell me, is it quietus?

Surely not so! for how could murder, even self-murder
ever a quietus make?

IV

O let us talk of quiet that we know,
that we can know, the deep and lovely quiet
of a strong heart at peace!

How can we this, our own quietus, make?

V

Build then the ship of death, for you must take
the longest journey, to oblivion.

And die the death, the long and painful death
that lies between the old self and the new.

Already our bodies are fallen, bruised, badly bruised,
already our souls are oozing through the exit
of the cruel bruise.

Already the dark and endless ocean of the end
is washing in through the breaches of our wounds,
already the flood is upon us.

Oh build your ship of death, your little ark
and furnish it with food, with little cakes, and wine
for the dark flight down oblivion.

VI

Piecemeal the body dies, and the timid soul
has her footing washed away, as the dark flood rises.

We are dying, we are dying, we are all of us dying
and nothing will stay the death-flood rising within us
and soon it will rise on the world, on the outside world.

We are dying, we are dying, piecemeal our bodies are dying
and our strength leaves us,
and our soul cowers naked in the dark rain over the flood,
cowering in the last branches of the tree of our life.

VII

We are dying, we are dying, so all we can do
is now to be willing to die, and to build the ship
of death to carry the soul on the longest journey.

A little ship, with oars and food
and little dishes, and all accoutrements
fitting and ready for the departing soul.

Now launch the small ship, now as the body dies
and life departs, launch out, the fragile soul
in the fragile ship of courage, the ark of faith
with its store of food and little cooking pans
and change of clothes,
upon the flood's black waste
upon the waters of the end
upon the sea of death, where still we sail
darkly, for we cannot steer, and have no port.

There is no port, there is nowhere to go
only the deepening blackness darkening still
blacker upon the soundless, ungurgling flood
darkness at one with darkness, up and down

and sideways utterly dark, so there is no direction any more.
and the little ship is there; yet she is gone.
She is not seen, for there is nothing to see her by.
She is gone! gone! and yet
somewhere she is there.
Nowhere!

VIII

And everything is gone, the body is gone
completely under, gone, entirely gone.
The upper darkness is heavy as the lower,
between them the little ship
is gone

It is the end, it is oblivion.

IX

And yet out of eternity a thread
separates itself on the blackness,
a horizontal thread
that fumes a little with pallor upon the dark.

Is it illusion? or does the pallor fume
A little higher?
Ah wait, wait, for there's the dawn,
the cruel dawn of coming back to life
out of oblivion.

Wait, wait, the little ship
drifting, beneath the deathly ashy grey
of a flood-dawn.

Wait, wait! even so, a flush of yellow
and strangely, O chilled wan soul, a flush of rose.

A flush of rose, and the whole thing starts again.

X

The flood subsides, and the body, like a worn sea-shell
emerges strange and lovely.

And the little ship wings home, faltering and lapsing
on the pink flood,
and the frail soul steps out, into the house again
filling the heart with peace.

Swings the heart renewed with peace
even of oblivion.

Oh build your ship of death. Oh build it!
for you will need it.
For the voyage of oblivion awaits you.

ALL SOULS' DAY

Be careful, then, and be gentle about death.
For it is hard to die, it is difficult to go through
the door, even when it opens.

And the poor dead, when they have left the walled
and silvery city of the now hopeless body
where are they to go, O where are they to go?

They linger in the shadow of the earth.
The earth's long conical shadow is full of souls
that cannot find the way across the sea of change.

Be kind, Oh be kind to your dead
and give them a little encouragement
and help them to build their little ship of death.

For the soul has a long, long journey after death
to the sweet home of pure oblivion.
Each needs a little ship, a little ship
and the proper store of meal for the longest journey.

Oh, from out of your heart
provide for your dead once more, equip them
like departing mariners, lovingly.

AFTER ALL SAINTS' DAY

Wrapped in the dark-red mantle of warm memories
the little, slender soul sits swiftly down, and takes the oars
and draws away, away, towards dark depths
wafting with warm love from still-living hearts
breathing on his small frail sail, and helping him on
to the fathomless deeps ahead, far, far from the grey shores
of marginal existence.

THE END, THE BEGINNING

If there were not an utter and absolute dark
of silence and sheer oblivion
at the core of everything,
how terrible the sun would be,
how ghastly it would be to strike a match, and make a light!

But the very sun himself is pivoted
upon a core of pure oblivion,
so is a candle, even as a match.

And if there were not an absolute, utter forgetting
and a ceasing to know, a perfect ceasing to know
and a silent, sheer cessation of all awareness
how terrible life would be!
how terrible it would be to think and know, to have conscious-
ness!

But dipped, once dipped in dark oblivion
the soul has peace, inward and lovely peace.

SLEEP AND WAKING

In sleep I am not, I am gone
I am given up.
And nothing in the world is lovelier than sleep,
dark, dreamless sleep, in deep oblivion!
Nothing in life is quite so good as this.

Yet there is waking from the soundest sleep,
waking, and waking new.

Did you sleep well?
Ah yes, the sleep of God!
The world is created afresh.

FATIGUE

My soul has had a long, hard day
she is tired,
she is seeking her oblivion.

O, and in the world
there is no place for the soul to find her oblivion
the after darkness of her peace,
for man has killed the silence of the earth
and ravished all the peaceful oblivious places
where the angels used to alight.

FORGET

To be able to forget is to be able to yield
to God who dwells in deep oblivion.
Only in sheer oblivion are we with God.
For when we know in full, we have left off knowing.

SHADOWS

And if tonight my soul may find her peace
in sleep, and sink in good oblivion,
and in the morning wake like a new-opened flower
then I have been dipped again in God, and new-created.

And if, as weeks go round, in the dark of the moon
my spirit darkens and goes out, and soft, strange gloom
pervades my movements and my thoughts and words
then I shall know that I am walking still
with God, we are close together now the moon's in shadow.

And if, as autumn deepens and darkens
I feel the pain of falling leaves, and stems that break in storms
and trouble and dissolution and distress
and then the softness of deep shadows folding, folding
around my soul and spirit, around my lips
so sweet, like a swoon, or more like the drowse of a low, sad song
singing darker than the nightingale, on, on to the solstice
and the silence of short days, the silence of the year, the shadow,
then I shall know that my life is moving still
with the dark earth, and drenched
with the deep oblivion of earth's lapse and renewal.

And if, in the changing phases of man's life
I fall in sickness and in misery
my wrists seem broken and my heart seems dead
and strength is gone, and my life
is only the leavings of a life:

and still, among it all, snatches of lovely oblivion, and snatches of
renewal
odd, wintry flowers upon the withered stem, yet new, strange
flowers
such as my life has not brought forth before, new blossoms of me

then I must know that still
I am in the hands [of] the unknown God,
he is breaking me down to his own oblivion
to send me forth on a new morning, a new man.

PHOENIX

Are you willing to be sponged out, erased, cancelled,
made nothing?
Are you willing to be made nothing?
dipped into oblivion?

If not, you will never really change.

The phoenix renews her youth
only when she is burnt, burnt alive, burnt down
to hot and flocculent ash.
Then the small stirring of a new small bub in the nest
with strands of down like floating ash
shows that she is renewing her youth like the eagle
immortal bird.

APPENDIX I

SHIP OF DEATH

I sing of autumn and the falling fruit
and the long journey towards oblivion.

The apples falling like great drops of dew
to bruise themselves an exit from themselves.

Have you built your ship of death, oh, have you?
Build then your ship of death, for you will need it!

Can man his own quietus make
with a bare bodkin?

With daggers, bodkins, bullets, man can make
a bruise or break of exit for his life
but is that a quietus, oh tell me, is it quietus?

Quietus is the goal of the long journey
the longest journey towards oblivion.

Slips out the soul, invisible one, wrapped still
in the white shirt of the mind's experiences
and folded in the dark-red, unseen
mantle of the body's still mortal memories.

Frightened and alone, the soul slips out of the house
or is pushed out
to find himself on the crowded, arid margins of existence.

Oh, it is not so easy, I tell you it is not so easy
to set softly forth on the longest journey, the longest journey.

It is easy to be pushed out of the silvery city of the body
through any breach in the wall,
thrust out onto the grey grey beaches of shadow
the long marginal stretches of existence, crowded with lost souls
that intervene between our tower and the shaking sea of the
    beyond.

Oh build your ship of death, oh build it in time
and build it lovingly, and put it between the hands of your soul.

Once outside the gate of the walled silvery life of days
once outside, upon the grey marsh beaches, where lost souls moan
in millions, unable to depart
having no boat to launch upon the shaken, soundless
deepest and longest of seas,
once outside the gate
what will you do, if you have no ship of the soul?

Oh pity the dead that are dead, but cannot take
the journey, still they moan and beat
against the silvery adamant walls of this our exclusive existence.
They moan and beat, they gnash, they rage
they fall upon the new outcoming souls with rage
and they send arrows of anger, bullets and bombs of frustration
over the adamant walls of this, our by-no-means impregnable
    existence.

Pity, oh pity the poor dead that are only ousted from life
and crowd there on the grey mud beaches of the margins
gaunt and horrible
waiting, waiting till at last the ancient boatman with the common
    barge
shall take them abroad, towards the great goal of oblivion.

Pity the poor gaunt dead that cannot die
into the distance with receding oars
but must roam like outcast dogs on the margins of life,
and think of them, and with the soul's deep sigh
waft nearer to them the bark of delivery.

But for myself, but for my soul, dear soul
let me build a little ship with oars and food
and little dishes, and all accoutrements
dainty and ready for the departing soul.

And put it between the hands of the trembling soul.
So that when the hour comes, and the last door closes behind him
he shall slip down the shores invisible
between the half-visible hordes
to where the furthest and the longest sea
touches the margins of our life's existence
with wincing unwilling waves.

And launching there his little ship,
wrapped in the dark-red mantle of the body's memories
the little, slender soul sits swiftly down, and takes the oars
and draws away, away, away, towards the dark depths
fathomless deep ahead, far, far from the grey shores
that fringe with shadow all this world's existence.

Over the sea, over the farthest sea
on the longest journey
past the jutting rocks of shadow
past the lurking, octopus arms of agonised memory
past the strange whirlpools of remembered greed
through the dead weed of a life-time's falsity,
slow, slow my soul, in his little ship
on the most soundless of all seas
taking the longest journey.

Pulling the long oars of a life-time's courage
drinking the confident water from the little jug
and eating the brave bread of a wholesome knowledge
row, little soul, row on
on the longest journey, towards the greatest goal

Neither straight nor crooked, neither here nor there
but shadows folded on deeper shadows
and deeper, to a core of sheer oblivion
like the convolutions of shadow-shell
or deeper, like the foldings and involvings of a womb.

Drift on, drift on, my soul, towards the most pure
most dark oblivion.
And at the penultimate porches, the dark-red mantle
of the body's memories slips and is absorbed
into the shell-like, womb-like convoluted shadow.

And round the great final bend of unbroken dark
the skirt of the spirit's experience has melted away
the oars have gone from the boat, and the little dishes
gone, gone, and the boat dissolves like pearl
as the soul at last slips perfect into the goal, the core
of sheer oblivion and of utter peace,
the womb of silence in the living night.

Ah peace, ah lovely peace, most lovely lapsing
of this my soul into the plasm of peace.

Oh lovely last, last lapse of death, into pure oblivion
at the end of the longest journey
peace, complete peace!
But can it be that also it is procreation?

Oh build your ship of death
oh build it!
Oh, nothing matters but the longest journey.

Ms B.

THE SHIP OF DEATH

Have you built your ship of death, Oh have you?
Oh build your ship of death, for you will need it.

Now in the twilight, sit by the invisible sea
Of peace, and build your little ship
Of death, that will carry the soul
On its last journey, on and on, so still
So beautiful, over the last of seas.
When the day comes, that will come.

Oh think of it in the twilight peacefully!
The last day, and the setting forth
On the longest journey, over the hidden sea
To the last wonder of oblivion.

Oblivion, the last wonder!
When we have trusted ourselves entirely
To the unknown, and are taken up
Out of our little ships of death
Into pure oblivion.

Oh build your ship of death, be building it now
With dim, calm thoughts and quiet hands
Putting its timbers together in the dusk,
Rigging its mast with the silent, invisible sail

That will spread in death to the breeze
Of the kindness of the cosmos, that will waft
The little ship with its soul to the wonder-goal.

Ah, if you want to live in peace on the face of the earth
Then build your ship of death, in readiness
For the longest journey, over the last of seas.

Lawrence's Typescript.

GLORY OF DARKNESS

Ink version:
Blue and dark
Bavarian gentians, tall ones
make a dark-blue gloom
in the sunny room

They have added blueness to blueness, until
it is dark: beauty
blue joy of my soul
Bavarian gentians
your dark blue gloom is so noble!

How deep I have gone
dark gentians
since I embarked on your dark blue fringes
how deep, how deep, how happy!

What a journey for my soul
in the dark blue gloom
of gentians here in the sunny room!

Pencil version:

. . . .
it is dark
and the door is open
to the depths

It is so blue, it is so dark
in the dark doorway
and the way is open
to Hades.

Oh, I know.
Persephone has just gone back
down the thickening thickening gloom
of dark-blue gentians to Pluto
to her bridegroom in the dark
and all the dead
and all the dark great ones of the underworld
down there, down there
down the blue depths of mountain gentian flowers
cold cold
are gathering to a
wedding in the winter dark
down the dark blue path

What a dark-blue gloom
of gentians here in the sunny room!

Ms B.

BAVARIAN GENTIANS

Not every man has gentians in his house
in soft September, at slow, sad Michaelmas.

Bavarian gentians, tall and dark, but dark
darkening the daytime torch-like with the smoking blueness of
Pluto's gloom,
ribbed hellish flowers erect, with their blaze of darkness spread
blue
Blown flat into points, by the heavy white draught of the day.

Torch-flowers of the blue-smoking darkness, Pluto's dark-blue
blaze
black lamps from the halls of Dis, smoking dark blue
giving off darkness, blue darkness, upon Demeter's yellow-pale
day
whom have you come for, here in the white-cast day?

Reach me a gentian, give me a torch!
let me guide myself with the blue, forked torch of a flower
down the darker and darker stairs, where blue is darkened on
blueness
down the way Persephone goes, just now, in first-frosted Sep-
tember
to the sightless realm where darkness is married to dark
and Persephone herself is but a voice, as a bride
a gloom invisible enfolded in the deeper dark
of the arms of Pluto as he ravishes her once again
and pierces her once more with his passion of the utter dark.
among the splendour of black-blue torches, shedding fathomless
darkness on the nuptials.

Give me a flower on a tall stem, and three dark flames,
for I will go to the wedding, and be wedding-guest
at the marriage of the living dark.

Ms A.

APPENDIX II

'Poetry of the Present' (Introduction to the American edition of New Poems)

It seems when we hear a skylark singing as if sound were running into the future, running so fast and utterly without consideration, straight on into futurity. And when we hear a nightingale, we hear the pause and the rich, piercing rhythm of recollection, the perfected past. The lark may sound sad, but with the lovely lapsing sadness that is almost a swoon of hope. The nightingale's triumph is a pæan, but a death-pæan.

So it is with poetry. Poetry is, as a rule, either the voice of the far future, exquisite and ethereal, or it is the voice of the past, rich, magnificent. When the Greeks heard the *Iliad* and the *Odyssey*, they heard their own past calling in their hearts, as men far inland sometimes hear the sea and fall weak with powerful, wonderful regret, nostalgia; or else their own future rippled its time-beats through their blood, as they followed the painful, glamorous progress of the Ithacan. This was Homer to the Greeks: their Past, splendid with battles won and death achieved, and their Future, the magic wandering of Ulysses through the unknown.

With us it is the same. Our birds sing on the horizons. They sing out of the blue, beyond us, or out of the quenched night. They sing at dawn and sunset. Only the poor, shrill, tame canaries whistle while we talk. The wild birds begin before we are awake, or as we drop into dimness, out of waking. Our poets sit by the gateways, some by the east, some by the west. As we arrive and as we go out our hearts surge with response. But whilst we are in the midst of life, we do not hear them.

The poetry of the beginning and the poetry of the end must have that exquisite finality, perfection which belongs to all that is far off. It is in the realm of all that is perfect. It is of the nature of all that is complete and consummate. This completeness, this consummateness, the finality and the perfection are conveyed in exquisite form: the perfect symmetry, the rhythm which returns upon itself like a dance where the hands link and loosen and link for the supreme moment of the end. Perfected bygone moments, perfected moments in the glimmering futurity, these are the treasured gem-like lyrics of Shelley and Keats.

But there is another kind of poetry: the poetry of that which is at hand: the immediate present. In the immediate present there is no perfection, no consummation, nothing finished. The strands are all flying, quivering, intermingling into the web, the waters are shaking the moon. There is no round, consummate moon on the face of running water, nor on the face of the unfinished tide. There are no gems of the living plasm. The living plasm vibrates unspeakably, it inhales the future, it exhales the past, it is the quick of both, and yet it is neither. There is no plasmic finality, nothing crystal, permanent. If we try to fix the living tissue, as the biologists fix it with formation, we have only a hardened bit of the past, the bygone life under our observation.

Life, the ever-present, knows no finality, no finished crystallisation. The perfect rose is only a running flame, emerging and flowing off, and never in any sense at rest, static, finished. Herein lies its transcendent loveliness. The whole tide of all life and all time suddenly heaves, and appears before us as an apparition, a revelation. We look at the very white quick of nascent creation. A water-lily heaves herself from the flood, looks around, gleams, and is gone. We have seen the incarnation, the quick of the ever-swirling flood. We have seen the invisible. We have seen, we have touched, we have partaken of the very substance of creative change, creative mutation. If you tell me about the lotus, tell me of nothing changeless or eternal. Tell me of the mystery of the inexhaustible, forever-unfolding creative spark. Tell me of the incarnate disclosure of the flux, mutation in blossom, laughter and decay perfectly open in their transit, nude in their movement before us.

Let me feel the mud and the heavens in my lotus. Let me feel the heavy, silting, sucking mud, the spinning of sky winds. Let me feel them both in purest contact, the nakedness of sucking weight, nakedly passing radiance. Give me nothing fixed, set, static. Don't give me the infinite or the eternal: nothing of infinity, nothing of eternity. Give me the still, white seething, the incandescence and the coldness of the incarnate moment: the moment, the quick of all change and haste and opposition: the moment, the immediate present, the Now. The immediate moment is not a drop of water running downstream. It is the source and issue, the bubbling up of the stream. Here, in this very instant moment, up bubbles the stream of time, out of the wells of futurity, flowing on to the oceans of the past. The source, the issue, the creative quick.

There is poetry of this immediate present, instant poetry, as well as poetry of the infinite past and the infinite future. The seething poetry of the incarnate Now is supreme, beyond even the everlasting gems of the before and after. In its quivering momentaneity it surpasses the crystalline, pearl-hard jewels, the poems of the eternities. Do not ask for the qualities of the unfading timeless gems. Ask for the whiteness which is the seethe of mud, ask for that incipient putrescence which is the skies falling, ask for the never-pausing, never-ceasing life itself. There must be mutation, swifter than iridescence, haste, not rest, come-and-go, not fixity, inconclusiveness, immediacy, the quality of life itself, without dénouement or close. There must be the rapid momentaneous association of things which meet and pass on the forever incalculable journey of creation: everything left in its own rapid, fluid relationship with the rest of things.

This is the unrestful, ungraspable poetry of the sheer present, poetry whose very permanency lies in its wind-like transit. Whitman's is the best poetry of this kind. Without beginning and without end, without any base and pediment, it sweeps past forever, like a wind that is forever in passage, and unchainable. Whitman truly looked before and after. But he did not sigh for what is not. The clue to all his utterance lies in the sheer appreciation of the instant moment, life surging itself into utterance at its very well-head. Eternity is only an abstraction from the actual present. Infinity is only a great reservoir of recollection, or a reservoir of aspiration: man-made. The quivering nimble hour of the present, this is the quick of Time. This is the immanence. The quick of the universe is the *pulsating, carnal self*, mysterious and palpable. So it is always.

Because Whitman put this into his poetry, we fear him and respect him so profoundly. We should not fear him if he sang only of the 'old unhappy far-off things', or of the 'wings of the morning'. It is because his heart beats with the urgent, insurgent Now, which is even upon us all, that we dread him. He is so near the quick.

From the foregoing it is obvious that the poetry of the instant present cannot have the same body or the same motion as the poetry of the before and after. It can never submit to the same conditions. It is never finished. There is no rhythm which returns upon itself, no serpent of eternity with its tail in its own mouth. There is no static perfection, none of that finality which we find so satisfying because we are so frightened.

Much has been written about free verse. But all that can be said, first and last, is that free verse is, or should be direct utterance from the instant, whole man. It is the soul and the mind and body surging at once, nothing left out. They speak all together. There is some confusion, some discord. But the confusion and the discord only belong to the reality, as noise belongs to the plunge of water. It is no use inventing fancy laws for free verse, no use drawing a melodic line which all the feet must toe. Free verse toes no melodic line, no matter what drill-sergeant. Whitman pruned away his clichés – perhaps his clichés of rhythm as well as of phrase. And this is about all we can do, deliberately, with free verse. We can get rid of the stereotyped movements and the old hackneyed associations of sound or sense. We can break down those artificial conduits and canals through which we do so love to force our utterance. We can break the stiff neck of habit. We can be in ourselves spontaneous and flexible as flame, we can see that utterance rushes out without artificial form or artificial smoothness. But we cannot positively prescribe any motion, any rhythm. All the laws we invent or discover – it amounts to pretty much the same – will fail to apply to free verse. They will only apply to some form of restricted, limited unfree verse.

All we can say is that free verse does *not* have the same nature as restricted verse. It is not of the nature of reminiscence. It is not the past which we treasure in its perfection between our hands. Neither is it the crystal of the perfect future, into which we gaze. Its tide is neither the full, yearning flow of aspiration, nor the sweet, poignant ebb of remembrance and regret. The past and the future are the two great bournes of human emotion, the two great homes of the human days, the two eternities. They are both conclusive, final. Their beauty is the beauty of the goal, finished, perfected. Finished beauty and measured symmetry belong to the stable, unchanging eternities.

But in free verse we look for the insurgent naked throb of the instant moment. To break the lovely form of metrical verse, and to dish up the fragments as a new substance, called *vers libre*, this is what most of the free-versifiers accomplish. They do not know that free verse has its own *nature*, that it is neither star nor pearl, but instantaneous like plasm. It has no goal in either eternity. It has no finish. It has no satisfying stability, satisfying to those who like the immutable. None of this. It is the instant; the quick; the very jetting source of all will-be and has-been. The utterance is like a spasm, naked contact with all influences at once. It does not want to get anywhere. It just takes place.

For such utterance any externally applied law would be mere shackles and death. The law must come new each time from within. The bird is on the wing in the winds, flexible to every breath, a living spark in the storm, its very flickering depending upon its supreme mutability and power of change. Whence such a bird came: whither it goes: from what solid earth it rose up, and upon what solid earth it will close its wings and settle, this is not the question. This is a question of before and after. Now, *now*, the bird is on the wing in the winds.

Such is the rare new poetry. One realm we have never conquered: the pure present. One great mystery of time is terra incognita to us: the instant. The most superb mystery we have hardly recognised: the immediate, instant self. The quick of all time is the instant. The quick of all the universe, of all creation, is the incarnate, carnal self. Poetry gave us the clue: free verse: Whitman. Now we know.

The ideal – what is the ideal? A figment. An abstraction. A static abstraction, abstracted from life. It is a fragment of the before or the after. It is a crystallised aspiration, or a crystallised remembrance: crystallised, set, finished. It is a thing set apart, in the great storehouse of eternity, the storehouse of finished things.

We do not speak of things crystallised and set apart. We speak of the instant, the immediate self, the very plasm of the self. We speak also of free verse.

All this should have come as a preface to *Look! We Have Come Through!* But is it not better to publish a preface long after the book it belongs to has appeared? For then the reader will have had his fair chance with the book, alone.

'Chaos in Poetry' (Introduction to Harry Crosby's Chariot of the Sun)

Poetry, they say, is a matter of words. And this is just as much true as that pictures are a matter of paint, and frescoes a matter of water and colour-wash. It is such a long way from being the whole truth that it is slightly silly if uttered sententiously.

Poetry is a matter of words. Poetry is a stringing together of words into a ripple and jingle and a run of colours. Poetry is an interplay of images. Poetry is the iridescent suggestion of an idea. Poetry is all these things, and still it is something else. Given all these ingredients, you have something very like poetry, something for which we might borrow the old romantic name of poesy. And poesy, like bric-à-brac, will forever be in fashion. But poetry is still another thing.

The essential quality of poetry is that it makes a new effort of attention, and 'discovers' a new world within the known world. Man, and the animals, and the flowers, all live within a strange and forever surging chaos. The chaos which we have got used to we call a cosmos. The unspeakable inner chaos of which we are composed we call consciousness, and mind, and even civilisation. But it is, ultimately, chaos, lit up by visions, or not lit up by visions. Just as the rainbow may or may not light up the storm. And, like the rainbow, the vision perisheth.

But man cannot live in chaos. The animals can. To the animal all is chaos, only there are a few recurring motions and aspects within the surge. And the animal is content. But man is not. Man must wrap himself in a vision, make a house of apparent form and stability, fixity. In his terror of chaos he begins by putting up an umbrella between himself and the everlasting whirl. Then he paints the under-side of his umbrella like a firmament. Then he parades around, lives and dies under his umbrella. Bequeathed to his descendants, the umbrella becomes a dome, a vault, and men at last begin to feel that something is wrong.

Man fixes some wonderful erection of his own between himself and the wild chaos, and gradually goes bleached and stifled under his parasol. Then comes a poet, enemy of convention, and makes a slit in the umbrella; and lo! the glimpse of chaos is a vision, a window to the sun. But after a while, getting used to the vision, and not liking the genuine draught from chaos, commonplace man daubs a simulacrum of the window that opens onto chaos, and patches the umbrella with the painted patch of the simulacrum. That is, he has got used to the vision; it is part of his house-decoration. So that the umbrella at last looks like a glowing open firmament, of many aspects. But alas! it is all simulacrum, in innumerable patches. Homer and Keats, annotated and with glossary.

This is the history of poetry in our era. Someone sees Titans in the wild air of chaos, and the Titan becomes a wall between succeeding generations and the chaos they should have inherited. The wild sky moved and sang. Even that became a great umbrella between mankind and the sky of fresh air; then it became a painted vault, a fresco on a vaulted roof, under which men bleach and go dissatisfied. Till another poet makes a slit onto the open and windy chaos.

But at last our roof deceives us no more. It is painted plaster, and all the skill of all the human ages won't take us in. Dante or Leonardo, Beethoven or Whitman: lo! it is painted on the plaster of our vault. Like St Francis preaching to the birds in Assisi. Wonderfully like air and birdy space and chaos of many things – partly because the fresco is faded. But even so, we are glad to get out of that church, and into the natural chaos.

This is the momentous crisis for mankind, when we have to get back to chaos. So long as the umbrella serves, and poets make slits in it, and the mass of people can be gradually educated up to the vision in the slit: which means they patch it over with a patch that looks just like the vision in the slit: so long as this process can continue, and mankind can be educated up, and thus built in, so long will a civilisation continue more or less happily, completing its own painted prison. It is called completing the consciousness.

The joy men had when Wordsworth, for example, made a slit and saw a primrose! Till then, men had only seen a primrose dimly, in the shadow of the umbrella. They saw it through Wordsworth in the full gleam of chaos. Since then, gradually, we have come to see primavera nothing but primrose. Which means, we have patched over the slit.

And the greater joy when Shakespeare made a big rent and saw emotional, wistful man outside in the chaos, beyond the conventional idea and painted umbrella of moral images and iron-bound paladins, which had been put up in the Middle Ages. But now, alas, the roof of our vault is simply painted dense with Hamlets and Macbeths, the side walls too, and the order is fixed and complete. Man can't be any different from his image. Chaos is all shut out.

The umbrella has got so big, the patches and plaster are so tight and hard, it can be slit no more. If it were slit, the rent would no more be a vision, it would only be an outrage. We should dab it over at once, to match the rest.

So the umbrella is absolute. And so the yearning for chaos becomes a nostalgia. And this will go on till some terrific wind blows the umbrella to ribbons, and much of mankind to oblivion. The rest will shiver in the midst of chaos. For chaos is always there, and always will be, no matter how we put up umbrellas of visions.

What about the poets, then, at this juncture? They reveal the inward desire of mankind. What do they reveal? They show the desire for chaos, and the fear of chaos. The desire for chaos is the breath of their poetry. The fear of chaos is in their parade of forms and technique. Poetry is made of words, they say. So they blow bubbles of sound and image, which soon burst with the breath of longing for chaos, which fills them. But the poetasters can make pretty shiny bubbles for the Christmas-tree, which never burst, because there is no breath of poetry in them, but they remain till we drop them.

What, then, of *Chariot of the Sun*? It is a warlike and bronzy title for a sheaf of flimsies, almost too flimsy for real bubbles. But incongruity is man's recognition of chaos.

If one had to judge these little poems for their magic of words, as one judges Paul Valéry, for example, they would look shabby. There is no obvious incantation of sweet noise: only too often the music of one line deliberately kills the next, breathlessly staccato. There is no particular jewellery of epithet. And no handsome handling of images. Where deliberate imagery is used, it is perhaps a little clumsy. There is no coloured thread of an idea; and no subtle ebbing of a theme into consciousness, no recognisable vision, new gleam of chaos let into a world of order. There is only a repetition of sun, sun, sun, not really as a glowing symbol, more as a bewilderment and a narcotic. The images in 'Sun Rhapsody' shatter one another, line by line. For the sun,

> it is a forest without trees
> it is a lion in a cage of breeze
> it is the roundness of her knees

great Hercules
and all the seas
and our soliloquies

The rhyme is responsible for a great deal. The lesser symbols are as confusing: sunmaids who are naiads of the water world, hiding in a cave. Only the forest becomes suddenly logical.

I am a tree whose roots are tangled in the sun
All men and women are trees whose roots are tangled in the sun
Therefore humanity is the forest of the sun.

What is there, then, in this poetry, where there seems to be nothing? For if there is nothing, it is merely nonsense.

And, almost, it is nonsense. Sometimes, as in the 'verse' beginning: 'sthhe fous on ssu eod', since I at least can make no head or tail of it, and the mere sound is impossible, and the mere look of it is not inspiring, to me it is just nonsense. But in a world overloaded with shallow 'sense', I can bear a page of nonsense, just for a pause.

For the rest, what is there? Take, at random, the poem called 'Néant':

Red sunbeams from an autumn sun
Shall be the strongest wall
To shield the sunmaids of my soul
From worlds inimical.

Yet sunflakes falling in the sea
Beyond the outer shore
Reduplicate their epitaph
To kill the conqueror.

It is a tissue of incongruity, in sound and sense. It means nothing, and it says nothing. And yet it has something to say. It even carries a dim suggestion of that which refuses to be said.

And therein lies the charm. It is a glimpse of chaos not reduced to order. But the chaos *alive*, not the chaos of matter. A glimpse of the living, untamed chaos. For the grand chaos is all alive, and everlasting. From it we draw our breath of life. If we shut ourselves off from it, we stifle. The animals live with it, as they live in grace. But when man became conscious, and aware of *himself*, his own littleness and puniness in the whirl of the vast chaos of God, he took fright, and began inventing God in his own image.

Now comes the moment when the terrified but inordinately conceited human consciousness must at last submit, and own itself part of the vast and potent living chaos. We must keep true to ourselves. But we must breathe in life from the living and unending chaos. We shall put up more umbrellas. They are a necessity of our consciousness. But never again shall we be able to put up The Absolute Umbrella, either religious or moral or rational or scientific or practical. The vast parasol of our conception of the universe, the cosmos, the firmament of suns and stars and space, this we can roll up like any other green sunshade, and bring it forth again when we want it. But we mustn't imagine it always spread above us. It is no more absolutely there than a green sunshade is absolutely there. It is casually there, only; because it is as much a contrivance and invention of our mind as a green sunshade is. Likewise the grand conception of God: this already shuts up like a Japanese parasol, rather clumsily, and is put by for Sundays, or bad weather, or a 'serious' mood.

Now we see the charm of *Chariot of the Sun*. It shuts up all the little and big umbrellas of poesy and importance, has no outstanding melody or rhythm or image or epithet or even sense. And we feel a certain relief. The sun is very much in evidence, certainly, but it is a bubble reality that always explodes before you can really look at it. And it upsets all the rest of things with its disappearing.

Hence the touch of true poetry in this sun. It bursts all the bubbles and umbrellas of reality, and gives us a breath of the live chaos. We struggle out into the fathomless chaos of things passing and coming, and many suns and different darknesses. There is a bursting of bubbles of reality, and the pang of extinction that is also liberation into the roving, uncaring chaos which is all we shall ever know of God.

To me there is a breath of poetry, like an uneasy waft of fresh air at dawn, before it is light. There is an acceptance of the limitations of consciousness, and a leaning-up against the sun-imbued world of chaos. It is poetry at the moment of inception in the soul, before the germs of the known and the unknown have fused to begin a new body of concepts. And therefore it is useless to quote fragments. They are too nebulous and *not there*. Yet in the whole there is a breath of real poetry, the essential quality of poetry. It makes a new act of attention, and wakes us to a nascent world of inner and outer suns. And it has the poetic faith in the chaotic splendour of suns.

It is poetry of suns which are the core of chaos, suns which are fountains of shadow and pools of light and centres of thought and lions of passion. Since chaos has a core which is itself quintessentially chaotic and fierce with incongruities. That such a sun should have a chariot makes it only more chaotic.

And in the chaotic re-echoing of the soul, wisps of sound curl round with curious soothing –

> Likewise invisible winds
> Drink fire, and all my heart is sun-consoled.

And a poem such as 'Water-Lilies' has a lovely suffusion in which the visual image passes at once into sense of touch, and back again, so that there is an iridescent confusion of sense-impression, sound and touch and sight all running into one another, blending into a vagueness which is a new world, a vagueness and a suffusion which liberates the soul, and lets a new flame of desire flicker delicately up from the numbed body.

The suffused fragments are the best, those that are only comprehensible with the senses, with vision passing into touch and to sound, then again touch, and the bursting of the bubble of an image. There is always sun, but there is also water, most palpably water. Even some of the suns are wetly so, wet pools that wet us with their touch. Then loose suns like lions, soft gold lions and white lions half-visible. Then again the elusive gleam of the sun of livingness, soft as gold and strange as the lion's eyes, the livingness that never ceases and never will cease. In this there is faith, soft, intangible, suffused faith that is the breath of all poetry, part of the breathing of the myriad sun in chaos. Such sun breathes its way into words, and the words become poetry, by suffusion. On the part of the poet it is an act of faith, pure attention and purified receptiveness. And without such faith there is no poetry. There is even no life. The poetry of conceit is a dead-sea fruit. The poetry of sunless chaos is already a bore. The poetry of a regulated cosmos is nothing but a wire bird-cage. Because in all living poetry the living chaos stirs, sun-suffused and sun-impulsive, and most subtly chaotic. All true poetry is most subtly and sensitively chaotic, outlawed. But it is the impulse of the sun in chaos, not conceit.

The Sun in unconcealèd rage
Glares down across the magic of the world.

The sun within us, that sways us incalculably.

At night
Swift to the Sun
Deep imaged in my soul
But during the long day black lands
To cross

And it is faith in the incalculable sun, inner and outer, which keeps us alive.

Sunmaid
Left by the tide
I bring you a conch-shell
That listening to the Sun you may
Revive

And there is always the battle of the sun, against the corrosive acid vapour of vanity and poisonous conceit, which is the breath of the world.

Dark clouds
Are not so dark
As our embittered thoughts
Which carve strange silences within
The Sun

That the next 'cinquain' may not be poetry at all is perhaps just as well, to keep us in mind of the world of conceit outside. It is the expired breath, with its necessary carbonic acid. It is the cold shadow across the sun, and saves us from the strain of the monos, from homogeneity and exaltation and forcedness and all-of-a-pieceness, which is the curse of the human consciousness. What does it matter if half the time a poet fails in his effort at expression! The failures make it real. The act of attention is not so easy. It is much easier to write poesy. Failure is part of the living chaos. And the groping reveals the act of attention, which suddenly passes into pure expression.

But I shall not be frightened by a sound
Of Something moving cautiously around.

Whims, and fumblings, and effort, and nonsense, and echoes from other poets, these all go to make up the living chaos of a little book of real poetry, as well as pure little poems like 'Sun-Ghost', 'To Those Who Return', 'Torse de Jeune Femme au Soleil', 'Poem for the Feet of Polia'. Through it all runs the intrinsic naïveté without which no poetry can exist, not even the most sophisticated. This naïveté is the opening of the soul to the sun of chaos, and the soul may open like a lily or a tiger-lily or a dandelion or a deadly nightshade or a rather paltry chickweed flower, and it will be poetry of its own sort. But open it must. This opening, and this alone, is the essential act of attention, the essential poetic and vital act. We may fumble in the act, and a hailstone may hit us. But it is in the course of things. In this act, and this alone, we truly *live*: in that innermost naïve opening of the soul, like a flower, like an animal, like a coloured snake, it does not matter, to the sun of chaotic livingness.

Now, after a long bout of conceit and self-assurance and flippancy, the young are waking up to the fact that they are starved of life and of essential sun, and at last they are being driven, out of sheer starvedness, to make the act of submission, the act of attention, to open into inner naïveté, deliberately and dauntlessly, admit the chaos and the sun of chaos. This is the new naïveté, chosen, recovered, regained. Round it range the white and golden soft lions of courage and the sun of dauntlessness, and the whorled ivory horn of the unicorn is erect and ruthless, as a weapon of defence. The naïve, open spirit of man will no longer be a victim, to be put on a cross, nor a beggar, to be scorned and given a pittance. This time it will be erect and a bright lord, with a heart open to the wild sun of chaos, but with the yellow lions of the sun's danger on guard in the eyes.

The new naïveté, erect, and ready, sufficiently sophisticated to wring the neck of sophistication, will be the new spirit of poetry and the new spirit of life. Tender, but purring like a leopard that may snarl, it may be clumsy at first, and make gestures of self-conscious crudity. But it is a real thing, the real creature of the inside of the soul. And to the young it is the essential reality, the liberation into the real self. The liberation into the wild air of chaos, the being part of the sun. A long course of merely negative 'freedom' reduces the soul and body both to numbness. They can feel no more and respond no more. Only the mind remains awake, and suffers keenly from the sense of nullity; to be young, and to feel you have every 'opportunity', every 'freedom' to live, and yet not to be able to live, because the responses have gone numb in the body and soul, this is the nemesis that is overtaking the young. It drives them silly.

But there is the other way, back to the sun, to faith in the speckled leopard of the mixed self. What is more chaotic than a dappled leopard trotting through dappled shade? And that is our life, really. Why try to whitewash ourselves? – or to camouflage ourselves into an artificially chaotic pattern? All we have to do is to accept the true chaos that we are, like the jaguar dappled with black suns in gold.

Preface to The Collected Poems of D. H. Lawrence

The volume of *Rhyming Poems* is collected from four little books, *Love Poems and Others*, *Amores*, *New Poems*, and *Bay*. Of these *Love Poems and Others* was the first, and was published in 1913.

I have now tried to arrange the poems, as far as possible, in chronological order, the order in which they were written. The first poems I ever wrote, if poems they were, was when I was nineteen: now twenty-three years ago. I remember perfectly the Sunday afternoon when I perpetrated those first two pieces: 'To Guelder-Roses' and 'To Campions'; in spring-time, of course, and, as I say, in my twentieth year. Any young lady might have written them and been pleased with them; as I was pleased with them. But it was after that, when I was twenty, that my real demon would now and then get hold of me and shake more real poems out of me, making me uneasy. I never 'liked' my real poems as I liked 'To Guelder-Roses'.

I have tried to establish a chronological order, because many of the poems are so personal that, in their fragmentary fashion, they make up a biography of an emotional and inner life. Many of the poems, again, are what one might call fictional, poems like 'Love on the Farm', 'Wedding Morn', 'Two Wives', and the dialect poems. They have no necessary chronological sequence. But the poems to Miriam, and to my Mother, and to Helen, and to the other woman, the woman of 'Kisses in the Train' and 'Hands of the Betrothed', they need the order of time, as that is the order of experience. So, perhaps, do the subjective poems like 'Virgin Youth'.

The first change in scene comes when for the first time I left Nottinghamshire, at the age of twenty-three, to go to teach in a new school on the fringes of South London. From the playground we could look north at the blue bubble of the Crystal Palace, fairy-like to me. Then the poems to Helen begin, and the school poems, and London.

Some of the earliest poems, like 'The Wild Common' and 'Virgin Youth', are a good deal rewritten. They were struggling to say something which it takes a man twenty years to be able to say. Some of the fictional poems are changed, to make the 'fiction' more complete. A young man is afraid of his demon and puts his hand over the demon's mouth sometimes and speaks for him. And the things the young man says are very rarely poetry. So I have tried to let the demon say his say, and to remove the passages where the young man intruded. So that, in the first volume, many poems are changed, some entirely rewritten, recast. But usually this is only because the poem started out to be something which it didn't quite achieve, because the young man interfered with his demon.

The crisis of Volume I is the death of the mother, with the long haunting of death in life, which continues to the end, through all the last poems, which come from *Bay*, and which belong to the war. *Bay* appeared in 1919, but the poems were written mostly in 1917 and 1918, after I left Cornwall perforce.

A big break in scene, however, had happened before then, in 1912, when I left England for the first time. In 1912 begins the new cycle of *Look! We Have Come Through!* Of this volume the first few poems belong to England and the end of the death-experience, but 'Bei Hennef', written in May, 1912, by a river in the Rhineland, starts the new cycle, which ends with 'Frost Flowers', written in Cornwall at the end of the bitter winter of 1916–17. It seems to me that no poetry, not even the best, should be judged as if it existed in the absolute, in the vacuum of the absolute. Even the best poetry, when it is at all personal, needs the penumbra of its own time and place and circumstance to make it full and whole. If we knew a little more of Shakespeare's self and circumstance how much more complete the Sonnets would be to us, how their strange, torn edges would be softened and merged into a whole body! So one would like to ask the reader of *Look! We Have Come Through!* to fill in the background of the poems, as far as possible, with the place, the time, the circumstance. What was uttered in the cruel spring of 1917 should not be dislocated and heard as if sounding out of the void.

The poems of *Birds, Beasts and Flowers* were begun in Tuscany, in the autumn of 1920, and finished in New Mexico in 1923, in my thirty-eighth year. So that from first to last these poems cover all but twenty years.

Scandicci,
12 May 1928.

Foreword to The Collected Poems of D. H. Lawrence

Instead of bewailing a lost youth, a man nowadays begins to wonder, when he reaches my ripe age of forty-two, if ever his past will subside and be comfortably bygone. Doing over these poems makes me realise that my teens and my twenties are just as much me, here and now and present, as ever they were, and that pastness is only an abstraction. The actuality, the body of feeling, is essentially alive and here.

And I remember the slightly self-conscious Sunday afternoon, when I was nineteen, and I 'composed' my first two 'poems'. One was to 'Guelder-Roses', and one to 'Campions', and most young ladies would have done better: at least I hope so. But I thought the effusions very nice, and so did Miriam.

Then much more vaguely I remember subsequent half-furtive moments when I would absorbedly scribble at verse for an hour or so, and then run away from the act and the production as if it were secret sin. It seems to me that 'knowing oneself' was a sin and a vice for innumerable centuries, before it became a virtue. It seems to me, it is still a sin and vice, when it comes to new knowledge. In those early days – for I was very green and unsophisticated at twenty – I used to feel myself at times haunted by something, and a little guilty about it, as if it were an abnormality. Then the haunting would get the better of me, and the ghost would suddenly appear, in the shape of a usually rather incoherent poem. Nearly always I shunned the apparition once it had appeared. From the first, I was a little afraid of my real poems – not my 'compositions', but the poems that had the ghost in them. They seemed to me to come from somewhere, I didn't quite know where, out of a me whom I didn't know and didn't want to know, and to say things I would much rather not have said: for choice. But there they were. I never read them again. Only I gave them to Miriam, and she loved them, or she seemed to. So when I was twenty-one, and went to Nottingham University as a day-student, I began putting them down in a little college note-book, which was the foundation of the poetic me. *Sapientiae Urbs Conditur*, it said on the cover. Never was anything less true. The city is founded on a passionate unreason.

To this day, I still have the uneasy haunted feeling, and would rather not write most of the things I do write – including this Note. Only now I know my demon better, and, after bitter years, respect him more than my other, milder and nicer self. Now I no longer like my 'compositions'. I once thought the poem 'Flapper' a little masterpiece: when I was twenty: because the demon isn't in it. And I must have burnt many poems that had the demon fuming in them. The fragment 'Discord in Childhood' was a long poem, probably was good, but I destroyed it. Save for Miriam, I perhaps should have destroyed them all. She encouraged my demon. But alas, it was me, not he, whom she loved. So for her too it was a catastrophe. My demon is not easily loved: whereas the ordinary me is. So poor Miriam was let down. Yet in a sense, she let down my demon, till he howled. And there it is. And no more *past* in me than my blood in my toes or my nose.

I have tried to arrange the poems in chronological order: that is, in the order in which they were written. The first are either subjective, or Miriam poems. 'The Wild Common' was very early and very confused. I have rewritten some of it, and added some, till it seems complete. It has taken me twenty years to say what I started to say, incoherently, when I was nineteen, in this poem. The same with 'Virgin Youth', and others of the subjective poems with the demon fuming in them smokily. To the demon, the past is not past. The wild common, the gorse, the virgin youth are here and now. The same: the same me, the same one experience. Only now perhaps I can give it more complete expression.

The poems to Miriam, at least the early ones like 'Dog-Tired' and 'Cherry-Robbers' and 'Renascence', are not much changed. But some of the later ones had to be altered, where sometimes the hand of commonplace youth had been laid on the mouth of the demon. It is not for technique these poems are altered: it is to say the real say.

Other verses, those I call the imaginative, or fictional, like 'Love on the Farm' and 'Wedding Morn', I have sometimes changed to get them into better form, and take out the dead bits. It took me many years to learn to play with the form of a poem: even if I can do it now. But it is only in the less immediate, the more fictional poems that the form has to be played with. The demon, when he's really there, makes his own form willy-nilly, and is unchangeable.

The poems to Miriam run into the first poems to my mother. Then when I was twenty-three, I went away from home for the first time, to the south of London. From the big new red school where I taught, we could look north and see the Crystal Palace: to me, who saw it for the first time, in lovely autumn weather, beautiful and softly blue on its hill to the north. And past the school, on an embankment, the trains rushed south to Brighton or to Kent. And round the school the country was still only just being built over, and the elms of Surrey stood tall and noble. It was different from the Midlands.

Then began the poems to Helen, and all that trouble of 'Lilies in the Fire': and London, and school, a whole new world. Then starts the rupture with home, with Miriam, away there in Nottinghamshire. And gradually the long illness, and then the death of my mother; and in the sick year after, the collapse of Miriam, of Helen, and of the other woman, the woman of 'Kisses in the Train' and 'The Hands of the Betrothed'.

Then, in that year, for me everything collapsed, save the mystery of death, and the haunting of death in life. I was twenty-five, and from the death of my mother, the world began to dissolve around me, beautiful, iridescent, but passing away substanceless. Till I almost dissolved away myself, and was very ill: when I was twenty-six.

Then slowly the world came back: or I myself returned: but to another world. And in 1912, when I was still twenty-six, the other phase commenced, the phase of *Look! We Have Come Through!* – when I left teaching, and left England, and left many other things, and the demon had a new run for his money.

But back in England during the war, there are the war poems from the little volume: *Bay*. These, beginning with 'Tommies in the Train', make up the end of the volume of *Rhyming Poems*. They are the end of the cycle of purely English experience, and death experience.

The first poems I had published were 'Dreams Old' and 'Dreams Nascent', which Miriam herself sent to Ford Madox Hueffer, in 1910, I believe, just when the *English Review* had started so brilliantly. Myself, I had offered the little poem 'Study' to the Nottingham *University Magazine*, but they returned it. But Hueffer accepted the 'Dreams' poems for the *English Review*, and was very kind to me, and was the first man I ever met who had a real and a true feeling for literature. He introduced me to Edward Garnett, who, somehow, introduced me to the world. How well I remember the evenings at Garnett's house in Kent, by the log fire. And there I wrote the best of the dialect poems. I remember Garnett disliked the old ending to 'Whether or Not'. Now I see he was right, it was the voice of the commonplace me, not the demon. So I have altered it. And there again, those days of Hueffer and Garnett are not past at all, once I recall them. They were good to the demon, and the demon is timeless. But the ordinary mealtime me has yesterdays.

And that is why I have altered 'Dreams Nascent', that exceedingly funny and optimistic piece of rhymeless poetry which Ford Hueffer printed in the *English Review*, and which introduced me to the public. The public seemed to like it. The MP for school-teachers said I was an ornament to the educational system, whereupon I knew it must be the ordinary me which had made itself heard, and not the demon. Anyhow, I was always uneasy about it.

There is a poem added to the second volume, which had to be left out of *Look! We Have Come Through!* when that book was first printed, because the publishers objected to mixing love and religion, so they said, in the lines:

> But I hope I shall find eternity
> With my face down buried between her breasts . . .

But surely there are many eternities, and one of them Adam spends with his face buried and at peace between the breasts of Eve: just as Eve spends one of her eternities with her face hidden in the breast of Adam. But the publishers coughed out that gnat, and I was left wondering, as usual.

Some of the poems in *Look!* are rewritten, but not many, not as in the first volume. And *Birds, Beasts and Flowers* are practically untouched. They are what they are. They are the same me as wrote 'The Wild Common', or 'Renascence'.

Perhaps it may seem bad taste to write this so personal foreword. But since the poems are so often personal themselves, and hang together in a life, it is perhaps only fair to give the demon his body of mere man, as far as possible.

Introduction to Pansies (*the unexpurgated edition*)

This little bunch of fragments is offered as a bunch of *pensées*, *anglicé* pansies; a handful of thoughts. Or, if you will have the other derivation of pansy, from *panser*, to dress or soothe a wound, these are my tender administrations to the mental and emotional wounds we suffer from. Or you can have heartsease if you like, since the modern heart could certainly do with it.

Each little piece is a thought; not a bare idea or an opinion or a didactic statement, but a true thought, which comes as much from the heart and the genitals as from the head. A thought, with its own blood of emotion and instinct running in it like the fire in a fire-opal, if I may be so bold. Perhaps if you hold up my pansies properly to the light, they may show a running vein of fire. At least, they do not pretend to be half-baked lyrics or melodies in American measure. They are thoughts which run through the modern mind and body, each having its own separate existence, yet each of them combining with all the others to make up a complete state of mind.

It suits the modern temper better to have its state of mind made up of apparently irrelevant thoughts that scurry in different directions, yet belong to the same nest; each thought trotting down the page like an independent creature, each with its own small head and tail, trotting its own little way, then curling up to sleep. We prefer it, at least the young seem to prefer it to those solid blocks of mental pabulum packed like bales in the pages of a proper heavy book. Even we prefer it to those slightly didactic opinions and slices of wisdom which are laid horizontally across the pages of Pascal's *Pensées* or La Bruyère's *Caractères*, separated only by *pattes de mouches*, like faint sprigs of parsley. Let every *pensée* trot on its own little paws, not be laid like a cutlet trimmed with a *patte de mouche*.

Live and let live, and each pansy will tip you its separate wink. The fairest thing in nature, a flower, still has its roots in earth and manure; and in the perfume there hovers still the faint strange scent of earth, the under-earth in all its heavy humidity and darkness. Certainly it is so in pansy-scent, and in violet-scent; mingled with the blue of the morning the black of the corrosive humus. Else the scent would be just sickly sweet.

So it is: we all have our roots in earth. And it is our roots that now need a little attention, need the hard soil eased away from them, and softened so that a little fresh air can come to them, and they can breathe. For by pretending to have no roots, we have trodden the earth so hard over them that they are starving and stifling below the soil. We have roots, and our roots are in the sensual, instinctive and intuitive body, and it is here we need fresh air of open consciousness.

I am abused most of all for using the so-called 'obscene' words. Nobody quite knows what the word 'obscene' itself means, or what it is intended to mean: but gradually all the *old* words that belong to the body below the navel, have come to be judged obscene. Obscene means today that the policeman thinks he has a right to arrest you, nothing else.

Myself, I am mystified at this horror over a mere word, a plain simple word that stands for a plain simple thing. 'In the beginning was the Word, and the Word was God and the Word was with God.' If that is true, then we are very far from the beginning. When did the Word 'fall'? When did the Word become unclean 'below the navel'? Because today, if you suggest that the word arse was in the beginning and was God and was with God, you will just be put in prison at once. Though a doctor might say the same of the word *ischial tuberosity*, and all the old ladies would piously murmur 'Quite!' Now that sort of thing is idiotic and humiliating. Whoever the God was that made us, He made us complete. He didn't stop at the navel and leave the rest to the devil. It is too childish. And the same with the Word which is God. If the Word is God – which in the sense of the human it is – then you can't suddenly say that all the words which belong below the navel are obscene. The word arse is as much god as the word face. It must be so, otherwise you cut off your god at the waist.

What is obvious is that the words in these cases have been dirtied by the mind, by unclean mental associations. The words themselves are clean, so are the things to which they apply. But the mind drags in a filthy association, calls up some repulsive emotion. Well, then, cleanse the mind, that is the real job. It is the mind which is the Augean stables, not language. The word arse is clean enough. Even the part of the body it refers to is just as much me as my hand and my brain are me. It is not for *me* to quarrel with my own natural make-up. If I am, I am all that I am. But the impudent and dirty mind won't have it. It hates certain parts of the body, and makes the words representing these parts scape-goats. It pelts them out of the consciousness with filth, and there they hover, never dying, never dead, slipping into the consciousness again unawares, and pelted out again with filth, haunting the margins of the consciousness like jackals or hyenas. And they refer to parts of our own living bodies, and to our most essential acts. So that man turns himself into a thing of shame and horror. And his consciousness shudders with horrors that he has made for himself.

That sort of thing has got to stop. We can't have the consciousness haunted any longer by repulsive spectres which are no more than poor simple scapegoat words representing parts of man himself; words that the cowardly and unclean mind has driven out into the limbo of the unconscious, whence they return upon us looming and magnified out of all proportion, frightening us beyond all reasons. We must put an end to that. It is the self divided against itself most dangerously. The simple and natural 'obscene' words must be cleaned up of all their depraved fear-associations, and readmitted into the consciousness to take their natural place. Now they are magnified out of all proportion, so is the mental fear they represent. We must accept the word arse as we accept the word face, since arses we have and always shall have. We can't start cutting off the buttocks of unfortunate mankind, like the ladies in the Voltaire story, just to fit the mental expulsion of the word.

This scapegoat business does the mind itself so much damage. There is a poem of Swift's which should make us pause. It is written to Celia, his Celia – and every verse ends with the mad, maddened refrain: 'But – Celia, Celia, Celia shits!' Now that, stated baldly, is so ridiculous it is almost funny. But when one remembers the gnashing insanity to which the great mind of Swift was reduced by that and similar thoughts, the joke dies away. Such thoughts poisoned him, like some terrible constipation. They poisoned his mind. And why, in heaven's name? The *fact* cannot have troubled him, since it applied to himself and to all of us. It was not the fact that Celia shits which so deranged him, it was the *thought*. His mind couldn't bear the thought. Great wit as he was, he could not see how ridiculous his revulsions were. His arrogant mind overbore him. He couldn't even see how much worse it would be if Celia didn't shit. His physical sympathies were too weak, his guts were too cold to sympathise with poor Celia in her natural functions. His insolent and sicklily squeamish mind just turned her into a thing of horror, because she was merely natural and went to the WC. It is monstrous! One feels like going back across all the years to poor Celia, to say to her: It's all right, don't you take any notice of that mental lunatic.

And Swift's form of madness is very common today. Men with cold guts and over-squeamish minds are always thinking those things and squirming. Wretched man is the victim of his own little revulsions, which he magnifies into great horrors and terrifying taboos. We are all savages, we all have taboos. The Australian black may have the kangaroo for his taboo. And then he will probably die of shock and terror if a kangaroo happens to touch him. Which is what I would call a purely unnecessary death. But modern men have even more dangerous taboos. To us, certain words, certain ideas are taboo, and if they come upon us and we can't drive them away, we die or go mad with a degraded sort of terror. Which is what happened to Swift. He was such a great wit. And the modern mind altogether is falling into this form of degraded taboo-insanity. I call it a waste of sane human consciousness. But it is very dangerous, dangerous to the individual and utterly dangerous to society as a whole. Nothing is so fearful in a mass-civilisation like ours as a mass-insanity.

The remedy is, of course, the same in both cases: lift off the taboo. The kangaroo is a harmless animal, the word shit is a harmless word. Make either into a taboo, and it becomes more dangerous. The result of taboo is insanity. And insanity, especially mob-insanity, mass-insanity, is the fearful danger that threatens our civilisation. There are certain persons with a sort of rabies, who live only to infect the mass. If the young do not watch out, they will find themselves, before so very many years are past, engulfed in a howling manifestation of mob-insanity, truly terrifying to think of. It will be better to be dead than to live to see it. Sanity, wholeness, is everything. In the name of piety and purity, what a mass of disgusting insanity is spoken and written. We shall have to fight the mob, in order to keep sane, and to keep society sane.

Foreword to Pansies

These poems are called *Pansies* because they are rather *Pensées* than anything else. Pascal or La Bruyère wrote their *Pensées* in prose, but it has always seemed to me that a real thought, a single thought, not an argument, can only exist easily in verse, or in some poetic form. There is a didactic element about prose thoughts which makes them repellent, slightly bullying. 'He who hath wife and children hath given hostages to fortune.' There is a thought well put; but it immediately irritates by its assertiveness. It applies too direct to actual practical life. If it were put into poetry it wouldn't nag at us so practically. We don't want to be nagged at.

So I should wish these *Pansies* to be taken as thoughts rather than anything else; casual thoughts that are true while they are true and irrelevant when the mood and circumstance changes. I should like them to be as fleeting as pansies, which wilt so soon, and are so fascinating with their varied faces, while they last. And flowers, to my thinking, are not merely pretty-pretty. They have in their fragrance an earthiness of the humus and the corruptive earth from which they spring. And pansies, in their streaked faces, have a look of many things besides heartsease.

Some of the poems are perforce omitted – about a dozen from the bunch. When Scotland Yard seized the MS in the post, at the order of the Home Secretary, no doubt there was a rush of detectives, postmen, and Home Office clerks and heads, to pick out the most lurid blossoms. They must have been very disappointed. When I now read down the list of the omitted poems, and recall the dozen amusing, not terribly important bits of pansies which have had to stay out of print for fear a policeman might put his foot on them, I can only grin once more to think of the nanny-goat, nanny-goat-in-a-white-petticoat silliness of it all. It is like listening to a Mrs Caudle's curtain lecture in the next house, and wondering whether Mrs Caudle is funnier, or Mr Caudle; or whether they aren't both merely stale and tedious.

Anyhow I offer a bunch of pansies, not a wreath of *immortelles*. I don't want everlasting flowers, and I don't want to offer them to anybody else. A flower passes, and that perhaps is the best of it. If we can take it in its transience, its breath, its maybe mephistophelian, maybe palely ophelian face, the look it gives, the gesture of its full bloom, and the way it turns upon us to depart – that was the flower, we have had it, and no *immortelle* can give us anything in comparison. The same with the pansy poems; merely the breath of the moment, and one eternal moment easily contradicting the next eternal moment. Only don't nail the pansy down. You won't keep it any better if you do.

Bandol,
March 1929.

Prefaces to Birds, Beasts and Flowers

FRUITS

'For fruits are all of them female, in them lies the seed. And so when they break and show the seed, then we look into the womb and see its secrets. So it is that the pomegranate is the apple of love to the Arab, and the fig has been a catch-word for the female fissure for ages. I don't care a fig for it! men say. But why a fig? The apple of Eden, even, was Eve's fruit. To her it belonged, and she offered it to the man. Even the apples of knowledge are Eve's fruit, the woman's. But the apples of life the dragon guards, and no woman gives them . . .'

'No sin is it to drink as much as a man can take and get home without a servant's help, so he be not stricken in years.'

TREES

'It is said, a disease has attacked the cypress trees of Italy, and they are all dying. Now even the shadow of the lost secret is vanishing from earth.'

'Empedokles says trees were the first living creatures to grow up out of the earth, before the sun was spread out and before day and night were distinguished; from the symmetry of their mixture of fire and water, they contain the proportion of male and female; they grow, rising up owing to the heat which is in the earth, so that they are parts of the earth just as embryos are parts of the uterus. Fruits are excretions of the water and fire in plants.'

FLOWERS

'And long ago, the almond was the symbol of resurrection. – But tell me, tell me, why should the almond be the symbol of resurrection? –

Have you not seen, in the mild winter sun of the southern Mediterranean, in January and February, the re-birth of the almond tree, all standing in clouds of glory? –

Ah yes! ah yes! would I might see it again!

Yet even this is not the secret of the secret. Do you know what was called the almond bone, the last bone of the spine? This was the seed of the body, and from the grave it could grow into a new body again, like almond blossom in January. – No, no, I know nothing of that. –'

'Oh Persephone, Persephone, bring back to me from Hades the life of a dead man. –'

'Wretches, utter wretches, keep your hands from beans! saith Empedokles. For according to some, the beans were the beans of votes, and votes were politics. But others say it was a food-taboo. Others also say the bean was one of the oldest symbols of the male organ, for the peas-cod is later than the beans-cod.'

'But blood is red, and blood is life. Red was the colour of kings. Kings, far-off kings, painted their faces vermilion, and were almost gods.'

THE EVANGELISTIC BEASTS

'Oh, put them back, put them back in the four corners of the heavens, where they belong, the Apocalyptic beasts. For with their wings full of stars they rule the night, and man that watches through the night lives four lives, and man that sleeps through the night sleeps four sleeps, the sleep of the lion, the sleep of the bull, the sleep of the man, and the eagle's sleep. After which the lion wakes, and it is day. Then from the four quarters the four winds blow, and life has its changes. But when the heavens are empty, empty of the four great Beasts, the four Natures, the four Winds, the four Quarters, then sleep is empty too, man sleeps no more like the lion and the bull, nor wakes from the light-eyed eagle sleep.'

CREATURES

'But fishes are very fiery, and take to the water to cool themselves.'

'To those things that love darkness, the light of day is cruel and a pain. Yet the light of lamps and candles has no fears for them; rather they draw near to taste it, as if saying: Now what is this? So we see that the sun is more than burning, more than the burning of fires or the shining of lamps. Because with his rays he hurts the creatures that live by night, and lamplight and firelight do them no hurt. Therefore the sun lives in his shining, and is not like fires, that die.'

REPTILES

'Homer was wrong in saying, "Would that strife might pass away from among gods and men!" He did not see that he was praying for the destruction of the universe; for, if his prayer were heard, all things would pass away – for in the tension of opposites all things have their being –'

'For when Fire in its downward path chanced to mingle with the dark breath of the earth, the serpent slid forth, lay revealed. But he was moist and cold, the sun in him darted uneasy, held down by moist earth, never could he rise on his feet. And this is what put poison in his mouth. For the sun in him would fain rise half-way, and move on feet. But moist earth weighs him down, though he dart and twist, still he must go with his belly on the ground. – The wise tortoise laid his earthy part around him, he cast it round him and found his feet. So he is the first of creatures to stand upon his toes, and the dome of his house is his heaven. Therefore it is charted out, and is the foundation of the world.'

BIRDS

'Birds are the life of the skies, and when they fly, they reveal the thoughts of the skies. The eagle flies nearest to the sun, no other bird flies so near.

So he brings down the life of the sun, and the power of the sun, in his wings, and men who see him wheeling are filled with the elation of the sun. But all creatures of the sun must dip their mouths in blood, the sun is for ever thirsty, thirsting for the brightest exhalation of blood.

You shall know a bird by his cry, and great birds cry loud, but sing not. The eagle screams when the sun is high, the peacock screams at the dawn, rooks call at evening, when the nightingale sings. And all birds have their voices, each means a different thing.'

ANIMALS

'Yes, and if oxen or lions had hands, and could paint with their hands, and produce works of art as men do, horses would paint the forms of the gods like horses, and oxen like oxen, and make their bodies in the image of their several kinds.'

'Once, they say, he was passing by when a dog was being beaten, and he spoke this word: "Stop! don't beat it! For it is the soul of a friend I recognised when I heard its voice."'

'Swine wash in mire, and barnyard fowls in dust.'

GHOSTS

'And as the dog with its nostrils tracking out the fragments of the beasts' limbs, and the breath from their feet that they leave in the soft grass, runs upon a path that is pathless to men, so does the soul follow the trail of the dead, across great spaces. For the journey is a far one, to sleep and a forgetting, and often the dead look back, and linger, for now they realise all that is lost. Then the living soul comes up with them, and great is the pain of greeting, and deadly the parting again. For oh, the dead are disconsolate, since even death can never make up for some mistakes.'

NOTES

Abbreviations

A. = *Apocalypse*; *AR* = *Aaron's Rod*; *F* = *Fantasia of the Unconscious*; L. = Lawrence; *LCL* = *Lady Chatterley's Lover*; *MEH* = *Movements in European History*; *MRN* = *Mr Noon*; *P* = *Phoenix*; *P II* = *Phoenix II*; *SCAL* = *Studies in Classic American Literature*; *SM* = *The Symbolic Meaning*; *SL* = *Sons and Lovers*; *TR* = *The Rainbow*; *TWP* = *The White Peacock*; *WIL* = *Women in Love*.

RHYMING POEMS

Written and rewritten between 1906 and 1912, these early poems are contemporary with the novels *TWP*, *The Trespasser* and *SL*, and with most of *The Prussian Officer* stories. They are set in Nottinghamshire and London and portray L.'s relationship with his mother and family, the friends of his youth and his days as a school teacher in Croydon. In June 1909 Jessie Chambers sent five poems to Ford Madox Hueffer (Ford), editor of the *English Review*, and these were published in the November issue: 'Dreams Old and Nascent' 1 & 2, 'Baby Movements' 1 & 2, 'Discipline'. See preface and foreword to *COLP*, Appendix II of this volume. For the finest and most complete account of L.'s life in these years, see John Worthen's *D. H. Lawrence: The Early Years*.

The poems in this selection were published in the following volumes: *Love Poems and Others* (1913): 'Dog-Tired', 'Cherry Robbers', 'The Collier's Wife' (as 'A Collier's Wife'), 'The Best of School' (first appeared in the *Saturday Westminster Gazette*, 1 June 1912), 'End of Another Home Holiday', 'Aware', 'Corot', 'Last Lesson of the Afternoon' (as 'The Last Lesson').

Amores (1916): 'The Wild Common', 'Discord in Childhood', 'Monologue of a Mother' (*Poetry*, January 1914, as 'The Mother of Sons'), 'Dreams Old and Nascent', 'Baby Running Barefoot', 'A Baby Asleep

After Pain' (as 'Trailing Clouds'), 'Discipline', 'The Bride', 'The Virgin Mother', 'Blueness' (as 'The Mystic Blue').

New Poems (1918): 'From a College Window', 'Gipsy', 'Letter from Town: The Almond-Tree', 'Piano', 'Seven Seals'.

The Wild Common (p. 35). A significantly different early version was printed in *Amores*. In the preface to *COLP* L. writes: 'It has taken me twenty years to say what I started to say, incoherently, when I was nineteen, in this poem.' For a comparison of the early and late versions see F. B. Pinion, *A D. H. Lawrence Companion*, pp. 93–4.

40. **all that is God takes substance!** L. had read and been influenced by Ernst Haeckel's *The Riddle of the Universe* (1899) which argues that God, as essence or spirit, pervades the universe of substance or matter. It was a notion L. retained throughout his life. Cf. 'The Body of God' in *Last Poems*. See also *Letters* i. 256.

From a College Window (p. 37). When he was eighteen L. went to Nottingham University College where he took his teaching certificate two years later. In *TR* he describes 'the big college built of stone, standing in the quiet street, with a rim of grass and lime-trees all so peaceful' (ch. xv).

Discord in Childhood (p. 38). Cf. *SL*: 'In front of the house was a huge ash-tree. The west wind, sweeping from Derbyshire, caught the houses with full force, and the tree shrieked again . . . To Paul it became almost a demoniacal noise . . . Having such a great space in front of the house gave the children a feeling of night, of vastness, and of terror. This terror came in from the shrieking of the tree and the anguish of the home discord. Often Paul would wake up, after he had been asleep a long time, aware of thuds downstairs. Instantly he was wide awake. Then he heard the booming shouts of his father, come home nearly drunk, then the sharp replies of his mother, then the bang, bang of his father's fist on the table, and the nasty snarling shout as the man's voice got higher. And then the whole was drowned in a piercing medley of shrieks and cries from the great, wind-swept ash-tree' (ch. iv). Cf. also Ada Lawrence and G. Stuart Gelder, *Young Lorenzo: the Early Life of D. H. Lawrence*, p. 18.

Cherry Robbers (p. 38). Cf. *SL*: 'Cherries touched his ears and his neck as he stretched forward, their chill finger-tips sending a flash down his blood . . . Miriam came out wondering . . . Beside her, on the rhubarb leaves, were four dead birds, thieves that had been shot . . . He threw a handful of cherries at her . . . She ran for shelter, picking up some cherries. Two fine pairs she hung over her ears; then she looked up again' (ch. iv). Cf. also an earlier version of this episode in *TWP*, part 1, ch. vi.

The Collier's Wife (p. 39). The familiar story of a miner brought home badly injured or dead is a recurrent one in L.'s works. See especially 'Odour of Chrysanthemums' and *SL* (ch. v).

7. **mard-arsed** Spoiled, soft; a namby-pamby (dialect).
19. **scraightin'** Crying (dialect).

Monologue of a Mother (p. 40). Essentially the story of Paul Morel and his mother (with a strong autobiographical element) in *SL*. See *Letters* i. 476–7: 'a woman of character and refinement goes into a lower class, and has no satisfaction in her own life. She has had a passion for her husband, so the children are born of passion, and have heaps of vitality. But as her sons grow up she selects them as lovers – first the oldest, then the second.'

12. **weird** Fate, destiny.

Dreams Old and Nascent: Old (p. 43). L. taught at Davidson Road School, Croydon (London) from 1908 to 1911. In *Letters* i. 83 he describes the school and its view: 'a great big new red-brick imposing handsome place, with a fair amount of open space – looking across in front over great stacks of timber, over two railways to Norwood where the musichall folk live in big houses among the trees, and to Sydenham where the round blue curves of the Crystal Palace swell out into view on fairly clear days.'

4. **Lorna Doone** R. D. Blackmore's popular romance (1869).
7. **palace at Sydenham** The Crystal Palace (destroyed by fire in 1936).
14. **romance of David and Dora** In Dickens' *David Copperfield* (1849–50) Dora's parents live at Norwood (see ch. xxvi).

Letter from Town: The Almond-Tree (p. 44). Jessie Chambers recalls that in 1909 'When spring came he wrote with delight about the flowering almonds, and sent me a box of the blossom because we had never seen the miracle of the flowering almond in our countryside', *A Personal Record*, p. 89.

Baby Running Barefoot (p. 46). L. lodged at 12 Colworth Road, Addiscombe, with Mr and Mrs J. W. Jones when he was teaching at Croydon and wrote several poems about Hilda Mary, their baby daughter. See *Letters* i. 39 and Jessie Chambers, *A Personal Record*, p. 157.

Aware (p. 47). For the story of L.'s relationship with Jessie Chambers see John Worthen, *D. H. Lawrence: The Early Years* and Jessie Chambers, *A Personal Record*: 'It was at Christmas, 1909, that he made the great attempt to resolve the conflict in himself. Soon after my return from London he sent me the verse 'Aware', but I had always been careful not to take his poems too literally. Now he came to me and told me that he had been mistaken all these years, that he must have loved me all along without knowing it. The idea of marrying the Croydon teacher was a mistake', p. 189.

Corot (p. 47). Jean Baptiste Corot (1796–1875), French landscape painter whose work L. admired and attempted to copy. See *Letters* i. 130 and 282; the reproduction of 'Landscape (after Corot)' in *Young Lorenzo* and Ada Lawrence's recollections pp. 66–7. See also Helen Corke 'D. H. Lawrence as I saw him', *Renaissance and Modern Studies*, IV, 1960, p. 12.

Discipline (p. 50). 'School is a conflict – mean and miserable – and I hate conflicts. I was never born to command; I do not want to command. So the lads and I have a fight, and I have a fight with my nature, and I am always vanquished . . . So I struggle with my nature and with my class, till I feel all frayed into rags', *Letters* i. 85. See also *Letters* i. 89 and ch. xiii in *TR* where L.'s experience (and his knowledge of Jessie Chambers's time as a teacher) is imaginatively transmuted into the story of Ursula.

The Bride (p. 52) and *The Virgin Mother* (p. 53). See preface to *COLP*, Appendix II, and Chambers, *A Personal Record*, p. 184. L. gave these poems to Jessie to read the day before his mother's funeral. Cf. *SL*: 'She lay like a maiden asleep . . . The mouth was a little open, as if wondering from the suffering, but her face was young, her brow clear and white as if life had never touched it. He looked again at the eyebrows, at the small, winsome nose a bit on one side. She was young again. Only the hair as it arched so beautifully from her temples was mixed with silver, and the two simple plaits that lay on her shoulders were filigree of silver and brown' (ch. xiv).

Piano (p. 54). Cf. *Young Lorenzo*, p. 52 and *TWP*, part I, ch. i.

Seven Seals (p. 55). In Revelation the opening of the seven seals signals the re-birth of the soul.

Dreams Old and Nascent: Nascent (p. 56). Cf. the last two pages of *TR* (ch. xvi) and Zola's vision of the miners' revolutionary power on the last page of *Germinal* (1885).

LOOK! WE HAVE COME THROUGH!

Written between May 1912 and 1914 this cycle of poems celebrates the early sexual love and conflict between L. and Frieda and chronicles 'the intrinsic experience of a man during the crisis of manhood when he marries and comes into himself' (foreword to *COLP*, Appendix II). For Frieda's account see *Not I*, and for an imaginative recreation of their time in Germany and Italy in fiction see *MRN* part 2. Something, too, of the sense of wonder and the difficulty of adjustment in married life between two highly individual people, is transmitted in the chapters of *TR* on the early married life of the first two Brangwen generations (see especially the end of ch. iii and the opening pages of ch. vi).

L. revised the poems for publication in January and February 1917 and in August Chatto and Windus accepted the manuscript conditionally: two poems were to be omitted ('Song of a Man Who is Loved' and 'Meeting Among the Mountains') and some lines rewritten as 'a process of refinement' (see *Letters* iii. 145; 148). The selection of poems here were all first published in *Look!* (1917) with the exception of: 'Bei Hennef' (*Love Poems and Others*, 1913); 'Green' (*Poetry*, January 1914; first collected in *Some Imagist Poets*, 1915); 'Gloire de Dijon' (*Poetry*, January 1914); 'Roses on the Breakfast Table' (*Poetry*, January 1914); 'Giorno dei Morti' (*New Statesman*, 15 November 1913 as 'Service of All the Dead'; first collected in *Georgian Poetry 1913–15* as 'Service of All the Dead').

Bei Hennef (p. 66). Written in May 1912 by a river in the German Rhineland and first published in *Love Poems* (1913) but, significantly, placed by L. in the 'Unrhyming Poems' volume of *COLP* as part of *Look! We Have Come Through!* to emphasise what he saw as the start of a new cycle in his life as a man and an artist. Perhaps the first of his truly free verse poems, it exemplifies his view of poetry as 'a direct utterance from the instant, whole man', a notion later developed in 'Poetry of the Present' (Appendix II). See also preface to *COLP* (Appendix II). In *Letters* i. 398 he records waiting for a train at Hennef 'beside a nice, twittering little river waiting for the twilight to drop . . . the promise of life with you is all richness'. *Letters* i. 440 also provides valuable insight into this cycle of poems: 'For ourselves Frieda and I have struggled through some bad times into a wonderful naked intimacy, all kindled with warmth, that I know at last is love'. See also *MRN* 184.

Mutilation (p. 67).

37. **Tuatha De Danaan** In Gaelic mythology, the people of the goddess Danu. The reference is an early example of L.'s belief in the dark gods, the forces of the unconscious and the unknown. He would have been familiar with Yeats's early poems; see especially *The Wind Among the Reeds* (1898).

I am Like a Rose (p. 72). Cf. *WIL* (ch. xix 'Moony') and the essay 'Love', written immediately after that novel, where the rose is the emblem of fulfilment in marriage: 'We are like a rose, which is a miracle of pure centrality, pure absolved equilibrium . . . We are like a rose. In the pure passion for distinctness and separateness, a dual passion of unutterable separation and lovely conjunction, the two in their perfect singleness, transported into one surpassing heaven of a rose-blossom' (*P* 153–4).

Giorno dei Morti (p. 74). 'Day of the Dead' (Italian); 2 November, All Souls' Day.

Song of a Man Who Has Come Through (p. 75). See introduction to this volume, p. 6.

10. **Hesperides** In Greek mythology, three nymphs, daughters of the Titan Atlas, who tended a golden apple tree in a remote land under the protection of Hera, Queen of Heaven.
17. **three strange angels** See Genesis xviii. Cf. *TR* describing the girlhood of Ursula when she is sexually awakened by Anton Skrebensky and likens his coming to the biblical myth: 'Once three angels stood in Abraham's doorway, and greeted him, and stayed and ate with him, leaving his household enriched forever when they went' (ch. xi 'First Love').

'*She said as well to me*' (p. 76).

15–38. **instrument** Cf. Gudrun's dangerously anti-life perception of Gerald in *WIL*: 'He was sheerly beautiful, he was a perfect instrument. To her mind, he was a pure, inhuman, almost superhuman instrument . . . she wished she were God, to use him as a tool' (ch. xxx).
45–6. **adder . . . princess** Cf. 'I saw a most beautiful brindled adder, in the spring, coiled up asleep with her head on her shoulder. She did not hear me till I was very near. Then she must have felt my motion, for she lifted her head like a queen to look, then turned and moved slowly and with delicate pride into the bushes. She often comes into my mind again, and I think I see her asleep in the sun, like a Princess of the fairy world' (*Letters* iii. 40). Cf. also *P* 680.

BIRDS, BEASTS AND FLOWERS

As the editors of *COMP* have noted, the title for this volume came from the second stanza of S. Baring Gould's 'Evening Hymn' (from *Hymns Ancient and Modern*):

> Now the darkness gathers,
> Stars begin to peep,
> Birds and beasts and flowers
> Soon will be asleep.

The poems were written between September 1920 and the spring of 1923 and the later ones, as several critics have noted, are a kind of poetic map of L.'s travels around the globe. Most of them were written at the Fontana Vecchia, Taormina, Sicily but 'Kangaroo' was written in Australia, and 'Mountain Lion', 'The Red Wolf' and 'Autumn at Taos' in New Mexico. L. corrected the proofs of the poems in August 1923 while in New York for his American publisher Thomas Seltzer and they were published on 9 October of that year.

The poems consider the mysterious life and wonder of the non-human universe, its distinctiveness and uniqueness as well as the poet's sense that life makes up a vast creative pattern of which man too is a part. L.'s vision is akin to Hopkins's in this respect – 'The world is charged with the grandeur of God' – and, again like Hopkins, he felt that the task of the poet was to attend to that wonder and convey in his art the 'otherness' of the natural object ('All the world is full of inscape'). But L. also saw man as at once part of and alienated from this pristine creation and this reveals itself in his two modes of consciousness. On the one hand there is what he termed 'blood knowledge', which is instinctive and intuitive; on the other hand there is the mental consciousness, the rational intellect, the 'nerve-brain' self. Some of the poems dramatise this division and are strenuous enquiries into the products of human intellectual consciousness, in particular doctrines such as Christianity and democracy which have at once creatively shaped but also, L. felt, distorted natural human impulses. Others combine the poet's close scrutiny of the natural world with an intuitive understanding of its processes of becoming (and dying); in these poems L. uses some of the resurrection myths of the ancient world as he was to do again in the 'Last Poems'.

The poems in this selection were first published by Thomas Seltzer (New York, 1923) with the exception of the following: 'Pomegranate' (first appeared in the *Dial*, March 1921); 'Medlars and Sorb-Apples' (the *New Republic*, 5 January 1921); 'Almond Blossom' (the *English Review*, February 1922); 'St Matthew' *Poetry*, 4 April 1923); 'St Mark' (the *Dial*, April 1921); 'St Luke' (the *Dial*, April 1921); 'St John' (the *Dial*, April 1921); 'Mosquito' (the New York *Bookman*, July 1921); 'Fish' (the *English Review*, June 1922); 'Bat' (the *English Review*, November 1922, and the *Literary Review*, 30 December 1922); 'Snake' (the *Dial*, July 1921, and first collected in *Georgian Poetry 1920–1922*); 'Turkey-Cock' (*Poetry*, November 1922); 'Humming-Bird' (the *New Republic*, May 1921); 'Autumn in Taos' (*Palms*, Autumn 1923, as 'Autumn in New Mexico'). Seltzer also published the five tortoise poems in a separate volume in 1921.

In the autumn of 1929 L. also wrote a series of prefaces for a new edition of the poems, but these were later thoughts, derived from his re-reading of Burnet's *Early Greek Philosophy* and contemporary with the writing of the 'Last Poems'. They therefore represent a different period in his writing and so, as retrospective illuminations of the poems, are reproduced in Appendix II rather than here.

FRUITS

Some of the poems in this sub-section – 'Pomegranate', 'Medlars and Sorb-Apples' and 'Grapes' – describe the natural process of ripening and subsequent decay of a fruit, which at the same time also contains the seeds of its renewal. In a wider sense this activity enacts the whole process of becoming and dissolution in the world of nature. L. called this power of destruction divine, in the sense of it being necessary, both for nature and for man: 'decay, corruption, destruction, breaking down is the opposite equivalent of creation'; 'when it breaks the ego and opens the soul to the wide heavens' it is a beneficent force (PII 402–3). He most fully articulated this doctrine in his essay 'The Crown' and a similar notion informs the relationships of the two main sets of characters in *WIL*. Eating the fruit and meditating on its nature becomes for the poet and reader an imaginative journey into the underworld, hence the references in these poems to mythological figures symbolising death and resurrection: Dionysos, Orpheus, Persephone.

Pomegranate (p. 81). In Greek mythology, Persephone (the daughter of Demeter, goddess of corn and harvests) was abducted by Hades and carried off to the underworld to be his queen. She was released but had to return each year for as many months as she had eaten pomegranate seeds while in the underworld. The pomegranate, then, is particularly associated with a resurrection and fertility myth and, with the fig, is seen as a characteristically feminine fruit. At the same time it was also sacred to Dionysos as an emblem of self-loss and renewal through possession by the god.

4–7. **Syracuse . . . Venice** The modulation is from the stone quarries of ancient Greek Syracuse 'where the Athenian youths, prisoners-of-war, died so horribly' (*Letters* iii. 509) to medieval and Renaissance Venice of the Doges. Byron also links the defeat of the Athenians at Syracuse to the fall of the Venetian Doges in *Childe Harold's Pilgrimage* iv. 16.

4. **viciousness of Greek women** Presumably the triumph of the women over the Athenians imprisoned and dying in the latomy, the stone quarry, but there is no reference in Thucidydes to any 'viciousness'.

Medlars and Sorb-Apples (p. 83). In its autumnal sense of departure for the underworld this anticipates some of the last poems (cf. the opening line of 'The Ship of Death': 'Now it is autumn and the falling fruit'). L. cites, and sometimes conflates, Dionysos and Orpheus (at other times Osiris and Hades and Satan) but the underworld god is always a symbol of resurrection, of the renewal of life.

5. **morbid** *Morbido* (Italian) means 'soft, tender'; L. also has in mind *morboso*, 'sensitive', and *morbo*, 'disease'.

25–6. **Orphic . . . Dionysos of the Underworld** The ancient Orphic cult believed in the immortality of the soul and elaborated a mythology with, variously, Dionysos or Orpheus as the central figure. In Greek mythology Dionysos was the god of wine and in Thrace his cult became synonymous with excess and wild abandon, but to other sects he was lord of souls in the underworld. Orpheus, a great musician, went down into the underworld to bring back his wife Eurydice. Hades agreed on condition that he should not look back before reaching the upper world. Traditionally, he does not resist the temptation and Eurydice's last cry as she fades away is *Iamque vale*, 'And now farewell'.

42–3 **ego sum . . . sono io** I am (Latin . . . Italian). Also a cry of praise to the god, an assertion of Dionysian life-force in the self.

Grapes (p. 88). L.'s rejection of the world of Christianity, of the intellectual consciousness, for the dark sensuality of the ancient Mediterranean world and its deities, especially Bacchus, originally another name for Dionysos (on Attic vases Dionysos is represented with vines and a drinking-horn).

1–2 **rose of all roses** See Yeats's '*Rose of all Roses, Rose of all the World!*' and 'The Rose of Battle', *Collected Poems* (1978), p. 42.
41. **God was all negroid** See note on 'Tropic'.
64. **fern-seed** Fern-seed conveys invisibility and the power to pass unseen into other worlds.

TREES

Here symbols of indestructibility and continuity, heralding new life and new blossoms out of winter and, by association, change and renewal in human civilisations.

Cypresses (p. 91). The cypresses are symbols of a more integrated consciousness and life-awareness which L. believed the civilisations of the ancient world possessed but which modern man has lost. It was a notion he developed more fully in the following year, 1921, when he wrote his foreword to *F*: 'the great pagan world . . . had a vast and perhaps perfect science of its own, a science in terms of life.' Civilisations such as the Etruscan (the earliest historical occupants of the area approximating to Tuscany in modern Italy) still treasure the fragments of that knowledge, once common throughout humanity, and 'taught the old wisdom, only in its half-forgotten, symbolic forms'. But modern man has lost this knowledge – 'tongues are dead and words are hollow' – and western civilisations, whether Roman or American, in destroying older cultures have crushed 'the delicate magic of life'. The modern world, L. argued, urgently needs to regain this lost sense of unison and living wholeness. For L.'s thoughts on this notion see especially *AR* ch. xix and Nehls ii. 49–50.

35. **Whom Rome called vicious.** The Etruscans formed a confederation of politically independent city-states and were Rome's principal early rivals for the hegemony of central Italy. They were at the height of their power *c.* 500 BC but were finally conquered and absorbed by the Romans. L.'s fascination with their culture is recorded in *Etruscan Places* where in the opening pages he writes: 'Besides, the Etruscans were vicious. We know it, because their enemies and exterminators said so. Just as we know the unspeakable depths of *our* enemies in the late war. Who isn't vicious to his enemy? . . . those pure, clean-living, sweet-souled Romans, who smashed nation after nation and crushed the free soul in people after people . . . they said the Etruscans were vicious.'

51. **Leonardo** da Vinci (1452–1519) whose famous portrait of Mona Lisa Pater described as 'older than the rocks among which she sits'.

76. **Montezuma** The Aztec priest-king (1466–1520) of Mexico killed at the time of the Spanish Conquest led by Cortez. In his essay 'The Spirit of Place', L. writes of the Spaniards' 'passion to destroy or mutilate life at its very quick, lusting in their dark power to annihilate all living impulses, both their own and their neighbour . . .' (*SM* 25). See also *SM* 23 on Montezuma.

Bare Almond-Trees (p. 93). Many of the prose writings of this period and the poems condemn the civilisation that produced the First World War but they are equally statements of L.'s belief in man's ability to emerge from that destruction. 'At present there is a vast myriad-branched human engine, the very thought of which is death. But in the winter even a tree looks like iron. Seeing the great trunk of dark iron and the swaying steel flails of boughs, we cannot help being afraid. What we see of buds looks like sharp bronze stud-points. The whole thing hums elastic and sinister and fatally metallic, like some confused scourge of swinging steel thongs. Yet the lovely cloud of green and summer lustre is within it . . . It only wants the miracle, the new, soft, creative wind: which does not blow yet. Meanwhile we can only stand and wait, knowing that what is, is not.' (*SM* 30–1). See also the opening pages of *Sea and Sardinia*.

Tropic (p. 94). In his essays 'The Spirit of Place' and 'The Two Principles' L. argued that every 'locality expresses itself perfectly, in its own flowers, its own birds and beasts, lastly its own men, with their perfected works' (*SM* 30) and that there exists 'a subtle and complex sympathy, correspondence between the plasm of the human body . . . and the material elements outside . . . the circumambient cosmos' (*PII* 227). He was fond of drawing a distinction between the northern consciousness of the white races – 'the milk of northern spume' – and the 'flood of black heat' in the dark races. Cf. *WIL*: 'The white races, having the arctic north behind them . . . the West Africans . . . had been fulfilled in sun-destruction' (ch. xix 'Moony'). In *Letters* iii. 538 he writes: 'We went to Malta, and it was so hot I feel quite stunned. I shouldn't wonder if my skin went black and my eyes went yellow, like a negro's. The south is so different from the north.' See also *Letters* ii. 520 (written in 1916 from Cornwall): '. . . there is left some of the old sensuousness of the darkness, a sort of softness, a sort of flowing together in physical intimacy, something almost negroid, which is fascinating.'

FLOWERS

Almond Blossom (p. 95). See note on 'Bare Almond-Trees'.

47–50. **Gethsemane . . . the Cross** Matthew xxvi. 36 ff. Christ's night of vigil and prayer in the garden of Gethsemane before his arrest and crucifixion. By extension, consciousness or knowledge of death. The lines explore the dual consciousness of man, the intuitional and the intellectual selves, a kind of crucifixion which must be transcended: 'The Cross sprouting its superb and fearless flowers'. Cf. L.'s essay 'Resurrection': 'The Cross has taken root again, and is putting forth buds. Its branches sprout out where the nails went in, there is a tuft of sprouts like tongues of flame at the top, where the inscription was.' (*P* 738).

Sicilian Cyclamens (p. 98). The dawn of human consciousness, the 'Mediterranean morning, when our world began' and grew into the wonder of Greek civilisation which produced the Parthenon temple and its marble sculptures by Phidias on the Athenian Acropolis (*c.* 447–432 BC) and the Erechtheum (*c.* 421–407 BC) with its wonderful friezes of marble and the famous porch of the maidens.

THE EVANGELISTIC BEASTS

The four beasts of the Apocalypse (Revelation vi–viii) became associated with the evangelistic writers – Matthew, Mark, Luke and John. These four poems voice L.'s criticism of Christian idealism and its emphasis on the spiritual which he saw as life-denying. For L. the division between body and spirit, the flesh and the word, was a pernicious falsehood. He argued for the end of the dominance of the Logos, the Word, and the re-establishing of a balance between the spiritual and sensual planes of existence that Greece, Rome and Christianity, with their emphasis on the spirit and mind, had destroyed. Only by such re-integration, he felt, could man attain inner harmony and a sense of living connection with the greater universe; only by recognising and transcending his own duality could man achieve that living wholeness which is the aim of human existence. L. argued that this creation of the self, this realising of human potential, was in itself an act of true reverence: 'the only form of worship is *to be*' (*SM* 137). Thus 'St Matthew' reminds us that man is a creature of the flesh as well as the spirit and both aspects must be nourished; the lion of 'St Mark' has denied his lion nature and diminished into a mere sheep-dog; the bull of 'St Luke' will explode into violence after two thousand years of suppression – 'the bull of the proletariat has got his head down' – and the eagle of 'St John', emblem of the Logos, now sits shabby and moulting, waiting for a new era when it can rise phoenix-like from the ashes of an outworn doctrine. See L. on the 'Four Evangels' in 'The Two Principles' (*P II* 233) and *A* (ch. i & ii).

St Matthew (p. 101).

4. **'And I . . . me'** John xii. 32. 'And I, if I be lifted up from the earth, will draw all men with me.'
8. **Filius Meus** Matthew iii. 17. 'And lo a voice from heaven, saying, This is my beloved Son, in whom I am well pleased.'
11. **Paraclete** advocate, intercessor as applied to Christ (1 John ii. 1); also the Holy Ghost (John xiv. 26).
53. *ΙΧΘΥΣ* In Christian art and literature the fish is the symbol of Christ. Its origin is obscure but may be derived from the acrostic ('Jesus Christ, Son of God, Saviour') which forms the Greek word for fish. See also L.'s essay 'The Proper Study'.
81. **a lark . . . singing** Cf. Shakespeare Sonnet 29: 'Like to the lark at break of day arising/From sullen earth sings hymns at heaven's gate.'

St Mark (p. 104).

4–6. **lion . . . Venice . . . Daniele Manin** The winged lion of St Mark, patron saint of Venice. Daniele Manin (1804–57), Venetian patriot who defended Venice against the Austrian army in 1849, and whose statue is in the Campo Manin with a winged lion at his feet.
32–3 **'Guard . . . morning'** Possibly a conflation of John xxi. 16 'Guard my sheep' and Psalm 139 'I take the wings of the morning'.
36. **Carpaccio** The Venetian painter (d. 1526) whose famous painting of the Lion of St Mark hangs in the Ducal Palace in Venice. But see also the delightful little woolly white dog in his painting of St Augustine in his study.

St Luke (p. 106).

9–11. **The golden horns of power . . . Moses had** Owing to an error in translation Moses is conventionally represented with horns. In Exodus xxiv. 29–30 when Moses came down from Mount Sinai 'the skin of his face shone'. The Hebrew for this 'shining' may be translated as 'sent forth *beams*' or 'sent forth *horns*' and the Vulgate took the latter as correct.
14. **Assyrian–wise** The man-headed, winged bulls of Assyrian sculpture.

St John (p. 108).

12–14. **'In the beginning . . . God'** John i. 1 '. . . Word was with God. And the word was God.' See also Revelation xix. 13.
43. **Patmos** St John of the island of Patmos is the author of the Book of Revelation, not to be confused with St John the Evangel of the Gospels. See *A* ch. iii.

CREATURES

The Mosquito (p. 112).

9. **Winged Victory** The marble statue of the Winged Nike or Victory of Samothrace (*c.* 200 BC) now in the Louvre, Paris.

Fish (p. 114).

37. **What price . . . bread upon the waters?** What do you think of? (slang) . . . See Ecclesiastes xi. 1.
61–2. **Quelle Joie de vivre/Dans l'eau!** What joy of living in the water! (French).
95. **Zeller lake** The poem was written at Zell-am-See in the Alps above Salzburg in the summer of 1921.
171. **Jesus . . . the Fish** See 'The Proper Study': 'The sea is a cosmic element, and the relation between the sea and the human psyche is impersonal and elemental'. L. explains that Jesus was called 'the Fish' because he had 'the other consciousness of the ocean which is the divine End of us all'. Men would be 'like fishes on a great wave of the God of the End, swimming together, and apart, in a new medium. A new relation, a new whole' (*P* 719–23). See note on 'St Matthew'. Cf. also *SCAL* 170.

Bat (p. 120).

6. **Ponte Vecchio** 'The Old Bridge', perhaps the most famous in Florence, lined with shops and houses. The present bridge dates from the mid-fourteenth century.
34. **Pipistrello** Bat (Italian).

Man and Bat (p. 121).

4. **Via de' Bardi** L. wrote the poem while staying at 32 Via dei Bardi, Florence, in August 1921 while on his way back to Sicily.
124. **a sghembo** erratically, tortuously (Italian).

REPTILES

Snake (p. 128). The poem's central image relies on several biblical and classical allusions – the snake in the Garden of Eden, the serpent of eternity, the snake as the ancient Mediterranean symbol for the underworld powers, emissary of the Chthonian deities (associated with both fertility and death). See also 'The Crown': 'The snake is the spirit of the great corruptive principle, the festering cold of the marsh. This is how he seems, as we look back. We revolt from him, but we share the same life and tide of life as he. He struggles as we struggle, he enjoys the sun, he comes to the water to drink, he curls up, hides himself to sleep. And under the low skies of the far past aeons, he emerged a king out of chaos, a long beam of new life.' (*PII* 407).

66. **the albatross** See Coleridge's (1772–1834) 'Rime of the Ancient Mariner' (1798) where the mariner sins against the natural order by wantonly shooting the albatross, creature of God.

TORTOISES

Baby Tortoise (p. 131).

55–9. **Ulysses . . . Titan** The baby tortoise is symbolic of life asserting itself against the vastness of the universe and, by extension, of humanity's adventure into the unknown: Greek Ulysses sailing for the horizon 'Over the edge of all things'; the immortal Titans, offspring of heaven and earth, the earliest master-craftsmen. Cf. 'The Odyssey of Homer is the story of the unfolding of the pristine soul of a race, in the potency and wonder of the surrounding unknown, until it consummates and perfects itself like a flower in spring' (*SM* 94).
57. **Buon viaggio** Italian for 'Bon voyage'.

Tortoise Shell (p. 133). The most lucid commentary on the number and cross symbolism in this poem is 'The Two Principles' where L. expands the dualistic vision of the cosmos which he had discussed in 'The Crown' and which derives from the pre-Socratic philosopher Heraclitos (*c.* 500 BC) whose writings he knew from Burnet. The cosmos is dual and all things exist by virtue of their opposition, in a ceaseless conflict of opposites, but beyond this the creative mystery is also fourfold: 'All creation depends on the fourfold activity. And on this root of four is all law and understanding established. Following the perception of these supreme truths, the Pythagoreans made their philosophy, asserting that all is number, and seeking to search out the mystery of the roots of three, four, five, seven, stable throughout all the universe, in a chain of developing phenomena. But our science of mathematics still waits for its fulfilment, its union with life itself. For the truths of mathematics are only the skeleton fabric of the living universe' (*P* 233).

1. **The Cross** The fourfold cruciform shape is both a symbol of creation and of the coming together of body and spirit in unison. 'If we conceive of the first division in Chaos . . . as being perpendicular, the inexplicable division into the first duality, then this next division, when the line of the firmament is drawn, we can consider as horizontal: thus

we have the ⊕, the elements of the Rosy Cross, and the first enclosed appearance of that tremendous symbol, which has dominated our era, the Cross itself' (*P* 228).

19. **Pythagoras** Credited with discovering numerical ratios and the principal intervals of the musical scale, Pythagoras (fl. *c.* 530 BC) interpreted the world through numbers. Burnet writes that he 'used to give the number of all sorts of things, such as horses and men, and . . . he demonstrated these by arranging pebbles in a certain way' (Burnet, 102).

22. **the Judean Lord** Christ.

28. **volte face** about face (Italian).

Tortoise Family Connections (p. 135).

13. **'Woman . . . thee?'** John ii. 4.

45. **Basta** Enough (Italian).

Lui et Elle (p. 137). He and She (French).

74. **Osiris** In Egyptian mythology, the god of the underworld whose son Horus was the god of renewed life (the Greeks equated Osiris with Dionysos). Osiris was dismembered by his evil brother deity Set, but his wife, Isis, gathered together all the pieces and Osiris was restored to life.

94. **Mère Tortue** Mother tortoise (French).

Tortoise Shout (p. 142).

9. **crucified into sex** Cf. 'On Being a Man' where L. writes that marriage 'is the invariable crucifixion. The Cross, as we know, stands for the body, for the dark self which lives in the body. And on the Cross of this bodily self is crucified the self which I know I am, my so-called *real* self. The Cross, as an ancient symbol, has an inevitably phallic reference. But it is far deeper than sex. It is the self which darkly inhabits our blood and bone, and for which the ithyphallus is but a symbol . . . and on this cross of division in the whole self is crucified the Christ. We are all crucified on it' (*P II* 619).

42. **Pentecost** The Greek name given to the Jewish harvest festival, the Feast of Weeks, so called because it fell on the fiftieth day after Passover. Because the Holy Ghost also descended on the Apostles on this day (Acts ii. 1–4) the Christian Church used the name to celebrate this event, popularly called Whitsunday.

85. **Christ . . . Osiris cry** See note above on Osiris. Also, Christ's last cry '*Consummatum est*' – it is finished or accomplished. The references symbolise the violation of the self or the abandoning of the self in the sexual act in order to achieve a new wholeness.

BIRDS

Turkey-Cock (p. 146).

61. **drum of Huichilobos** Possibly Huitailopochtli, the Aztec wargod and god of the sun, fire and sacrifices who is said to have led the Aztecs to the site of Mexico City. See *The Plumed Serpent*.
89. **Dross-jabot** A frill formerly worn by men in the front or bosom of the shirt edging the opening (OED).

Humming-Bird (p. 149). Cf. L.'s essay 'Hector St John de Crevecoeur' in *SM* 63–5.

The Blue Jay (p. 149).

12. **What voice . . . smoke?** See Exodus iii. 2 where God speaks to Moses from the burning bush, but also 'If we look for God, let us look in the bush where he sings. That is, in living creatures' (*P* 708). See also *SM*: 'The religious truth is the same now as it has ever been . . . that the universe is a bush which burns for ever with the Presence, consuming itself and yet never consumed' (38).

ANIMALS

The Ass (p. 151). Cf. *Sea and Sardinia* (ch. i): 'Cocks crowing and the long, howling, hiccupping, melancholy bray of an ass. "All females are dead, all females – och! och! och! – hoooo! Ahaaa! – there's one left." So he ends on a moaning grunt of consolation. This is what the Arabs tell us an ass is howling when he brays.' L.'s contrast in this poem between the wild ass and the domestic donkey is paralleled to the conflict between the body and spirit of Christian doctrine.

32. **noli me tangere** Touch me not (Latin). See John xx. 17.
48. **Triumphant Entry** Christ's entry into Jerusalem on the back of an ass. See Matthew xxi. 7; John xii. 4.
60. **Gorgon's head** Medusa, a terrible monster in Greek mythology, whose eyes turned people to stone.

He-Goat (p. 154).

15 **sierra roqueña** Rocky mountain range (Spanish).

She-Goat (p. 157).

12. – **Tace, tu, crapa, bestia** Shut up, you she-goat, you animal! (Italian). The editors of *COMP* point out that '*crapa* is Sicilian dialect for *capra* by metathesis' (1004).
24. **bête** Stupid (French).
27. **Le bestie non parlano, poverine** The beasts can't speak, poor things (Italian).

34. **God the Father . . . Blake** A reference to Blake's painting 'The Ancient of Days' where God the Creator is portrayed with flowing hair and beard.

Mountain Lion (p. 162).

16–17. **Qué tien, amigo? León** What are you carrying, friend? Lion (Spanish). The context of the poem however suggests this should be *leona*, lioness.
31. **Hermoso es** Beautiful.
44–6. **room . . . miss them** Cf. Birkin in *WIL* (ch. xi): 'You yourself, don't you find it a beautiful clean thought, a world empty of people, just uninterrupted grass, and a hare sitting up?'

The Red Wolf (p. 164). Cf. 'Indians and an Englishman': 'The soul is as old as the oldest day, and has its own hushed echoes, its own far-off tribal understandings sunk and incorporated. We do not need to live the past over again. Our darkest tissues are twisted in this old tribal experience, our warmest blood came out of the old tribal fire. And they vibrate still in answer, our blood, our tissue. But me, the conscious me, I have gone a long road since then . . . I don't want to go back to them . . . I don't want to live again the tribal mysteries my blood has lived long since . . . I have a dark-faced, bronze-voiced father far back in the resinous ages . . . And I have not forgotten him. But he, like many an old father with a changeling son, he would like to deny me. But I stand on the far edge of their firelight, and am neither denied nor accepted. My way is my own, old red father; I can't cluster at the drum any more' (*P* 99). See also *Mornings in Mexico*.

GHOSTS

Autumn at Taos (p. 167).

13. **golden hawk of Horus** In Egyptian mythology, the hawk was the emblem of the god Horus, son of Osiris and Isis.

PANSIES

L. wrote *Pansies* in November and December 1928 when he was in Bandol, France. 'He would write them in bed in the mornings . . . There was something perky and birdlike about him thus, and he was intensely happy and proud of the *Pansies*; he would read out the newest ones with delight, accentuating the wicked sharp little pecks in them. He little thought of the ridiculous heavy-handed official interference these vivid little lizards of poems were about to endure. Yet in the end they emerged triumphant, with their tails up' (Nehls iii. 274). After the typescript of *Pansies* was seized by the postal authorities – 'Scotland Yard seized the

MS in the post' (Moore 1006) – L. revised and retyped them in February 1929 and they were published by L.'s English publisher Martin Secker in July 1929. Secker omitted fourteen of the poems however (see Roberts) and L. arranged for a privately printed, unexpurgated edition to be published in London in August 1929. The poems in this selection were first published in the two first editions with the exception of the following which appeared in the *Dial* for July 1929: 'When I Went to the Circus', 'Things Men Have Made', 'Whatever Man Makes', 'Sea-Weed' and 'Lizard'. For a general discussion of the manuscript sources of *Pansies* and the subject matter of these poems see note below on 'Last Poems'.

Leda (p. 174). In Greek mythology, daughter of the king of Aetolia, wife to Tyndareus and mother of the Dioscuri (the twins Castor and Pollux, the Gemini) and Helen. Zeus approached her in the shape of a swan and begat Helen and Pollux; Castor was begotten by Tyndareus the same night. For L. the swan was a symbol for new vitality; he painted this subject himself and was familiar with Michelangelo's 'Leda and the Swan' (1530: however, this painting has only survived in copies). In 'The Crown' L. writes: 'The spirit of destruction is divine, when it breaks the ego and opens the soul to the wide heavens. In corruption there is divinity . . . the swan is one of the symbols of divine corruption . . . when Leonardo and Michael Angelo represent Leda in the embrace of the swan, they are painting mankind in the clasp of the divine flux of corruption, the singing death' (*P II* 402–3).

Elemental (p. 187). The four original elements were thought to be Earth, Air, Fire and Water. L. uses this myth symbolically in many of his essays and poems – see especially 'The Two Principles' and his poem 'The Four' in 'Last Poems' – to articulate his belief that 'life depends on duality and polarity' (*SM* 186), and that in mankind there is a division between the spiritual and sensual being which needs to be overcome. The 'elements' need to be brought into a more delicate harmony. Cf. *A*: 'With Empedocles in the fifth century the Four of Fire, Earth, Air and Water established themselves in the imagination of men for ever, the four *living* or cosmic elements, the radical elements . . . the four cosmic roots of all existence' (134).

Dies Irae (p. 188) and *Dies Illa* (p. 189). 'The Day of Wrath', the opening words of the greatest of medieval Latin hymns attributed to Thomas of Celano (fl. *c.* 1225).

Democracy (p. 192). Cf. L.'s essays 'Aristocracy', 'Blessed are the Powerful', 'Democracy' and 'Return to Bestwood'. In *SM* he writes: 'Every man knows that intrinsically men are not equal' (84) and in his last book *A*: 'Mankind falls forever into the two divisions of aristocrat and democrat . . . We are speaking now not of political parties, but of the two sorts of human nature: those that feel themselves strong in their souls and those that feel themselves weak' (65). See also note on 'Last Poems'.

14. **Tiberius** (42 BC–AD 37) Roman emperor (AD 14–37) infamous for his debaucheries and atrocities against the people, though recent historical scholarship has cast doubts on the authenticity of these stories.

NETTLES

These poems were written in July and August 1929, principally in response to the censorship difficulties with *Pansies* and the confiscation of L.'s paintings from the Warren Gallery, London: 'I've done some nice stinging nettles, and let's hope they'll sting the arses of all the Meads and Persians of slimy London' (Moore 1174). He prepared *Nettles* for publication in December 1929 – 'I am getting the *Nettles* ready' (Moore 1220) – and the volume was published posthumously by Faber on 13 March 1930.

Innocent England (p. 197).

7. **virginal, pure policemen** The six police officers who raided the Warren Gallery on 5 July 1929 and carried off a number of L.'s pictures. See Moore 394 and Nehls iii. 326 ff.
11. **Mr Mead** Frederick Mead (1847–1945) the 82-year old London magistrate who presided over the impounding of L.'s pictures and before whom the case was brought on 8 August 1929. See Nehls iii. 381–7; Moore 413–14.
19. **cache sexe** Something which conceals the sexual organs (French).

Modern Prayer (p. 198).

1. **Mammon** The Aramaic word for 'riches', occurring in the Greek text of Matthew vi. 24 – 'Ye cannot serve God and mammon' – and Luke xvi. 9–13. The word was taken by medieval writers as the name of the false god of greed and covetousness. See also Milton, *Paradise Lost* Book 1, ll 678–92. Cf. Mellors in *LCL*: 'Mammon: which I think, after all, is only the mass-will of people, wanting money and hating life' (ch. xix).

Leaves of Grass, Flowers of Grass (p. 198). The reference is to Walt Whitman's (1819–92) *Leaves of Grass* (1855). In Chant 6 a child comes to the poet holding a bunch of grass, the central image of the poem:

> 'A Child said, What is grass? fetching it to me with full hands.
> How could I answer the child? . . . I do not know what it is
>   any more than he.'

The grass symbolises both the miracle of continuing life in the world of nature and the divinity which suffuses human kind, a theme that is to become increasingly important in L.'s 'Last Poems'. But see also L.'s disagreement with Whitman's ideas on democracy and equality: 'All men must be mown level with the grass, because most men, the average, are leaves of grass, and therefore it would be impertinent and arrogant to rise above the grass. So we mow life down' (*SM* 85).

LAST POEMS

In his introduction to the *Last Poems* (1932), Richard Aldington points out that the draft manuscript material for some of the later *Pansies* poems (which were subsequently extensively revised and retyped for publication) and most of the *Nettles* poems come from one of two manuscript notebooks found among L.'s papers after his death. Aldington labelled these two notebooks MS A and MS B. The latter apparently had a page, now lost, bearing the date 23 Nov. 1928 and entitled *Pensées*. When he came to publish L.'s late poems, therefore, Aldington passed over the *Pansies* and *Nettles* poems which had already been published and divided the rest into two sections: the poems in MS B became 'More Pansies'; those in MS A 'Last Poems', and the two were published together in one volume, *Last Poems*. It seems that the composition of some of the late *Pansies* and *Nettles* poems, then, is intertwined with 'More Pansies' and perhaps some of the 'Last Poems', for it is likely that L. moved freely from one notebook to another when he was writing them. His friends the Brewsters recall: 'One afternoon we were with him and Frieda at Villa Beau Soleil, he began selecting some of his "*Nettles*" for a small volume. There were to be others called "Dead Nettles", because they were to have no sting in them. He turned the pages of his notebook, adding that he had been writing some verses about death and would read them; then, shaking his head wistfully, he closed the book, saying, "I can't read them now"' (Nehls iii. 421). Although Aldington's division of the late poems into 'More Pansies' and 'Last Poems' is understandable, it is arbitrary given that their composition was interwoven. The present selection simply groups all the final poems together under one heading, 'Last Poems', with the MS B poems first and the MS A poems on death second. Aldington's edition sought to reproduce L.'s final writings faithfully, but it is an inaccurate text notwithstanding. The editor and printer misread words and in places unaccountably omitted whole lines and all subsequent editions have perpetuated these errors. The present selection is based on the two manuscript notebooks of the poems in the Harry Ransom Humanities Research Center collection and is the first to reproduce the poems accurately, as L. wrote them.

The 'Last Poems', then, written in the concluding months of L.'s life, represent a final attempt to convey his vision of man and the universe to posterity. They span the entire range of his thought on the nature of God and man, religion, myth, art, civilisation, politics. Like his last book, *A*, they are both a vigorous criticism of our technological and materialistic age and also a symbolic blueprint for humanity's future regeneration. In this last year of his life L. returned with renewed urgency to his condemnation of western civilisation and to the fundamental question that had always seemed to him to face humanity in every age: 'How shall Man put himself into relation with God, into a living relation?' (*P* 726–7). In our era, he felt, 'the long light of Christianity is guttering to go out and we have to get at new sources in ourselves' (*PII* 628). His late writings, and his re-reading of Burnet's *Early Greek Philosophy* and Gilbert Murray's *Five Stages of Greek Religion* which influenced them, were a renewed search for the archetypal myths and symbols which would help humanity find those 'new sources'. Above all, the crucial question for him was always how to come into living contact with the unknown, how to live to the fullest of one's capacity. He believed that this could be achieved not through specific political doctrines or religious creeds, but by awakening 'the religious element inherent in all life . . . the sense of wonder' (*PII* 599).

As the poems, fiction and essays show, L. condemned what he saw as the failure of Christian and democratic ideals in western civilisation. Like Nietzsche before him, he criticised Christianity's emphasis on renunciation, love and equality because he felt they denied individual potential and ignored the deep impulse to power in mankind. Poems like 'Democracy is Service', 'Retort to Whitman', 'Commandments' and 'Retort to Jesus' point to the falsity of Christian and democratic doctrines on love and equality, for man is a highly complex creature driven by the impulse to achieve power as well as to love, with a fundamental need 'to get a living balance between his nature of power and his nature of love, without denying either' (*A* 163). In *A* he defined these two modes as the collective power mode and the individual love mode and argued that in denying the power mode and focusing only on love, Christ inevitably relinquished power to the mediocre, the second-rate: 'Mankind falls forever into the two divisions of aristocrat and democrat . . . we are speaking now not of political parties, but of the two sorts of human nature: those that feel themselves strong in their souls and those that feel themselves weak' (*A* 65). The aristocrat is he who can put humanity in touch with the cosmos, who can interfuse the earthly and the spiritual for the enrichment of the self. A poem like 'Worship' expresses this sense of divinity informing humanity:

> And worship is the joy of the gleam from the eyes of the gods
> and the robot is denial of the same,
> even the denial that there *is* any gleam.

It is a belief strikingly similar to Blake's: 'The Worship of God is: Honouring his gifts in other men, each according to his genius, and loving the greatest men best. Those who envy or calumniate great men, hate God; for there is no other God' (*The Marriage of Heaven and Hell*, plates 22–4). L.'s distinction between aristocrat and democrat, however, has no overtones of what we nowadays loosely term fascism. He detested all forms of political authoritarianism 'whether it represent one man . . . or a whole mass of people, a Demos' (*P* 381) which deny or seek to limit the freedom of the individual. Essentially, his view of man is not political at all but spiritual, based on the undeniable differences that do exist between human beings: 'Your democracy is an absolute lie' says Birkin in *WIL*. 'One man isn't any better than another, not because they are equal, but because they are intrinsically *other*, that there is no term of comparison. The minute you begin to compare, one man is seen to be far better than another, all the inequality you can imagine is there by nature' (ch. viii). What humanity must achieve is a state where each individual can fully realise his own potential and recognise it in others (see *A* 164–8).

Throughout his life as an artist, L. explored some of the ways in which humanity might achieve this. And he came to see that central to human consciousness and endeavour is the activity of the imagination, that creative functioning of the mind which awakens us, which puts us in touch with the universe around. L. called it 'the poetic intelligence' (*A* 49) and argued that any expansion of that awareness was, in the deepest sense, a religious act, for humanity can only attain a sense of living connection and wholeness through the cultivation of imaginative and spiritual values. Through the act of imagining reality, then, the psyche can create those moments of intuitive understanding that are its closest approach to that unknown power which informs the universe and which all cultures and times have seen as divine. These notions are of course a development of ideas L. had suggested earlier in his writings, but they find their final and most complete expression in the poems and essays of 1929. In his review of Eric Gill's *Art Nonsense and other Essays*, written in February 1930 only days before his death, L. spoke of such moments of imaginative integration and awakening as 'the state of absorption into the creative spirit, which is God' (*P* 395). These last poems are that spirit made manifest.

There are Too Many People (p. 203). Cf. Birkin in *WIL* (ch. viii) and the opening paragraph of L.'s story 'The Man Who Loved Islands' (1926).

Future Relationships, Future Religion, Future States, Future War (pp. 205–6). Cf. Mellors in *LCL*('I stand for the touch of bodily awareness between human beings . . . and the touch of tenderness' (ch. xviii).

Non-Existence and *All-Knowing* (p. 206). Cf. *SM*: 'The quick and issue of our being stands previous to any control, prior to all knowledge. The centre of creative mystery is primal and central in every man, but in each man it is unique and incommutable . . . When we know that the unique, incommutable creative mystery of the Self is within us and precedes us, then we shall be able to take our full being from this mystery. We shall at last learn the pure lesson of knowing not-to-know' (49).

Lucifer (p. 206). Lucifer, 'Bringer of Light', the greatest of the fallen archangels. See a second version of this poem below and note on 'When Satan Fell'.

1. **Angels . . . fell** *Macbeth* IV, iii. 22.

Fallen Leaves (p. 206).

4. **mills of God** An echo of Friedrich von Logau (1604–55) *Sinngedichte* (transl. Henry Wadsworth Longfellow): 'Though the mills of God grind slowly, yet they grind exceeding small.' Cf. 'Leaves of Grass, Flowers of Grass' above.

Forte Dei Marmi (p. 211). L. had visited this holiday resort on the Ligurian coast, Italy, with Aldous Huxley in June 1927 and again in July 1929: 'beastly as a place; flat, dead sea, jellyfishy, and millions of villas' (Moore 406).

Dark Satanic Mills (p. 212). Blake's 'Preface' to *Milton*: 'And was Jerusalem builded here/Among these dark Satanic mills?'

15. **Retro me, Satanas** Get thee behind me, Satan (Latin). See Matthew xvi. 23.
22. **What is man . . . him?** See Psalms viii. 4.

We Die Together (p. 212).

16. **'Il Signore'** Sir (Italian).
18. **the Black Country** The heart of the English industrial Midlands.

Oh Wonderful Machine! (p. 215).

7. **Nirvana** In Buddhist doctrine, the attainment of enlightenment, the cessation of the self as a personality and the absorption into the supreme spirit.

Love Thy Neighbour (p. 215). Matthew vi. 43. Cf. *A*: 'To love your neighbour as yourself means loving him, not as an individual, because he isn't one, but as a fragment of an unformed whole: and then trying to bring to life the organic "whole", which is nation or community or state, wherein the individual fragment can feel itself fulfilled. It needs love and power both, in perpetual interplay' (147).

4. **cachinnate** To laugh loudly or immoderately (OED).

Worship (p. 218). See general note on 'Last Poems'.

Name the Gods! (p. 220). L. found the pre-Socratic vision of the cosmos – 'All things are full of Gods' (Thales, cited in Burnet 48) – naturally congenial and the notion informs many of these late poems. See especially notes on 'All Sorts of Gods', 'For a Moment' and 'God is Born' below.

11. **Priapus** In Greek mythology a god of fertility whose symbol was the phallus.

Retort to Whitman (p. 221). In his essay on Whitman (*SM* 258), L. quotes the American poet: 'And whoever walks a furlong without sympathy/walks to his own funeral, dressed in his [own] shroud.' Though he admired his poetry, L. came to disagree emphatically with Whitman's ideas on equality and democracy. See his chapter on Whitman in *SCAL* and his essay 'Democracy' where he rejects Whitman's notions as a pernicious denial of the intrinsic uniqueness and otherness of each individual: 'So the Whitman One Identity, the *En-Masse*, is a horrible nullification of true identity and being' (*P* 709).

Race and Battle (p. 222). Ecclesiastes ix. 9: 'I returned, and saw under the sun, that the race *is* not to the swift, nor the battle to the strong.'

Terra Incognita (p. 224). The unknown land (Latin).

16. **Know Thyself** The inscription on the temple of Apollo at Delphi. See 'The Proper Study' (*P* 719–23) and 'On Being a Man' (*PII* 616–22).

All Sorts of Gods (p. 224). Cf. 'The gods are only ourselves, as we are in our moments of pure manifestation' (*COMP* 673) and Whitman's 'In the faces of men and women I see God, and in my own face in the glass' (*Leaves of Grass* i., 1278). Cf. also Blake: 'All deities reside in the human breast' (*The Marriage of Heaven and Hell*, plate 11).

6. **Buddha . . . Ra** 'The Enlightened One', title given to the great religious teacher Gautama (also known as Sakyamuni and Siddhartha) who flourished in n. India in the fifth century BC. In ancient Egyptian mythology Ra was the sun-god and supreme deity, often equated with Horus whose emblem is the hawk.

For a Moment (p. 225). See note on 'All Sorts of Gods'. Hyacinthus was a pre-Hellenic god, but in later Greek mythology he was a beautiful boy whom the god Apollo loved. He was accidentally killed by a discus and from his spilt blood sprang the hyacinth. Io, a priestess of Hera, was loved by the god Zeus who turned her into a heifer to conceal her from his jealous wife. Among Io's descendents was Danaus (not Danäe as L. incorrectly says). The goddess Isis was the wife of Osiris in Egyptian mythology but in later centuries she became Hellenised and identified with many other Mediterranean goddesses. The Centaurs, part-horse and part-human, were representative of wild life and animal desires but some of them, notably Chiron, were famous for their wisdom and great healing powers.

Thought (p. 226). The manuscript notebook contains a fragment after this poem which is not published in the *Last Poems* but is included in *COMP*:

> 'The gods are all things, and so are we.
> The gods are only ourselves, as we are in our moments of
> pure manifestation.'

Cf. 'The Spirit of Place', *SM* 19.

So Let Me Live (p. 226). Perhaps an echo of the opening phrase of 'Thanatopsis' (1817), a poem on death by the American poet William Cullen Bryant (1794–1878): 'So let me live . . .'

God is Born (p. 228). Cf. *A*: 'To the ancient consciousness, Matter, Materia, or Substantial things are God. A great rock is God. A pool of water is God . . . Then those things that move are doubly God. That is, we are doubly aware of their godhead: that which is, and that which moves: twice godly . . . the universe is a great complex activity of things existing and moving and having effect. And all this is God' (95). L. derived some of the ideas in this paragraph and in this cycle of poems from Murray's *Five Stages of Greek Religion*: 'We must notice the instinctive language of the poets, using the word *Θεός* in many subtle senses for which our word "God" is too stiff, too personal, and too anthropomorphic' (see 27 ff.).

The Argonauts (p. 230). The human adventure into the unknown is here symbolised by the references to the Argonauts and Odysseus. One of the oldest Greek myths tells the story of Jason's quest for the golden fleece. His ship was called the 'Argo' and hence his followers were the Argonauts. Odysseus, the Greek hero, wandered the seas for ten years after the end of the Trojan war.

10. **pain grillé** Toasted bread (French).

Middle of the World (p. 231). 'Do you remember that little round picture at the beginning of *Hesiod*, of Dionysos crossing the sea? . . . Dionysos in a ship with a white sail and the mast a tree with grapes, sailing over a golden sea, with dark, keen, joyful fish?' (*Letters* ii. 517). 'Dionysos Crossing the Sea' is the frontispiece to *Hesiod, the Homeric Hymns and Homerica*, transl. H. G. Evelyn-White (1915) which L. read in January 1916. See also letter dated 4 October 1929: 'I still love the Mediterranean, it still seems young as Odysseus, in the morning . . . When the morning comes, and the sea runs silvery and the distant islands are delicate and clear, then I feel again, only man is vile' (Moore 1205–6).

8–17. **Cnossos . . . Minoan Gods . . . Gods of Tiryns** Minoan denotes the Bronze age civilisation of Crete whose capital in this period was Cnossos. Tiryns, in the Argive plain, became an important Greek city in the Bronze age.

For the Heroes are Dipped in Scarlet (p. 231). Red symbolises life and vitality – 'It was the colour of glory' (*A* 128). In *Etruscan Places* L. writes: 'There you have the ancient idea of kings, kings who are gods by vividness, because they have gathered into themselves core after core of vital potency from the universe, till they are clothed in scarlet, they are bodily a piece of the deepest fire . . . They are the vivid key to life, the vermilion clue to the mystery and the delight of death and life . . . scarlet royal as a piece of living life, pure vermilion' (ch. iii). See also *A* 128–9.

1. **Plato** (*c.* 427–348 BC) the great Athenian philosopher who became a pupil and devoted admirer of Socrates whose teachings he recorded in his *Dialogues*. L. had read Jowett's translation of the *Dialogues* (1871). Plato came to represent for him the beginning of western civilisation's emphasis on the division between mind and body and the cultivation of the former at the expense of the latter. He disagreed with Plato's doctrine of Forms or Ideas, i.e. that there are objective essences of universal realities which have a transcendental existence of their own, apart from particular, sensible things.
3. **Samson** In the OT (Judges xvi) the source of Samson's great strength was said to be his long hair, which his wife Delilah treacherously cut off, rendering him powerless before his enemies, the Philistines.

Demiurge (p. 232). 'Demiurge' meaning 'craftsman' was used of the Divine Being by Plato (see note above) in his account of the formation of the visible, material world.

[Religion] (p. 233). In the manuscript notebook these five lines, hitherto published as part of 'Demiurge', are actually separate and would appear to be an independent, though untitled, poem.

The Body of God (p. 234).

4. **Helen . . . Ninon:** Helen was the daughter of the God Zeus and Leda (see note on 'Leda'). In Homer's *Iliad* and *Odyssey* she is the wife of Menelaus whom Paris abducts for her beauty and carries off to Troy, precipitating the Trojan war. Ninon de Lenclos (1620–1705), Frenchwoman of legendary beauty and wit.

11. **demi-urge** See note on 'Demiurge'.

Maximus (p. 234). The Greatest One (Latin). Cf. 'All Sorts of Gods'.

11. **Hermes!** In Greek mythology the messenger or herald of the gods; also the guide of souls to the underworld.

The Man of Tyre (p. 235). Tyre was an important city on the Phoenician coast during Hellenistic and Roman times.

19. **Aphrodite** The Greek goddess of beauty and love whose name, according to Hesiod who tells of her emergence from the sea, means 'foam-born'.

They Say the Sea is Loveless (p. 236). See note on 'Middle of the World'.

Whales Weep Not! (p. 236). Cf. L.'s essay in *SCAL* on Hermann Melville's *Moby DICK*: 'There a sleek, pure calm reigns. There the females
swam in peace, and the young whales came snuffling tamely at the boat, like dogs. And there the astonished seamen watched the love-making of these amazing monsters, mammals, now in rut far down in the sea – . . . Some of the subtlest secrets of the seas seemed divulged to us in this enchanted pool. We saw young Leviathan amours in the deep. And thus, though surrounded by circle upon circle of consternation and affrights, did these inscrutable creatures at the centre freely and fearlessly indulge in all peaceful concernments; yea – serenely revelled in dalliance and delight –' (164).

19–28 **archangels . . . Cherubim . . . Seraphim** The three highest orders of angels.

32. **Aphrodite** See note on 'the Man of Tyre' above.

Invocation to the Moon (p. 237). The moon as symbol of the often corrosive and destructive feminine principle (see *TR* ch. xi and *WIL* ch. xix 'Moony') here takes on a different resonance. In *F* L. had written of his dualistic philosophy: 'There are two sheer dynamic principles in our universe, the sun-principle and the moon-principle' (ch. xiii). In *A* he defines these principles further, as the hot blood and the cool spirit, that which binds us to all created life and that by which we achieve our individuality and distinction: 'The sun, like a lion, loves the bright red blood of life, and can give infinite enrichment if we know how to receive it. But we don't. We have lost the sun . . . And we have lost the moon, the cool, bright, ever-varying moon. It is she who would caress our nerves, smooth them with the silky hand of her glowing, soothe them into serenity again with her cool presence. For the moon is the mistress and mother of our watery bodies, the pale body of our nervous consciousness and our moist flesh' (77). The moon also is an emblem of death, of not-being, as the sun is of life, so approaching death a man must make his peace with this aspect of his nature: 'Now I must enter your mansion, and by your gift Moon, O Moon, great lady.' L. likens this to a journey, leaving 'the golden house of the sun'. The 'six' are Venus 'of the twilight', the lion sun 'with golden paws' and the 'four great lords' are the planets Mercury, Mars, Jupiter and Saturn.

Butterfly (p. 238). See introduction to this volume p. 17.

Bavarian Gentians (p. 239). Written in Bavaria in September 1929, when Frieda recalled: 'We left the heat of Florence for the Tegersee . . . I remember some autumn nights when the end seemed to have come. I listened for his breath through the open door, all night long, an owl hooting ominously from the walnut trees outside. In the dim dawn an enormous bunch of gentians I had put on the floor by his bed seemed the only living thing in the room' (*Not I*, 213). As with many of the last poems on death and resurrection L. used ancient Mediterranean myths, here the familiar one of Persephone, daughter of Demeter, goddess of corn and harvests, who was abducted by Hades, god of the underworld (later conflated with Pluto, god of wealth). According to legend she must spend part of each year in the underworld (Dis) but may return to earth each spring. See Appendix I for other drafts of this poem. Cf. also Frieda's recollection of her early days with L. in May 1912: 'When Lawrence first found a gentian, a big single blue one, I remember feeling as if he had a strange communion with it, as if the gentian yielded up its blueness, its very essence, to him. Everything he met had the newness of a creation just that moment come into being' (*Not I*, 33).

Lucifer (p. 240). See note on the other version of this poem above and on 'When Satan Fell'.

In The Cities (p. 242).

13. **In Minos, in Mycenae** Minos, a king of Crete, but the name may also refer to a dynastic title. Mycenae, a city in the n.e. corner of the Argive plain, rose to power and splendour in the Bronze Age.

Lord's Prayer and *Mana of the Sea* (p. 243). Murray defines 'mana' as 'that primitive word, which comprises force, vitality, prestige, holiness, and power of magic, and which may belong equally to a lion, a chief, a medicine-man, or a battle-axe' (19).

Salt (p. 244). L. was attracted by the teaching of the pre-Socratic philosophers that the cosmos exists only by virtue of opposition. Anaximander (*c.* 610–540 BC), a disciple of Thales, taught that the first principle, a primary substance, is eternal matter (the Boundless or the Infinite) containing within itself all contraries such as heat and cold, moist and dry, and that the phenomenal universe has been evolved through the separation of these contraries and the creative union of those elements which have an affinity for each other. Thus, salt is created by the 'opposition' of fire and water.

The Four (p. 244) and *Walk Warily* (p. 245). Empedokles (*c.* 493–33 BC) maintained that everything in the world is composed of four primary 'roots' or 'elements' – air, earth, fire, water – which mingle and separate under the contrary impulses of 'love' and 'strife', thus causing the creation and dissolution of all things. So, too, life follows a continual, cyclical pattern: 'When the elements have been mingled in the fashion of a man and come to the light of day, or in the fashion of the race of wild beasts or plants or birds, then men say that these come into being; and when they are separated, they call that, as is the custom . . . death' (Burnet 220). 'And these things never cease, continually changing places, at one time all uniting in one through Love, at another each borne in different directions by the repulsion of Strife' (Burnet 221). Cf. note on 'Elemental'.

Anaxagoras (p. 246). Anaxagoras (*c.* 500–*c.* 428 BC) taught that however far matter (which is itself infinitely divisible) is divided, there is never a particle so small that it does not contain a certain portion of all qualities in it. Thus: 'That which is hot is also to a certain extent cold. Even snow, Anaxagoras affirmed, was black; that is, even the white contains a certain portion of the opposite quality' (Burnet 288).

Kissing and Horrid Strife (p. 247). See note on 'The Four'. Empedokles' doctrine that generation and decay are nothing but the compounding and dissolution of eternally unchanging elements held a great fascination for L.: 'At one time all the limbs that are the body's portion are brought together into one by Love, and flourish in the high season of life; and again, at another time they are severed by cruel Strife, and wander each in different directions by the breakers of the sea of life' (Burnet 229). Cf. 'The Ship of Death' and see note below on 'Strife'.

When Satan Fell (p. 248). Cf. *The Marriage of Heaven and Hell* where Blake teaches that reason (heaven) and energy (hell) are active contraries and equally necessary for human existence. In this respect L., like Blake (and Milton) was of the devil's party – and also a true poet. See also the doctrine of Heraclitus on cyclical balance in the nature of things: 'Mortals are immortals and immortals are mortals, the one living the other's death and dying the other's life' (Burnet 138).

The Wandering Cosmos (p. 248). Anaximander taught that 'the heavenly bodies are a wheel of fire' (Burnet 69) and that the universe is subject to a single law. Cf. *A* 82.

Death is Not Evil, Evil is Mechanical (p. 249). In a letter dated 29 October 1929 L. wrote: 'I say, as the ancient said, there is an evil world-soul which sometimes overpowers one, and with which one has to struggle most of the time to keep oneself clear. I feel so strongly as if my illness weren't really me – I feel perfectly well and all right, in *myself*. Yet there is this beastly torturing chest super-imposed on me, and it's as if there was a demon lived there, triumphing, and extraneous to me' (Nehls iii. 405).

7. **Dante** Alighieri (1265–1321), the famous Italian poet, author of *The Divine Comedy*. See *MEH* ch. xiii and L.'s essay 'The Novel' where he discusses Dante.
9. **Know thyself** See note on 'Terra Incognita'.

Strife (p. 250). The deep influence of Heraclitus' teachings can be seen in this cycle of poems on 'strife'. Heraclitus maintained that all things are in a state of flux, a ceaseless conflict of opposites, coming into existence and passing away. 'Homer was wrong in saying "Would that strife might perish from among gods and men!" He did not see that he was praying for the destruction of the universe; for, if his prayer were heard, all things would pass away' (Burnet 136). Cf. L.'s fullest working out of this doctrine in 'The Crown' and the distinction he draws there (as here) between the creative conflict of active contraries, and single dominance, which is evil.

The Ship of Death (p. 250). L.'s long meditative poem on dissolution and death takes for its central symbol the ancient Egyptian ship which ferries the soul across the underworld. This becomes also the 'ark of faith', suggesting Noah's ark and also the ark as a symbol for the womb and of spiritual rebirth. See Appendix 1 for two draft versions of the poem.

17–18. **quietus . . . bodkin?** 'When he himself might his quietus make with a bare bodkin?' *Hamlet* III, i. 75–6.

All Souls' Day (p. 254). 2 November.

After All Saints' Day (p. 255). 1 November.

Shadows (p. 256). Cf. L.'s essay 'Life' (first published February 1918) for an uncanny foreshadowing of this poem: 'Do I fear the strange approach of the creative unknown to my door? I fear it only with pain and unspeakable joy. And do I fear the invisible dark hand of death plucking me into the darkness, gathering me blossom by blossom from the stem of my life, into the unknown of my afterwards? I fear it only in reverence and with strange satisfaction. For this is my final satisfaction, to be gathered blossom by blossom, all my life long, into the finality of the unknown which is my end' (*P* 698).

APPENDIX 1

For details of these poems and their composition see Richard Aldington's 'Introduction' to *Last Poems*; *COMP* 1047; Keith Sagar 'The Genesis of "Bavarian Gentians"', *D. H. Lawrence Review* 8 i (1975).

INDEX OF FIRST LINES